New Tricks for Old Bureaucracies

New Tricks for Old Bureaucracies

Improving Policy Outcomes in the Public Sector

Joshua Schank with Emma Huang
and Marla Westervelt Berg

New Tricks for Old Bureaucracies:
Improving Policy Outcomes in the Public Sector

Cover Design by Nico Chavez

Illustrations by Vytis Snarskis

Interior design by S4Carlisle Publishing Services, Chennai, India

First published in 2026 by
Business Expert Press, LLC
222 East 46th Street, New York, NY 10017
www.businessexpertpress.com

ISBN-13: 978-1-63742-944-0 (paperback)
ISBN-13: 978-1-63742-945-7 (e-book)

Economics and Public Policy Collection

First edition: 2026
10 9 8 7 6 5 4 3 2 1

EU SAFETY REPRESENTATIVE
Mare Nostrum Group B.V.
Doelen 72
4831 GR Breda
The Netherlands
gpsr@mare-nostrum.co.uk

Dedication

Joshua: To Lindsey, who made me fall in love with her and Los Angeles.

Emma: For Ryan, my partner through it all and always up for the ride.

Marla: To Greg, my rock, who helped me find time to write even when life got busy.

Description

New Tricks for Old Bureaucracies explores why public agencies so often resist innovation and how to change that. Drawing on the authors' direct experience inside Los Angeles Metro's Office of Extraordinary Innovation, the book examines the structural, political, and cultural forces that make governments slow to adopt new ideas. It offers a pragmatic playbook for public servants, policymakers, and civic entrepreneurs who want to deliver lasting reform. Through candid storytelling and actionable strategies, the authors show how to navigate internal resistance, build coalitions, and design reforms that achieve meaningful change within complex systems.

Contents

List of Acronyms

ABLE   Automated Bus Lane Enforcement
ACS   American Community Survey
ACLU   American Civil Liberties Union
ADA   Americans with Disabilities Act
ATSAC   Advanced Transportation System and Coordination
ATU   Amalgamated Transit Union
BOS   Board of Supervisors
BRT   Bus Rapid Transit
BRU   Bus Riders Union
CAHSR   California High-Speed Rail
CE   The California Endowment
CEO   Chief Executive Officer
CFO   Chief Financial Officer
COG   Council of Governments
COO   Chief Operations Officer
CPUC   California Public Utilities Commission
DB   Design-Build
DBB   Design-Bid-Build
DBFOM   Design-Build-Finance-Operate-Maintain
DC   Washington, District of Columbia
ENA   Exclusive Negotiating Agreement
EPA   Environmental Protection Agency
EPW   U.S. Senate Committee on Environment and Public Works
FTA   Federal Transit Administration
FTE   Full-Time Equivalent
FY   Fiscal Year
GM   General Manager
HOT   High Occupancy Toll
HR   Human Resources
ILO   Innovation in Large Organizations
JFK   John F. Kennedy International Airport

KCATA	Kansas City Area Transportation Authority
LA	Los Angeles
LACTC	Los Angeles County Transportation Commission
LACMOA	Los Angeles County Municipal Operators Association
LACMTA	Los Angeles County Metropolitan Transportation Authority
LADOT	Los Angeles Department of Transportation
LAPD	Los Angeles Police Department
LA Metro (Metro)	Los Angeles County Metropolitan Transportation Authority
LAWA	Los Angeles World Airports
LRTP	Long Range Transportation Plan
Maglev	Magnetic levitation
MIT	Massachusetts Institute of Technology
MOD	Mobility on Demand
MSA	Metropolitan Statistical Area
MTI	Mineta Transportation Institute
NAACP	National Association for the Advancement of Colored People
NEPA	National Environmental Policy Act
NOFO	Notice of Funding Opportunity
OEI	Office of Extraordinary Innovation
OMB	Office of Management and Budget
OSI	Office of Strategic Innovation
P3	Public-Private Partnership
PDA	Project Development Agreement
PR	Public Relations
PRT	Personal Rapid Transit
PSTA	Pinellas Suncoast Transit Authority
QCP	Qualified Candidate Pool
ROI	Return on Investment
ROW	Right of Way
RTD	Regional Transportation District

RTF	Recovery Task Force
SANDAG	San Diego Association of Governments
SCAG	Southern California Association of Governments
SCRTD	Southern California Rapid Transit District
SGL	Southeast Gateway Line
SMART	International Association of Sheet Metal, Air, Rail, and Transportation Workers
SLT	Senior Leadership Team
TAP	Transit Access Pass
TNC	Transportation Network Company
TRS	Traffic Reduction Study
TVM	Ticket Vending Machine(s)
UCLA	University of California Los Angeles
USC	University of Southern California
UP	Unsolicited Proposal
USDOT	United States Department of Transportation
VPPP	Value Pricing Pilot Program
WSAB	West Santa Ana Branch

List of Figures

Preface

This book is for anyone who has tried to make change from within a public institution and wondered if it was worth it. It's for the frustrated policy analyst, the bold transportation executive, the young planner who dreams big, and the career public servant who still cares deeply—despite everything. It can also benefit the elected official navigating political pressures, the new board member seeking to make an impact, the transportation advocate fighting for better service, and even the unabashed transit enthusiast who wants a peek behind the curtain.

New Tricks for Old Bureaucracies is written from Joshua Schank's perspective but is based on the collective experiences of Joshua, Emma Huang, and Marla Westervelt Berg working inside Los Angeles Metro's Office of Extraordinary Innovation (OEI), an experiment in reimagining what changes are possible within a large transit agency. We helped launch pilots, challenge assumptions, and test new approaches to public sector problem-solving. Some efforts failed. Others succeeded beyond what we thought was possible. All of them taught us something about how change happens, or doesn't, in government.

This book is not just about ideas or plans—it's about politics, personalities, process, and power. We share our experience not because it's perfect, but because it's real. We hope it helps the next generation of innovators inside public agencies find their own ways to push forward, even when the system pushes back.

The tools are in your hands now.

Acknowledgments

The authors would like to above all recognize the support of Karen Philbrick and Hilary Nixon of the Mineta Transportation Institute (MTI) at San Jose State University. Without their support, both financial and motivational, this endeavor and this book would not have been possible.

Rose Conway and Scott Isenberg were critical in enabling this book to come to fruition. Rose helped us navigate a complicated world of publishers with great ease, and Scott saw potential for this book and allowed us to fulfill our vision of what we wanted to write.

We want to especially thank Phil Washington, who not only reviewed an early draft but gave us the opportunity to work at LA Metro, supported our efforts to make change, and continues to serve as an inspirational leader and model for us and so many others in the transportation industry.

We would also like to thank David Bragdon, Robert Puentes, Elliot Regenstein, Michael Schneider, Matthew Barrett, Adam J. Epstein, and Tham Nguyen for their thoughtful input and reviews of earlier drafts, as well as Brian D. Taylor for his review and touching foreword.

We also want to acknowledge all of the people who were a part of OEI and contributed to its work even if they are not specifically mentioned: Avital Shavit, Colin Peppard, Ryan Wolfe, Ray Kan, Eileen Hsu, Marie Sullivan, Tamar Fuhrer, Rani Narula-Woods, Cassie Halls, Glendora Walker, Nadine Lee, Mark Vallianatos, Sharyne Ng, Nolan Borgman, Shaun Miller, Yousef Salama, Andrew Carrasco, Luis Zazueta, Darryl Carter, Andrew Quinn, Naz Habib, doreen Morrissey, and Dennis Arnold.

Also, a special thanks to Carolina Coppolo, without whom we probably would have accomplished very little, Greg Levine and Teddy Lowe for their legal assistance, and to Stephanie Wiggins, who helped us overcome challenges time and again. Thanks also to other Metro executives who supported the mission of change: Rick Clarke, Jim Gallagher, Shalonda Baldwin, Greg Kildare, and Jonaura Wisdom.

Finally, thanks to Marty Wachs—may his memory be a blessing—who inspired all of us to do better work in transportation.

Foreword

It's been said that successful venture capitalists back failed ventures 80 percent of the time. In other words, if just one out of five of their investments pans out, they will more than recoup their losses on other four unsuccessful endeavors. Such go-big-or-go-home strategies have fostered the "move fast and break things" mantra of many of the most successful, and disruptive, start-up firms over the past three decades.

While decrying the inefficiency of clumsy, calcified government bureaucracies has been a hobby horse of politics for well over a century, do voters really want public agencies to break lots of things and fail 80 percent of the time? Perhaps not. So if not, are sclerotic, unimaginative bureaucracies our unavoidable fate?

In this book, Joshua Schank, Emma Huang, and Marla Westervelt Berg answer that latter question with a resounding no!

In eight engaging and insightful chapters, Schank, Huang, and Westervelt tell the, well, extraordinary seven-year story of their time at the Office of Extraordinary Innovation (OEI) at the Los Angeles Metropolitan Transportation Authority, or LA Metro. Theirs is far from a simple, one idea story of heroic innovators battling unimaginative, obstructionist bureaucrats.

Instead they tell a far more interesting and reflective story of why government agencies like LA Metro tend to be cautious and slow-moving, and why the people in them learn to be risk averse. This understanding leads to a series of clear lessons and strategies for managing that inherent risk aversion in order to nudge, push, and occasionally drag organizations toward meaningful, positive change. They do this through a series of very specific stories about the successes and failures of many OEI efforts.

Indeed, many of the most salient lessons they offer come from their refreshing candor in discussing failed OEI initiatives, and how they draw on those lessons learned in subsequent efforts. This collective story of aiming to make a positive difference, running into one brick wall or another, and then recalibrating to be smarter and more effective the next time around should be an inspiring lesson on growing throughout one's career.

While their focus is on their experiences at a single transportation agency in Los Angeles County, the lessons they draw about how to effect meaningful change in government bureaucracies are in no way confined to either transportation agencies or Southern California. Instead, any aspiring change agent in local, regional, state, or national government can learn much from the case studies told and lessons learned by the authors.

I began my career as planner/analyst at a regional planning agency, have spent most of my professional life as a policy and planning academic studying about and arguing for many of the changes Schank, Huang, and Westervelt pushed for at OEI, and I was fortunate to serve on the OEI Advisory Board during their time there and so got to see firsthand just how quietly radical OEI was in attempting to disrupt and change the status quo. So *New Tricks for Old Bureaucracies* is neither a run-of-the-mill "war stories from the trenches" nor a "tell all" book. It is instead a lively "how to" guide to making the public sector more agile and innovative in bureaucracies that were explicitly designed to be neither.

And what could be more *extraordinary* than that?

Brian D. Taylor, PhD

Review Quotes

"Anyone dedicated to reforming public agencies and modernizing transit service in cities should read New Tricks for Old Bureaucracies. *You will not only enjoy an engaging book but you will also gain valuable insights about the methods and pitfalls of prodding and coaxing bureaucratic organizations to improve processes, performance and outcomes for their constituents."*—**David Bragdon, Former Executive Director of Transit Center**

"Making change in public institutions is hard! Schank, Huang, and Westervelt recount amusing stories of their successes and failures at LA Metro to illustrate how we can make things happen!"—**Nadine Lee, President and Chief Executive Officer of Dallas Area Rapid Transit**

"Cities face big transportation problems, and they cannot be solved without innovative thinking and major policy change. I love that in higher numbers, people are bringing their entrepreneurial spirit to the public sector. But as Joshua, Emma, and Marla outline, it is still not easy or guaranteed to succeed. Fortunately, they took some hard knocks that you can learn from, vs. making the same mistakes. The authors' persistence created positive change, and in this book, they distill some helpful lessons learned for anyone looking to do the same."—**Gabe Klein, Former Director of the Chicago and Washington, DC Departments of Transportation**

Introduction: "Why Are You Even Here?"

Not long after I arrived in Los Angeles, I got a call from a friend of mine.

"Hey, I'm sitting in traffic right now, so I thought of you. When exactly are you going to fix this?"

He was asking because I had recently accepted a position as Chief Innovation Officer of the Office of Extraordinary Innovation (OEI) at the Los Angeles County Metropolitan Transportation Authority (LA Metro or Metro), the lead transportation agency for Los Angeles County, and I suppose he expected quick results.

At the time, Los Angeles had a rare trifecta of visionary leadership, sufficient resources, and public support critical for driving lasting change in the public sector. OEI easily attracted some of the most talented folks from across the country. Going in, I thought that the biggest obstacles would be Political, with a capital "P." I felt that if we (OEI) could effectively make the case for change, it would be embraced. But I eventually learned that most of the barriers to change lay within the organization itself. Before our team could enact real policy change, we would have to change the processes and incentives within the organization.

Ultimately, we proved that meaningful change is not just possible in government bureaucracy—it's achievable, repeatable, and worth pursuing. However, change in government does not come because someone has a good idea or a new exciting technology. We found that change can occur only through the challenging and laborious task of building consensus, fixing broken processes, and picking your battles.

Welcome to Los Angeles

"Why are you even here?" LA Metro's Chief Financial Officer (CFO) asked me. "What value do you bring?"

I had never been asked such a question by anyone, much less a new colleague. It was so surprising that I could not offer a carefully thought-out answer. Instead, I felt incredulous, which was likely the intended reaction. I later figured out she hadn't asked this question to inform her decision making. She had asked me because I was intruding on her turf, and she was intent on showing me her boundaries.

In retrospect, though, her question was—if it had been genuine—one with legitimate value. She had been working at LA Metro for 30 years, reaching her pinnacle as CFO. I was many decades her junior, had no executive experience at a public agency or in Los Angeles, and was largely ignorant of the intricacies of her responsibilities and the agency itself. Yet here I was, trying to insert myself into her work, questioning her decision making, and thinking I knew better.

Such is the life of an outsider brought in to foster innovation at a public agency. My job was to question everything. My job was to ask why Metro wasn't doing it differently. My job was to tell people with many years of experience and more expertise that they were doing it wrong.

I was not a popular employee.

In May 2013, Eric Garcetti was elected mayor of Los Angeles. While the mayor of Los Angeles does not appoint the head of LA Metro—the countywide transportation agency that plans, builds, funds, and operates transportation in the largest county in the United States—he or she serves on the LA Metro Board, appoints three other board members, and chairs the Board every three years.[i]

In July 2014, the mayor became chair of that Board and soon had the opportunity to replace the CEO of LA Metro with someone new. Unlike his predecessors, Mayor Garcetti chose not to rely on someone with experience in Los Angeles and instead went after the best available CEO in the business. That person was Phillip A. Washington, the CEO of Denver's Regional Transportation District (RTD) and widely recognized as perhaps the most talented executive in the industry.

The choice of an outsider—known as an agent of change and a builder of great infrastructure—would have substantial ramifications for LA Metro and the region. Mr. Washington (Phil) made this immediately apparent when he boldly announced the creation of the OEI in the summer of 2015.[ii]

His intention in creating this office was for OEI to "champion new ideas for improving mobility."[iii] It turned out that in practice, that would mean championing ideas that the rest of Metro (1) didn't want to do, (2) thought they were already doing, and/or (3) did not have the resources to do. This set up an inherent conflict within the agency, and I was at the center of it.

I came to LA Metro with two decades of experience in transportation policy and politics. I had run a nonpartisan transportation policy think-tank in Washington, DC, advised then-Senator Hillary Clinton on transportation, and worked for state and federal agencies. I had a PhD in Urban Planning and Transportation and a book on federal transportation policy under my belt.[iv] In these previous positions, I worked toward making change from within the various systems in which I worked by using my expertise and research skills to advocate for improved policies, so I thought I knew what awaited me. But I had no idea.

Going West as a Youngish Man

Los Angeles is huge. As in really, really, big. People may think they understand the size of the area intuitively, but it helps to put things in perspective to fully grasp how large it is. Los Angeles is the second largest city in the country, but Los Angeles County is the most populous county in the nation with more people than 40 states. There are 88 cities in Los Angeles County, and the City of Los Angeles is just one of them. Moreover, Los Angeles County is just one of five counties covering the Los Angeles Metropolitan Statistical Area (MSA), which is the second largest MSA[1] in the country in population (just under 13 million).

And yet, as large and awe-inspiring as the region is, the political world of Los Angeles can feel irrelevant to many, especially compared to Washington, DC, where I had spent the previous 13 years. Despite operating in the nation's largest county, and an annual budget of over $9 billion, LA Metro and most of the politics of the region can often fly

---

[1]An MSA is a standardized classification created by the Census Bureau for large urban centers and their surrounding areas to compare the characteristics and sizes of different regions in the United States.

under the radar.ᵛ As parodied on the show *Mr. Mayor,* a short-lived series about the mayor of LA, most Angelenos don't even know who the
mayor is at any given moment, and even fewer know who the county
supervisors are.

When I first began commuting from Studio City, my new inner-ring
suburban home in Los Angeles, to downtown 12 miles away, it often felt
like switching between worlds every day. I lived in an area near the heart
of the entertainment industry, with both struggling and successful writers
and actors, homogeneity, suburban Americana, and a plethora of store-
fronts offering aesthetic surgery, foot massages, weed, and sushi. Every
day, I got onto the Red Line subway (now the B Line) and emerged in a
downtown area where there was rampant poverty, tremendous diversity,
and a focus on politics and power brokers. It was hard to believe these
were the same city.

While I was extremely excited to move to the West Coast, I found the
transition from Washington, DC, jarring. In DC, it seems that everyone
is in politics. Even people in professions unrelated to politics cannot
escape the obsessive political infatuation that pervades the city and most
of the region. While you're there, it's also easy to develop arrogance with
respect to politics and policy. It feels as if the best, smartest, and most
competitive people in public policy come to DC to make a difference
and/or seek their fame, if not fortune. This is one of the reasons that DC
is often known as "Hollywood for ugly people." At the time, I figured
it would be easy to use my learned policy and political skills on the LA
bureaucrats.

I also had something of an advantage growing up as a child of two
psychologists. Besides the impact that may have had on my development
(and future therapy bills), having a psychotherapist mom and a professor
of psychology dad meant that from an early age, I was trained in how to
consider what's driving people's behavior—which probably explains why
I psychoanalyze everyone I meet. Throughout my childhood, my parents
couldn't help but constantly analyze my (and everyone else's) behavior,
which in turn taught me how to read people, listen intently, and dis-
cern their motivations. These skills had proven quite useful in DC, and
it seemed like they might be even more effective in the stereotypically
therapeutic world of Los Angeles.

When I left DC, I was well-known among the small transportation policy community there. I had strong relationships in federal transportation policy and nationally, including current and former secretaries of transportation, heads of major trade associations, and public transit agency CEOs. But, upon arriving in LA, I found that most, if not all, of my previous political and policy accomplishments impressed few people.

What I did not anticipate, and soon found out, was that the biggest barrier to change and improvements in transportation in Los Angeles was bureaucracy[2] and how it functioned, and that I had no clue how to deal with it. While local politics were complicated and challenging, the bureaucracy was so entrenched that it often prevented me from even getting into the political issues. If I was going to be successful in Los Angeles, I'd have to learn how to work within that system, and fast.

Part of the difficulty was that the system wasn't designed to adapt. Bureaucracies like Metro's are built for order, predictability, and control, often at the expense of nuance and agility. Political scientist James C. Scott refers to this dynamic as "legibility": the impulse to simplify the world into tidy categories that make sense from the top down, even when they overlook what works on the ground.[vi] That mindset wasn't just frustrating, it was foundational. And until I understood it, I had no shot at changing anything that mattered.

LA Metro is not Just a Metro

LA Metro itself is challenging to understand, but perhaps the easiest way to grasp the organization is to understand that it is enormous and unwieldy in part because of the way it was created. The official name is the Los Angeles County Metropolitan Transportation Authority (LACMTA), a name that reflects the fact that it is the result of the

---

[2]Bureaucracies answer to diverse stakeholders across government and society, including Boards and constituencies. Unlike business firms, they also function as democratic institutions where accountability and fairness are paramount. The resources required to maintain these principles often conflict with performance objectives. Steven J. Balla and William T. Gormley write about this extensively in their 2017 book *Bureaucracy and Democracy*.

merger—or perhaps more accurately a "shotgun marriage"—of two organizations: the Southern California Rapid Transportation District (SCRTD
or RTD), which operated buses across much, but not all, of the region;
and the Los Angeles County Transportation Commission (LACTC), the
countywide planning and funding organization. They were merged under
state legislation in 1993.[vii]

Studio City is not a City

Every metropolitan landscape has its governance oddities. Just as every
unhappy family is unhappy in its own way, every metropolitan area
has its own insanity. These are some of Los Angeles' eccentricities.

- Five county supervisors, each representing approximately 2 million
  people, are executives for the county. They have so much power
  that former Congresswomen Janice Hahn and Hilda Solis, the
  latter also the former U.S. Secretary of Labor, both decided to become Los Angeles County Supervisors after their federal positions.[3]
- Thirteen city council members run the City of Los Angeles,
  the smallest ratio of members to population for any large city
  in the United States, each focused on their own sizable constit-
  uency and largely without accountability to the larger city.
- The mayor of Los Angeles has little power other than a bully
  pulpit, which often gets limited press coverage. The mayor is
  unable to even hire or fire most city officials.
- There are 88 cities in LA County, and there are also 99 neighborhood councils and hundreds of other unofficial neighborhoods in the City of Los Angeles.
- Some cities in LA County are surrounded by the City of Los
  Angeles, including Beverly Hills and Santa Monica.
- Studio City is not a city; it is a neighborhood. Harbor City
  is not a city; it is a neighborhood. East LA is not a city; it is

---

[3]In fact, so many people agreed that having five people run an area that is more
populous than some states needs reform that Measure G was passed by LA
County voters in November 2024 to increase the number of supervisors from
five to nine beginning in 2032, following a redistricting process.

> unincorporated LA County. Venice is not a city; it is a neigh-
> borhood. Culver City is a city.
>
> • North Hollywood is a neighborhood. East Hollywood is a
>   neighborhood. Hollywood is a neighborhood. West Holly-
>   wood is a city.
> • The City of Duarte has 22,000 people. The City of Los Angeles
>   has 4 million people. For most of the last two decades, both
>   have had seats on the LA Metro Board, which controls transpor-
>   tation planning, funding, and operations for the entire county.
> • Los Angeles is in California, which means stricter environ-
>   mental regulations, frequent direct democracy in the form of
>   ballot measures, and a Democratic party super-majority.

The merger was painful and combative, and the difference in perspective between the operations and planning functions still pervades the
agency. In terms of people, most of the over 12,000 employees of LA
Metro are in the Operations Department. But in terms of the annual
budget, most of the $9.5 billion[4] goes toward Planning and Construction
Departments, as prescribed by various ballot measures approved over the
years.[4] This means that there is internal conflict between Finance and
Operations, with Operations always feeling starved of cash. It also creates
conflict between Construction and Operations, wherein projects can be
built without consideration of how well they can be operated.

LA Metro is like this for a reason—in all democracies across the world,
it is politically challenging to get people to vote for what they already have.
If you ask people to vote on a ballot measure to tax themselves to provide
funds to operate and maintain a transit system, you are likely to lose. Making it even more challenging, tax increases in California must be passed
by ballot measures receiving two-thirds vote.[5] In general, this is a tough
sell, but it is even harder in LA County, where most people don't ride the

---

[4]Metro's FY26 budget was approximately $9.5 billion. When I came to the
agency in FY16, the budget was approximately $5.5 billion.
[5]In 1996, Californians adopted Proposition 218, a constitutional initiative that
specifies that any local tax imposed to pay for a specific government program, like
transportation, must be approved by two-thirds of the voters.

transit system much or at all—per the 2023 American Community Survey (ACS, one-year), only 4 percent of Angelenos commute to work via transit. But if instead you promise them new rail and bus services that cross every part of the county, you are much more likely to win. This means that most of the ballot measures passed by LA County voters primarily fund new construction rather than operating and maintaining the existing system. It also means that the projects LA Metro builds must appeal to the whole county, not just the places where mass transit is likely to be useful.[viii]

The LA Metro Board has 14 members. Five of them are the LA County Supervisors. One is the mayor of Los Angeles, and the LA mayor also appoints three other directors (typically city council members or other elected officials). The other seats go to representatives from four sectors of the county through a political process known as the "City Selection Committee"[ix] largely hidden from view but led by their councils of government (COGs). The 14th person is a nonvoting member. The chairperson of the board rotates on a three-year cycle between the mayor of LA, a county supervisor, and the COG representatives.

Without the LA Metro Board members' support, sales tax ballot measures are unlikely to achieve the two-thirds vote requirement for passage. So even though the City of Los Angeles and other densely developed cities in the county are places where mass transit can thrive, a political compromise is required to get all the board members to support a ballot measure. This usually means funding either highway projects, which some of the outlying areas prefer to mass transit, or new transit lines that are likely to carry very few people. It also means less funding is available for the projects that offer the best return on investment. For example, Measure M, the sales tax ballot measure passed in 2016, spread $120 billion like peanut butter over LA County to ensure passage.

The result of this governance structure is a system that has very little funding flexibility. With most of the money coming from sales tax increment increases passed via ballot measures, LA Metro finds itself tightly restricted in how that money can be spent. Each of the four half-cent sales tax increase ballot measures includes a carefully constructed political compromise that specifies exactly when and where that money must be spent. Any proposed changes cause great consternation among metro staff and board members and are unlikely to be considered.

This structure also means that the relatively small amount of money available for operations is hotly contested. Within LA Metro there is fierce competition for that money, as it is the most flexible funding. It is also the only funding available for new ideas. And it is controlled, largely, by the CFO.[6]

Metro also has a somewhat ignominious history that colors much of how it behaves today. First, there was the National Association for the Advancement of Colored People (NAACP) Legal Defense and Education Fund civil rights lawsuit brought on behalf of the Bus Riders Union (BRU) and other plaintiffs, which pushed Metro to agree to a 10-year consent decree administered by federal court that, among other things, effectively suspended rail construction in the 1990s.[x] The NAACP painted this issue as one of civil rights, arguing that raising fares while neglecting buses and adding rail was effectively neglecting people of color in the hopes of attracting wealthier riders. This history meant that many in Los Angeles viewed Metro as an organization with a history of racism.

Second, there was a history of corruption among board members.[xi] Shortly after my arrival, I was given a long lecture about this history by Karen Gorman, who served at the time as both the inspector general and the ethics officer, and reported directly to the Board of Directors and the CEO by virtue of holding both of those titles. Karen had been with the agency for 30 years and saw herself as responsible for not only avoiding conflicts of interest but also any "perceived" conflicts of interest. If an issue arose about a potential conflict, her office could and would investigate and make a ruling on the subject.

Despite the enormity of Metro's budget, the fact that LA County is more populated than 40 states, and this history of corruption, much of what LA Metro does still winds up flying under the radar. The LA Times had a transportation reporter who regularly covered the agency for many years, but that was curtailed over time such that the stories that were published during my time were rarely in-depth. Streetsblog, a nonprofit advocacy group, has a reporter who attends Metro Board meetings and

---

[6]The CEO and the Board must approve the budget, of course, but the CFO does the initial draft, controls the data, and has access to more information than any other player.

live tweets from them, which provides some transparency, but that organization presents a highly biased point of view wherein bikes reign supreme.[7] Most Angelenos are largely unaware of local politics and tend to focus more on the entertainment industry news or national political issues. This limits demand for serious investigations of local issues, such as how Metro spends $9.5 billion.

However, there is one strange and well-known exception to this lack of coverage, known by those in the know as "Numble."

Numble is the social media handle of an individual who maintains— and I am not making this up—a secret identity. While someone may know who he or she is, it has never been publicly revealed. But whoever it is not only follows Metro meticulously and religiously but also has an incredible knowledge of everything Metro has ever done, and a knack for unbiased reporting and analysis of Metro machinations that is truly incredible.

Numble says on their X (formerly Twitter) handle that they "read Metro documents for fun," but they do much more. They seek out and use public information requests to obtain Metro documents. They then analyze those documents with a precision that, when occasionally challenged in a public forum, always turns out to have been correct. This is because no one knows more about Metro, or reads Metro documents with more care, than Numble. In fact, it was not uncommon for Metro employees to learn about developments through Numble before hearing from their own leadership. Numble wielded enough influence that Metro leaders often would make decisions about when and how to release information because they knew Numble would catch things.

Numble represents the nerdiest, and often the most accurate, voice in the larger transit community of Los Angeles. But there are many others who play critical roles, such as Move LA, an advocacy group focused on passing ballot measures to fund transportation. There is also Investing in Place, a nonprofit focused on transit and other public spaces, and FAST—Fixing Angelenos Stuck in Traffic, a group led by a highly connected and politically savvy individual who has quietly been involved in transportation decisions across the county and state.

---

[7] I love bikes, and I ride one all over LA. But for most trips in Los Angeles and for most people, bikes are often not the optimal transportation choice.

And then there are advocates who mobilize on a specific issue. Often, this can be a community group looking to stop or change a planned project. Other times, it could be advocates for specific policies such as lower fares, better policing, or services for people with disabilities. All these groups would work to influence Metro behind the scenes and with the Board. But their primary influence was often with another group—Board Staff.

Metro Board Staff

As the board members all have other primary jobs serving their constituents in various jurisdictions across the county, they delegate much of their work to people affectionately known as "Board Staff." Board Staff are typically employed by the city represented by the board member, by the county if the board member is a supervisor, or by the local Council of Governments (COG) if the member is a city selection committee member. They are like legislative staff for a Member of Congress. They are not typically employed by LA Metro, but they are assigned office space in the LA Metro building, and many go on to work for LA Metro.

When I first came to LA Metro, I was warned about Board Staff, but I did not at the time fully grasp what interacting with them was going to be like. My relationship with Board Staff began with a phone call from one staffer who began by mockingly asking me, "So what have you done that is so extraordinary?" She then proceeded to criticize, with very limited understanding, the one idea she heard me propose.

Then there were the Board Staff Briefings, a concept so absurd that it is difficult for me to describe. Thanks to the Brown Act,[8] in general, three or more board members cannot meet collectively to discuss LA Metro business unless it is in a public meeting. But hammering out issues in

---

[8]Passed in 1953, the Brown Act is a California law that requires that meetings of local legislative bodies are open to the public, held in an accessible place, and publicly noticed. Per the act itself, a "meeting" is defined as anytime a majority of members of the legislative body are present. In an abundance of caution, LA Metro's written policy also applies this logic to committees and subcommittees— which are typically between six to seven members. As a result, in general, if three or more board members are convening, it's likely to be in violation of the Brown Act and Metro policies. The Brown Act fundamentally shapes how LA Metro Board meetings are structured, conducted, and strategized.

public can be a recipe for disaster and can also take a substantial time. Therefore, each month, before the Board committee meetings, LA metro staff collectively brief the Board Staff on all items that will come before the Board that month. In theory, this is a time for Board Staff to flag any issues that might be of concern to their bosses and help LA metro staff improve their Board items.

In reality, it is an agonistic, *Game-of-Thrones*-style battle for power that at times serves as an obstacle to those pushing change. Board Staff run the three-to-five-hour meetings that include breakfast and lunch for them but not for LA Metro staff (this is true—Metro staff who try to eat may be publicly chastised by Board Staff). The Board Staffer working for the current board chair runs the meeting as if he or she is the chair of the actual Board. They work with the CEO's office to set the agenda for the meeting. Any item that is super-controversial may not even make it to the actual board agenda or can be delayed, and as a result the Board Staff often purposefully craft the agenda based on their—and not metro staff's—priorities.

During most of the time I was there, Board Staff Briefings were held in a very small conference room near the Board Staff's LA Metro offices. The LA Metro CEO attends the entire meeting, as does his or her Senior Leadership Team (the chiefs of Metro's various departments). Only the CEO and the Board Staff may sit at the conference room table—everyone else must scramble for a seat on the perimeter in tight quarters.

A parade of LA metro staff must then enter to present at this preliminary meeting when their item is up for consideration by the Board Staff. For example, when an item from the Planning Department is up for discussion, the staff from Planning working on that item (typically executives but not chiefs[9]) will present. But there is barely enough room in the conference room for Board Staff and the chiefs, so these folks must wait awkwardly in the hallway until they are called. A meeting agenda is sent out in advance so that they can potentially time it appropriately, but of course that agenda is rarely kept on time, so top executives from an agency responsible for transportation in the largest county in America wind up idling in a hallway waiting to be summoned.

---

[9]During Phil's tenure, chiefs ran the entire department, while executives ran a portion or subsection of the department.

When the staff present, it's painful. Keep in mind that most of these executives have spent decades studying and working in their respective fields. They have years of experience, extensive expertise, and an array of staff and consultants working for them. However, when they appear before the Board Staff, they are powerless. Board Staff question them relentlessly and often obnoxiously or ignorantly, with a few basic assumptions behind their questions, which I would characterize as follows:

1. Metro staff are fundamentally misinformed and must be corrected by Board Staff.
2. If metro staff appear cautious or uncertain, they must be lazy or unprepared.
3. And if things really go off the rails, some Board Staff seem to believe that replacing metro staff might solve the problem, and feel they have the power to do it.

My first time presenting to the Board Staff, I was threatened with losing my job. This is not atypical. Board Staff spend most of their time trying to influence Metro policy. But ultimately, they have no real power to do so because they are not Metro executives, nor are they board members. So, they vent their frustrations by chastising metro staff, and one another, and largely get away with it.

What's worse is that the CEO must sit through this nonsense. Being CEO of LA Metro is no easy task. The demands on your time are relentless as you manage a staff of 12,000 people, 12+ chiefs with huge egos, five labor unions, and 14 board members. But the CEO needs to be there, because if he or she is absent, the behavior only gets worse. The CEO protects their flock from abuse and harassment and keeps the Board Staff from preemptively pushing back on their key agency initiatives.

The fights play out in this small backroom so that they don't have to take place publicly. This benefits the board members as it reduces challenging or embarrassing arguments in public. But it also makes policy change more difficult as it sets up yet another barrier to get through, while simultaneously reducing transparency for the public. It is just these sorts of informal and asymmetric obstacles to meaningful change, and how to effectively manage them, that are the focus of this book.

How to Use This Book

When I arrived in Los Angeles, I had a strong background in transportation and public policy change. But I did not have experience putting that knowledge into practice at a public agency. The academic literature exploring why innovation is difficult in bureaucracies is plentiful, but there are fewer sources on how to get things done despite the dysfunction.

I've now been through that process and have the battle scars and insights to prove it. My experiences, both successes and challenges, have made me even more committed to engaging in the hard work required to drive toward positive policy change in the public interest. While my lessons were hard-earned, they don't have to be for you. To support my fellow change makers, I've packaged my lessons learned into this book.

My hope is that when given an opportunity to drive positive change within a government agency, you'll have a head start and be equipped with the tools necessary to be successful. Even if you have a demanding Board Staff or an extremely complex regional structure, or you don't have a dynamic leader who creates an "extraordinary" office, you can still make a difference.

The book is organized by the lessons I learned, as follows:

Chapter 1: Pick Your Battles and Win Them

This chapter describes my initial mindset setting up OEI—bright-eyed and bushy-tailed, ready to change everything—colliding with the reality of working in a large government agency. The initial barriers were different and much more challenging than I expected. Instead of being a change agent out of the gate, early on I was learning what it would take to be successful, and while I still had no idea what lay ahead of me, I learned quickly that I had to be selective about what I wanted to change. I learned there is finite political capital to leverage when calling in your chits, so you must do so judiciously. If you do get a yes, then be sure to apply your resources accordingly, otherwise, you risk losing reputational power and legitimacy.

Chapter 2: You Need to Make Friends to Fix Processes

This chapter explores some initial failures and how they taught me about the need to collaborate and deal more directly with processes, which OEI eventually used with great success. Over time, I created and changed processes in meaningful ways, but first, I had to learn that short-term fixes rarely hold. I found that discussing ideas in terms of costs and benefits, rather than how to overcome obstacles, was an effective strategy. But for lasting change, intentionally building relationships and processes was the most critical building block.

Chapter 3: Recognize Impenetrable Fiefdoms

This chapter shows how I learned, sometimes painfully, about the limits of my power as a leader to create change. While the CEO would typically support me in these efforts, he had his limitations, and therefore so did I. Moreover, I learned that each time the CEO had to overrule other executives in the agency, this would exact a price as their resentment toward OEI would grow. So, I had to recognize early on when something was a lost cause.

Chapter 4: It's a Marathon and a Sprint

Fundamentally changing how an agency operates or does business can't be achieved through a pilot or brute force from one department. This chapter exemplifies what it takes to implement big, lasting changes through the story of bringing on-demand transit to LA Metro. Introducing on-demand transit required creating new kinds of partnerships with the private sector, but this was challenging to do in a bureaucracy that is designed around a very different kind of business model. Bringing on-demand transit to LA Metro required building an extensive network of supporters and a new procurement process to support the idea. It also took far longer than anticipated, as did most everything OEI tried to do.

Chapter 5: Both Naivete and Experience Are Required

Innovation requires constructing a new vision, and that can be a painful process. This chapter explores the challenges of having outsiders come into an agency and attempt to build a strategic plan. But it also shows how incredibly valuable that can be in fostering innovation when it is successful. OEI was successful in putting together a new vision for Metro because we had the right combination of naivete and experience.

Chapter 6: Beware Your Expiration Date

This chapter shows how limited the opportunity for real change can be in the public sector. A crisis or a change in leadership can drastically alter the best-laid plans. That said, if the groundwork has been laid, some final improvements can be made even on the way out, potentially leaving a critical legacy.

Chapter 7: How to Overcome Resistance in Public Agencies

While each chapter is developed to highlight applicable lessons learned, this chapter introduces broader tactical strategies for success. The hope is that these strategies and tactics can inform future teams seeking to effect change through government.

CHAPTER 1

Pick Your Battles and Win Them

Los Angeles is famous for fantastic hikes with beautiful views. One of my favorites is Burbank Peak in Griffith Park. It is a short but very steep climb, often full of tourists going to the back of the Hollywood Sign. But before the sign, there is the Wisdom Tree, which sits atop a point of view where you can see almost all of Los Angeles, allowing for meaningful contemplation. When I first moved to Los Angeles, I would climb to this spot with my kids and point to my office downtown, a high rise that stood apart from the LA skyline. It was here that I imagined the change I would bring to this city (Figure 1.1).

Many people come to Los Angeles with a dream of a career in entertainment. As an urban planner, I arrived with a different dream—to help reshape the city from one centered around cars to one where mass transit was a more viable alternative. I had prepared my whole career for such an opportunity. When I was in graduate school at MIT, my classmates voted me the person most likely to become a power broker in the tradition of Robert Moses.[10] I had worked my whole life on the East Coast, where cities were far less car-centric. Los Angeles would be the ultimate challenge.

Looking out from Burbank Peak, it seemed anything was possible. LA Metro had great leadership, ample funding, a brand-new office focused entirely on innovation, and what seemed like genuine openness to change. But reality set in rather quickly. Even under the best circumstances, change is exceedingly challenging. OEI would eventually accomplish many things, but we would also learn of our limitations; we would learn to pick our battles and win them.

---

[10]I promise this award was given with love. My classmates saw me as someone who wanted to get things done in transportation, not as a racist, anti-transit, highway builder. At least I hope they did.

Figure 1.1 Photograph of Joshua Schank's son contemplating the future of Los Angeles from Burbank Peak

Source: Photograph by Joshua Schank.

Welcome to Metro—You Don't Have Two Years

When I first started visiting Los Angeles, even before moving there, I discovered Langer's Delicatessen. As a child of New Yorkers, I had long been led to believe that the best pastrami sandwich in the world can be found in Katz's Deli in Manhattan. But it turns out (sorry New York) it is at Langer's Deli in Los Angeles, a short subway ride away from my new office. Despite the deliciousness, I tried to keep my visits there to a minimum in the hopes of avoiding triple-bypass surgery.

Still, I was thrilled when early on in my tenure, the CEO's executive assistant asked me what I wanted from Langer's for an upcoming meeting with the CEO and the chair of the Board. I hadn't yet met the board chair, so I was excited for that too, but it was also a great opportunity for a #1 (pastrami on rye with coleslaw and Russian dressing) and some matzo ball soup.

The Board Chair at the time was Mark Ridley-Thomas, also known as MRT. He was a monumental figure in LA politics.[11] At the time he was a member of the Board of Supervisors for LA County, an extremely powerful position. But he had a long career prior to that pinnacle having served in the LA City Council, State Assembly, and State Senate. He was also a prominent figure in civil rights in Los Angeles, having represented South Los Angeles during the Rodney King era.

So, I was a little intimidated when I walked into the conference room to meet him along with my boss. While my delicious food was there as well, I didn't dare touch it, as I was immediately peppered with questions. He also gave me his perspective. There would be limited patience for this innovation experiment, so I would need to show results fast. His exact words were, "You don't have two years."

The implication was that this great experiment in innovation was fine and all, but he wasn't going to allow it unless it showed results and quickly. With that message conveyed, I was asked to leave the room so that he could speak with the CEO alone before I had even touched my sandwich. I picked up my food and slinked out to go and eat in my office, alone. I had to wonder—*Did I make the right move coming here?*

The meeting with the board chair was hardly the only unfriendly greeting. My first meetings with my colleagues were instructive in that most of them made it clear how unenthusiastic they were to meet me.

One new colleague, the interim head of procurement, explained to me everything that went into the procurement process. But as I questioned him about it, he seemed to get frustrated. At one point, I asked whether his department had ever looked back to analyze why some major construction projects went over time or budget to develop lessons learned. He answered that "LA Metro has never had a project go over budget."

That statement was laughable, as Metro had had many projects go well over budget for many years, which is a problem plaguing many transportation projects across the United States. But from his standpoint, his assertion was technically true. Procurement would never allow a contract to go over the budget allowed in the contract. If more money was needed,

---

[11]This was well before his political downfall. In August 2023, Mark Ridley-Thomas was convicted of fraud and bribery schemes and sentenced to 42 months in federal prison.

the contract would be amended before that money could be made available, or a new contract procured. The concept of a "cost overrun" was not his issue, it was someone else's problem. This classic bureaucratic issue wherein one department focuses only on covering their own portion of an issue, and no one looks at the big picture, would pervade everything OEI encountered at LA Metro.

You might think the aforementioned CFO would be looking at the big picture and embracing the idea of innovation. You would be wrong. She was an agency veteran who had figured out how to play the game and solidify her support on the Board and within the agency through a combination of rewarding loyalty, punishing defectors, and coming through for board members. She had little interest in collaborating with a disrupter.

Not long after my arrival, the CFO unaffectionately branded OEI the "Office of Extreme Irritation." She explicitly forbade her staff from working with us. Unfortunately for OEI and the people of Los Angeles, her office not only controlled the agency budget but also happened to be responsible for fare collection, an issue that was ripe for innovation. I would have to figure a way around her.

The Chief Operations Officer (COO) Jim Gallagher was a tall, gruff man who had a face that seemed frozen in the "annoyed" position. He was a sharp, experienced transportation veteran who LA Metro CEO Phil Washington had hired. He was quick to anger and often seemed like he might be itching for a fight. He had an old-school militaristic perspective on public transit, with little patience for pontification. He was, in other words, the perfect person to run transit operations. Jim had little patience for my "academic" views on public transit and how to make it better, and we would clash frequently.

What we "eggheads"[12] in OEI did not understand is that Operations, like many other departments, did not effectively communicate with itself. So just because we had an agreement with someone in that department on a project, that did not mean it had been run up the chain of command. So, when Jim found out something was happening involving Operations that he didn't know about, he would routinely blow his stack.

---

[12] This was something Phil called us as a term of endearment. We think.

After one of our clashes, I reached out with an olive branch and apologized. I then offered to buy Jim a beer so we could talk. His response was, "I don't believe in that 'let's have a beer together' stuff. But I wouldn't be opposed to a Chablis if it came my way."[13]

Must-Win Battles

There is a theory in business management called "must-win battles" or MWB. These are "three to five key battles that your organization must win to achieve its key objectives."[xii] My first battles weren't so thoughtful. For example, I picked a battle with Human Resources (HR) about the hiring process. While hiring at Metro was indeed ripe for innovation, I (relatively) quickly learned that it wasn't a MWB for OEI, and that I could figure out how to get the outcomes I was looking for within the process that already existed.

The first two full projects OEI took on, however, did become MWBs. While the projects themselves—a podcast on Metro and a marketing partnership with Uber for the opening of the Expo Line—were not existential to transportation in the region, they became must-wins because they were the first two projects we chose to push forward. It was critical to demonstrate to our colleagues that we could see things through to the end and were not going to back down easily. We picked these, so we had to win them.

Hiring—or Fun with Bureaucracy

When I arrived at LA Metro, I had little experience with large bureaucratic public agencies. This was, in theory, a feature, not a bug. I had worked at a low level in public agencies earlier in my career, but I had been largely shielded from the challenges of bureaucracy, like hiring.

As a consultant in my post-Metro life, I now work with transit agencies nationwide. Without fail, when you ask transit agency personnel what challenges they face in their daily lives, they will almost always

---

[13]We did eventually have drinks together, and also became friends and effective colleagues, though those things were not necessarily related.

mention hiring. The hiring process at most public agencies is challenging in part due to legal regulations, civil service requirements, and fear of lawsuits. Their processes are focused on fairness and avoiding bias, and they usually try to do this by adding, but rarely subtracting, steps in the process. Whether this accomplishes the goal of removing bias is highly questionable. HR Departments will inevitably complain that they are understaffed, which is probably true given the cumbersome workload associated with any given hire.

The first step for OEI was to bring on staff for the new start-up office. Phil Washington publicly announced that OEI Staff would be drawn "from every corner of the world." He pushed me to come out to LA and start the new office quickly, and had my appointment approved by the Metro Board. I figured my first move would be to hire some of the top people in the field as quickly as possible—especially since I didn't have two years.

Naively, I assumed I would have the power to hire people I wanted. And I did, kind of. The CEO of LA Metro has the power to appoint people to a position without Board approval if their salary is under $200,000/ year. Phil told me I could hire three people to start. I decided to bring in a deputy with impressive transit agency experience in Denver, whom he had recommended, plus two of the smartest people I knew in transportation in Washington, DC. I asked Phil to appoint them.

Ironically, being the innovation office in this case led to a lack of innovation, or at least a lack of speed, which is critical for innovation. The announcement of the office, along with its "extraordinary" name, had unwittingly created a challenging dynamic. Employees at LA Metro knew that this office would be working on the most exciting initiatives at the agency and would wield unprecedented and even exceptional power. They immediately either wanted to be a part of it or hated it. This meant that any attempt to appoint three people from outside the agency was likely to stir up tension from the rank and file. Phil therefore made the suboptimal but wise decision to put these jobs out for competition rather than simply appointing the folks I wanted.

For those who have not worked in a public agency, you may not fully understand what it is like to hire someone there. First, the process is typically structured to favor existing employees. If you confine your search only to people currently employed by the agency, it will go much faster, by design, as HR is set up to accommodate this process, employees understand the intricacies of the process, and there are fewer restrictions.

Second, at LA Metro and many other public agencies, internal candidates interview for jobs all the time, even if they are not necessarily interested in that specific job or are unlikely to be selected. This is because of the Qualified Candidate Pool (QCP). All employees, current or prospective, must first get into a QCP by interviewing and "qualifying" for a job, even if they are not ultimately selected for that job. Employees within the agency are in a QCP for a given job level. As promotions are not technically permitted, getting into a QCP is the best way to move up within the agency. This means that any job announcement for a higher-level position will get a flood of internal candidates.

Meanwhile, HR is not set up to recruit external candidates. The byzantine platform HR used to accept applications was challenging for anyone to navigate, but easier for those who do it all the time. The way HR determines qualifications is largely based on internal classifications and nomenclature, so they struggle to effectively assess outside experience.

LA Metro and most public agencies also do little if any effective advertising of most of their available positions. The process is also incredibly slow, so if you do not have a job already or need to switch jobs quickly, and you are well qualified, you'll likely get offers from private organizations and take them before you get one from a public agency.

Third, HR in the public sector is far more focused on projecting fairness than on recruiting the best candidate for the job. One way to project fairness is to have specific salary ranges based on years of experience. For example, if you have "x" years of experience doing "y," you qualify for salary band "z." The problem with this structure is that the "y" is debatable (and sometimes so is the "x"). Does an unpaid internship count toward years of experience? A master's degree does. How about part-time experience? What counts as management? Does it matter how many people you were managing? What if your title was "manager" but you didn't manage any people or any projects? Also, do years of experience automatically guarantee capability? The subjectivity here meant that arguments over these decisions were inevitable.

Another way HR can project fairness is to have interview panels wherein people are required to act like robots. Instead of a normal job interview, where you might prepare some questions in advance but then proceed to have a conversation, for a Metro interview you must prepare all questions in advance and adhere to them rigidly. Some of those questions are predetermined by HR, and all must be approved by HR. Then you must alternate who on the panel reads each question. Follow-up questions are discouraged.

HR was far more concerned with having a paper trail and a policy to justify decisions than helping to make good decisions. And how can you blame them? If instead they were to focus on outcomes—say, getting the best candidate—they would stand to benefit very little and take on much more risk for themselves.

Finally, because HR is so concerned with avoiding being sued, they are also relatively unconcerned about speed. Again, their job is to make sure you follow the process, not to get the best outcome. Every document going through HR needs to be run up the chain of command for the whole department, and there are lots of documents and lots of people in the chain. Typically, the sign-off process requires actual wet signatures on an actual piece of paper. If someone is out of the office at any step, that will cause a delay. If someone has a question about the document, that could cause a delay. And then heaven forbid if you disagree with one of their decisions—about salary levels for example—you will need to appeal that process and, sometimes, start over.

As a bonus, in the name of fairness and diversity, every interview panel consists of three people meeting specific requirements. At least one person had to be a different gender than the other panelists, at least one person had to be from outside of your department, and at least one member of a recognized minority group had to be on the panel.

However, panelists also needed to be at a level within the agency that was as high or higher than the position being hired. This means that if you were interviewing for a top executive job, the pool of people who could conduct the interview was small, and the pool of minority and female executives was even smaller. This created substantial demand for all high-level minority and female executives to participate in interviews for jobs outside of their department, which takes several hours over multiple days. It also resulted in substantial challenges in scheduling interviews, as these in-demand people had only so many hours in the day.

My initial reaction, upon being confronted with this process, was to fight against the process itself every time HR did something ridiculous such as telling me that no, they could not get rid of the standard requirement that applicants must have a California driver's license.[14] Or telling me that we could not interview anyone for months because of scheduling. Or telling me that the person assigned to my hiring process hadn't responded to my proposed interview questions for weeks because they were overwhelmed. Or telling me sarcastically, as they eventually did, that they were working on a new hiring strategy called the "Joshua Schank method" wherein everything could be done differently.

Fortunately, I eventually pushed back on my instinct, knowing that if I spent my first few months trying to reform HR, I would likely not only fail but also would not wind up with the staff I needed to succeed. I knew this was a battle I couldn't win in the short term and decided to defer. And fixing this process wasn't my must-win battle, and only hiring the best staff was.

This was the right decision. Instead of appointing people to positions in my office, we followed the "competitive process" in the name of fairness. It was often frustrating and took more time than I wished it would. But somehow, despite this incredibly "fair" process, and checking all the boxes we needed to check, the people we hired in the end were the same ones I had wanted originally.

Podcasts—Shots Fired

Not long after I finally hired the beginnings of a team, we tried to get our first wins. Upon assuming my new job, I met a lot of people from the private sector. Most were trying to sell me something, but that was ok because I was open to new ideas, and I saw meeting with them as worth my time. But some folks wanted to meet because they were just excited about transit in Los Angeles and wanted to be a part of the coming revolution.

---

[14]To work at a public transit agency. Where most riders were riders largely because they did not have cars and could not drive.

One of those people was Neille Ilel. Neille was an Information Architect whose expertise was in revamping websites, with some media/communications experience. But she was also a proud transit nerd who wanted to be involved with LA Metro. When we met, she told me that she had developed podcasts, and we came up with an idea for a podcast series we could do for LA Metro.

Our thinking was simple—there was a tremendous amount of dialogue in the transit community about needing to build a culture of transit in Los Angeles. So, what if we could do a series that was entertaining, honest, and got people excited about riding public transit? The idea was to cover transportation in Los Angeles generally, telling stories that the average person might not know but might find interesting. We came up with a few on the spot—the story of the private Pink Line bus that used to run to the ocean, the story of the first female bus driver, and the obvious story of how LA transit lines became dismantled (also inaccurately portrayed in *Who Framed Roger Rabbit*).[15]

It was not an idea that would revolutionize transportation in Los Angeles. But we thought it might catch on and convince a few Angelenos to try public transit. It would be inexpensive and a decent piece of PR that wouldn't even look like PR. Most importantly, we thought it would be a quick and easy win.

"What's so extraordinary about a podcast?" said our Chief of Communications. This was followed by several other reasons for rejection from that department:

"Podcasts are not new. That's an old idea."

"We have our own podcast studio being built right now. We can just do this ourselves without outside help, when that is complete."

"We have a bench of communications professionals who can do this. Why do we need Neille?"

"We are developing our communications strategic plan. Can you wait until that is finished so we know where this fits in?"

---

[15] The conspiracy to destroy transit in LA is more urban myth than reality. The truth is that almost no one protested the loss of rail in Los Angeles, as highways and private cars were seen as the future and buses were a technology improvement over the rail lines at the time.

And the always classic response that we would find ourselves hearing constantly, "We don't have the resources to devote to this."

We tried numerous approaches. We were happy to let them take the lead on execution, while we would just advise. Or if they preferred, we could take the lead and run the product by them. We tried being passive. We tried being aggressive. We tried being passive-aggressive (kidding). Despite offering multiple forms of partnership, we couldn't find alignment.

The choice was simple: Was this a battle we wanted to fight, or not? Is a podcast worth it? Didn't we have bigger fish to fry? But this was our first shot out of the gate. If other departments knew that we would back down in the face of any resistance, we would inevitably face resistance every step of the way. In retrospect, it might be easy to say we picked the wrong first battle. We jumped on this idea because it seemed like an easy early win, without considering that it might be a fight, which means that we probably picked a fight we didn't need to. But once we picked it, we knew we had to win it.

It is helpful to think of this situation as analogous to how you might behave as a parent (and this whole concept comes from my closest friend, when I asked for advice on parenting). If you have too many rules, you will be fighting with your family all the time. If you do not have enough rules, your kids will run roughshod over your life. The right balance is to find the minimum number of rules (pick your battles) and then never, ever, let them get away with breaking them (win them). Because if they break the rule and get away with it once, they know that you can be vanquished and will always try to defy you.

The strategy used to achieve victory was another indication that we probably should have been more selective. We had to go to Phil and have him overrule the Chief Communications Officer. He also had to overrule procurement, as they did not want to do this as a sole source (more on that later). As I would soon learn, we could only go to our most powerful weapon (Phil) so many times to win our battles. While it might have been necessary no matter what we chose first, in hindsight, we could have been more selective.

That said, the podcast episodes (called *Off Peak*) were great.[xiii] Communications grudgingly took the lead in developing them with Neille, while we advised and offered suggestions. The stories were compelling, and the series was well produced. The series did just ok, though it obviously didn't start a revolution.

But that doesn't mean we hadn't accomplished something important. OEI had shown the agency that we could not be easily ignored or pushed away, and Phil showed that he had our back. And I had learned that next time I picked a fight, I would be careful to pick something that mattered more.

Procurement and Unsolicited Proposals

Lest you think that HR is the most bureaucratic component of a public agency, let me be the first to introduce you to Procurement.

A keen observer once noted that most people's job at a public agency is just managing consultants. This is true of many public agencies and has been noted in the literature as potentially being one reason everything they do costs so much.[xiv] Public agencies struggle to hire people and often lack the budget to do so. Hiring someone is a long-term commitment of costs, which include benefits, and is difficult to reverse. Hiring a consultant or otherwise outsourcing the work is much easier and, in many cases, makes more sense. For example, transit agencies must occasionally reorganize their bus networks. Having someone on staff to do this, when it only happens every 5 to 10 years (if that), would be extremely inefficient. When a transit agency is looking to do something innovative in which they have little expertise, and they might not do it forever, such as creating a new podcast, for example, it makes sense to outsource.

This incentive to go to the market for goods and services means that procurement is a huge part of what makes a transit agency work. But it also means that there is a huge amount of money being spent on consultants, especially at agencies with large, complex budgets due to a variety of funding sources, including sales tax measures, and therefore plenty of scrutiny surrounding who gets that money and for what purpose.

Procurement, like HR, has adopted numerous rules and policies over the years intended to engender fairness and a competitive process and prevent cronyism, nepotism, and all the other -isms. This idea is based on good intentions. A fair and competitive process will theoretically ensure not only the best options possible for the agency but also that anyone can be eligible to get access to the funds in the public coffers (in exchange for goods and services, of course). In theory this is a good idea. In reality, it creates a procurement process that is exceedingly slow, often uncompetitive, and far too focused on price.

The process is slow because to ensure fairness, public agencies add extensive steps and requirements. For example, at Metro all purchases over $100,000 must be made available for competition even if you know which vendor you want to use or if there is only one vendor available. Even something less than $100,000 (and over $2,500), if sole sourced, must be justified and authorized by the CEO. Procurements must be posted long enough to provide sufficient time for everyone to respond, and they always include a requirement for small businesses, disadvantaged businesses, and minority businesses. Posting a procurement requires not just writing a scope but then painstaking and time-consuming work using antiquated procurement software. Despite this software, most of the procurement process is performed on paper with wet signatures and snail mail deliveries.

Exhausted yet? We are not done. Once a procurement is posted, no conversations about it are allowed outside of the organization except through official procurement channels, known as the blackout period. This makes adjustments to the procurement based on market feedback impossible during this time and can result in a procurement with no responses. Furthermore, the procurement office is also walled off from the rest of the agency. No one can enter without an escort, hindering communication and delaying progress.

Then we review the submissions. All procurements must have review panels that include a diversity of gender, race, and departments. All reviewers must read and rate all submitted proposals, which can be voluminous and numerous, and then conduct interviews. When reviewers select a winner, it must then be approved by the department's chief, which also takes time. Then the recommendation for the award must be approved by either CEO, if the amount is under $500,000, and the Board of Directors, if the amount is higher (assuming Board Staff permits it to move forward). The Board meets once per month but skips two months every year, which can cause delays. The Board may choose to reject or postpone a procurement for numerous reasons, but most often because they are disappointed with the small or minority business threshold, there were insufficient bidders, or they just don't like that the firm they wanted wasn't selected. If the Board does not accept the staff recommendation for the award, they can reject the procurement, and the entire process begins again.

Oh, and at any point in this process, even after it is complete, procurement or anyone else can raise an ethics concern about the award, which results in an internal ethics roundtable to determine if the procurement can proceed. After the procurement is awarded, private companies that feel they were not given a fair shake in the process can protest the procurement, resulting in an adjudication process. If there is a finding that the procurement was unfair, it must be restarted.

Procurement (the department) lives in fear of a protest. As a result, they do everything possible to avoid one, which means practicing an (over)abundance of caution. For example, on one of our procurements, one of the proposers submitted their proposal five minutes after the deadline, and it was rejected. If procurement had accepted their proposal, any of the other proposers might have filed a protest. But rejecting the proposal, of course, reduced competition and the potential for innovation for the project. Another time, the ethics officer determined after the award that even though there was no ethical violation, there could be a perception of one, and thus the entire procurement was discarded and restarted. This potential perception was regarding a subcontract worth $50,000 on a multimillion-dollar contract.

It was in this context, and without full understanding of this situation, that OEI undertook an unsolicited proposals (UPs) program. The UP process—a way for the private sector to submit ideas directly to Metro—was something Phil had used effectively at RTD in Denver for capital projects. But with an office in place to evaluate ideas coming in as UPs, LA Metro could potentially get any private-sector idea through this process, not just those for capital projects. During an era when new technologies were taking over or at least playing at taking over transportation (think Uber, autonomous vehicles, and navigation apps), opening the door to new ideas was critical for an office focused on innovation.

The process we designed was simple. The private sector would submit ideas, and OEI would assemble review teams to analyze them. The review teams would include people from the relevant departments that would be part of any implementation. If the review team liked the idea, they could ask for a second, more detailed proposal. Then if that one was approved, the idea could move forward.

What we were doing was effectively turning the procurement process on its head. Typically, procurements would be initiated by LA metro staff, meaning that staff recognized the need for a product or service, and then developed a scope that detailed what kind of product or service this would be, and engaged in a competitive process that would drag out as described above. These solicitations often left the private sector guessing what Metro wanted. What we were proposing was instead letting the private sector suggest the ideas.

Procurement was not amused. They argued that this process would break several federal laws. We could not show preference and award a contract to a private-sector company just because they had an idea we liked. And of course, procurement did not want to be circumvented.

In moving this UP policy forward, which would become a signature and core function of OEI, we wisely decided not to pick a battle. Instead of fighting procurement, we teamed up with them. We found they were receptive to working together on designing a policy that could accommodate new ideas and facilitate conversations with the private sector without blowing up the existing process. While this meant that things wouldn't move as fast as we had hoped, it also meant that procurement was now invested in this process. They became an ally instead of an enemy.

In another instance of battle avoidance, the attorneys for LA Metro advised Phil that for the UP policy to take effect, it would need to be approved by the Board of Directors. Phil wisely ignored their legal advice (as he would numerous times). He knew that if we presented this to the Board, they would pick at it and change it and maybe even resist it. Instead, Phil decided to just approve the policy himself and post it on our website. The Board never objected.

We still had to get the word out about this new policy. Phil decided we would present it to the world at an industry forum (snarkily termed a "coming out" party for OEI by other departments). Metro invited businesses from around the world—"the usual and unusual suspects," as Phil liked to say—to hear what we were trying to do and how they could play a role. It represented a sea change in how Metro had historically worked with the private sector and included speeches by top elected officials, including the Mayor of Los Angeles and the Chair of the Transportation Committee in the California State Senate.

The industry forum was a big success. People will rarely turn down a free lunch, but they are especially amenable to it when a huge agency like LA Metro with lots of existing and anticipated resources is also offering them an opportunity to peek inside and understand how they can win work in the future. This is exactly what the forum did, as we released and discussed the UP policy, and had each LA Metro Department Head speak about the issues they had coming up and kinds of ideas that might be useful to them. It was a groundbreaking, extraordinary, and innovative event.[xv]

Uber-Expo

Podcasts were a good start, but we picked our first substantial battle based on an early UP from Uber. This proposal was not from the Uber we know and love today. This was the OG Uber—the ruthless, sexist, move fast and break things Uber. In 2016, Uber was riding high as a darling of venture capital investors and seemed poised to take over the world. They were promoting an autonomous future where everyone would use Uber for everything, they were doing things like reinventing the bus, and they were still largely ignoring or flouting regulations.[xvi]

Meanwhile, their main competitor, Lyft, was trying to market itself as a kinder, gentler Uber. Lyft was talking up partnerships with cities and transit agencies, and in some cases maybe even executing on those partnerships. Uber took note and proposed providing discounted Uber-POOL (shared) rides to and from newly opened stations on our Expo Line, for two weeks, as a promotion.

Our team thought this was a great opportunity to begin to explore how to effectively collaborate with the new on-demand transportation services, and to test whether the provision of first and last mile services would help incentivize new riders or make current riders happier. However, we quickly learned that the rest of Metro did not see the opportunity that we saw. In fact, the rest of the agency fought back as hard as they could.

To put this in context, at the time there was an underlying fear that services like Uber could put transit agencies out of business. And, indeed, research eventually did show that the advent of services like Uber correlated with the decline of public transit ridership.[xvii] Uber was also providing heavily subsidized rides and leveraging investors to keep their new services in hypergrowth mode indefinitely. This meant that they could capture a growing market share without having to make a profit or even cover costs—they were losing billions every year. Transit agencies and cities, who had largely been blindsided by Uber, were not exactly eager to roll out the red carpet.

Moreover, the approach that Lyft and, especially, Uber took politically to navigate local regulations was even more toxic. The taxicab industry was being decimated, and political power was their only way to stay alive.[xviii] In some cities the taxi industry successfully fought Uber off, not through competition, but via regulatory changes favorable to taxicabs—primarily at the local level which had long regulated the cab industry. But California was both the first and arguably the most critical market for the ridehail companies. Relatively early in their existence, their leaders realized that they would be better positioned to introduce regulations at the state level, preempting cab-regulating cities and making it much easier for Lyft and Uber to scale.

Uber wasn't navigating politics so much as bulldozing through it. As political strategist Bradley Tusk later detailed in *The Fixer*, the goal wasn't to ask permission—it was to create so much public momentum that regulation had to scramble to catch up.[ix]

Indeed, the California Public Utilities Commission (CPUC) agreed to regulate ridehail companies, making it impossible for local governments like Los Angeles to stop Uber. Nonetheless, some elected officials had the back of the taxicab industry. Ridehail opponents often had union support, as they were broadly opposed to this new, rapidly growing industry of nonunionized and unusually (and often poorly) compensated drivers who mostly drove their own cars and were paid by the trip and not by the hour. Further, the unions had strong influence over LA Metro Board members, which increased the Board's hostility toward Uber. While Uber was street legal, local political sentiment was not in their favor.

Despite these obstacles, and perhaps unaware of some of them, I decided that OEI should pick this battle for the following reasons:

1. It was obvious that the on-demand technology developed by Uber was providing a higher level of customer experience than anything transit or traditional taxicabs had to offer and wasn't going anywhere. Trying to compete directly with this burgeoning new service seemed insane, but working together could be mutually beneficial and might even bring in new transit customers.

2. We needed a win to show how UPs and OEI could work, and this one did not require any funding, would be promoting a huge milestone (connecting rail to Santa Monica) for LA Metro, and would open the door to more private-sector partnerships.

3. It seemed winnable. In fact, it seemed easy. Oops.

The opposition came from all directions—even though this partnership was only a marketing partnership. For two weeks, Metro would help facilitate the pickup and drop-off of riders at Metro's existing Culver City station and new Expo Line stations opening in West LA and Santa Monica with wayfinding materials. This included promoting the UberPOOL option for Metro customers through traditional and digital media channels, as well as via promotional signs at each station. In exchange, Uber would provide ride discounts of $15 for new riders and $5 for all other riders on UberPOOL trips that began or ended at Metro's new Expo stations and the existing Culver City station; in addition, they would promote newly available Metro Expo Line services to UberPOOL customers through the Uber app.[xx]

One of the things we hadn't realized upon taking this on was that an idea like this would involve multiple Metro Departments and cities, each with a different reason to say no:

Legal—This partnership is too risky for us (because we have never done anything like it). What will happen when someone gets in an accident—who will be liable? Are we liable for where passengers are dropped off? We will be sued.

Procurement—This is a sole-source procurement that will engender a protest. It also violates the American Disabilities Act (ADA) and it could cause us to lose all federal funding.

Public Relations—Expo is the biggest new rail line opening we have ever had, and you are ruining it! We've been planning this rollout for months; it is going to be a spectacle, and we planned this meticulously and never anticipated anything like this so just forget it. Stay away from promotions!

Marketing—Why would we help the competition? Also, we have an existing advertising contract and all of it is spoken for so you cannot have any space to advertise this partnership.

Civil Rights—Uber is not accessible for people in wheelchairs and if you do not offer a parallel service for disabled customers, you are the equivalent of a racist.[16] Plus, we will be sued.

Operations—Go away (I am paraphrasing here). We have buses to take people to and from the stations and those are operated by unions who will be pissed off. Plus, where will people be dropped off? And we'd have to lock up any signs every night and have no space to do that. Do not even try this.

Safety—Do not advertise this initiative at stations because the signs could cause an obstruction for passengers. If we see this being advertised at a station, we will remove it.

City of Santa Monica—You are legally prohibited from advertising this initiative on city property. If we see any notices about this initiative, the police will remove them.

All of this despite a motion from Metro's Board of Directors instructing metro staff to pursue a partnership of this type for technology to improve customer service and integrate modes![xxi]

---

[16]The head of civil rights often made the very valid point that providing a service for people that did not accommodate those with disabilities was the equivalent of providing inferior, segregated services a la Jim Crow. He therefore felt justified in saying skirting ADA regulations was the same as being racist. In this case, it was a marketing partnership with a company that was flaunting ADA regulations by failing to provide adequate numbers of ADA compliant vehicles.

Then there was Uber, a private company that had no idea how to deal with the public sector. In negotiations, they told us that everything in the agreement had to be confidential and this was nonnegotiable. We patiently explained to them that, as a public agency, this wasn't theoretically, legally, or practically possible.

Fortunately, one of the people I had hired to work in OEI, Colin Peppard, was a DC veteran who knew how to *Politic*. He was given responsibility for executing this UP and overcoming each of these obstacles. Not to mention negotiating the actual contract with Uber, which was no picnic either. One of the key issues for him was differentiating between people making a lot of noise, and people who could stop the partnership from going into effect or cause it to fail.

For example, people raising concerns were just that. Legal and Civil Rights could yell and scream and throw a tantrum, but unless Phil agreed with them, their power was merely advisory. We didn't know how Phil would ultimately decide, but if we tried within reason to accommodate their concerns, we felt comfortable that the program would move forward.

And the people at Uber lived up to their reputation by being difficult and arrogant. But coming from DC, Colin was used to people being difficult and arrogant. He eventually got them to realize that if they wanted to work with public agencies at all, they were going to have to give a little. They signed the deal.

But promotion was key. If we couldn't promote this thing, it would go nowhere. The promotion was the only thing we were offering to Uber. We were not offering any funds, just in-kind advertising of the partnership itself. Uber wouldn't partner with us without advertising.

Fortunately, Colin had already built strong relationships with many of the key players. Perhaps since he was formerly staff to a U.S. Senator, he quickly, and perhaps naturally, cultivated relationships with Board Staff. While the Board Staff could be difficult in Board Staff Briefings, in private they could be helpful, especially when they knew their bosses would want something to happen. They were also younger and free from many of the preconceived notions of how transit had to be operated, and less likely to despise OEI (yet). So, when Colin and I called and asked for help, they were happy to oblige. They helped us work with the cities and negotiate through the challenges there. They also helped us calm down some of the internal folks.

But operations still refused to help or provide any resources to make this work. Colin persisted and literally drove around Los Angeles putting up signs about the partnership, like he was promoting a bake sale. He also had to move and/or replace signs when security removed them.

The *coup de grace* was when Phil had to literally sign off on several theoretical legal and procurement risks to allow it to move forward. Phil consistently told us, "Legal is here to advise. They do not make the decisions." He would often add his signature instruction, "Just keep a brother out of jail."

Legal presented Phil with a list of risks that he would be taking if he moved forward with this initiative. He signed his name acknowledging all the risks, allowing legal to say they did their job. After much back and forth, we signed the contract with Uber.

While there was a price to pay, if we hadn't pushed forward, this project would not have come to fruition, and we would likely never have moved on to bigger and better things (including more evolved on-demand transit applications discussed later). The experience showed (most of) the rest of the organization that the UP process was here to stay, and they needed to play ball. We went out and celebrated. OEI had arrived!

How did the project turn out? Not bad! People used the UberPOOL rides and enjoyed the discount. Did it change the world forever? No. But it broke the seal and, in many ways, allowed everything we did later to happen. It was a tough battle, and it bruised us, but it was one worth picking, and we made sure to win it.

Picking Your Battles and Winning Them

OEI's launch was more turbulent than I would have imagined. Coming from the world of DC politics, we thought the hardest fights would be external—navigating politics, regulations, or public perception. But the real resistance was from inside the organization itself. From the moment we arrived, we encountered internal opposition—not necessarily because people were against innovation, but because we were perceived as disrupting the delicate equilibrium of a massive bureaucracy.

At first, we didn't even realize that we were picking battles. We thought we were just doing our job. We wanted to hire fast and keep moving. What I didn't fully appreciate was that in a civil service environment, these seemingly simple decisions had a lot of political and institutional meaning.

This early hiring misstep was instructive and taught us that not every battle is worth picking, even if you're technically right. We tried to back off and recalibrate to learn how to work within the system without surrendering our goals. This eventually worked, but it happened slowly and didn't happen without a few battle scars.

Other fights—over podcasts and the Uber-Expo pilot—weren't chosen per se but rather stumbled into. But once we were in them, we realized that we couldn't afford to lose. So, we tried to win them the only way that we knew how to at the time, through brute force. While we did win, we paid the price in trust and relationships.

These early lessons were important and helped us to evolve. Colin Peppard started to demonstrate how to get things done not by just fighting harder, but by also building alliances. He played the long game, built credibility, and slowly earned buy-in. We learned that winning in a public agency isn't just about being right, it's about knowing when to fight, when to wait, and who to work with when you do.

CHAPTER 2

You Need to Make Friends to Fix Processes

"Bob says it's a bad idea."

That was Chief Operations Officer Jim Gallagher's response when I suggested that we consider using drones to inspect our rail lines. We had gotten this idea from an unsolicited proposal (UP), and it seemed worth exploring. Humans walking the length of the tracks of the longest single seat light-rail line in the United States looking for flaws seemed inefficient and risky compared to using a drone with sophisticated detection technology that doesn't get tired or bored. Why not check it out?

I didn't know who Bob was, why his opinion mattered, or what the basis was for this opinion. And I would never find out because at this point, Jim had already made his decision and had no desire or incentive to explain to me why it had been made. Jim was being asked about a solution to a problem that no one had asked him about. He and I were not (yet) friends, so a curt explanation without further exploration was just fine with him. Bob got the last word, whether he knew it or not.

The UP process generated some great ideas, but often those ideas would wind up leading us to find many other processes that were broken within the organization. Through the UP process, we learned key lessons that helped us better understand the organization and how to use processes as a tool to drive innovation:

1. Processes are the problem.
2. Technology alone does not fix processes.
3. You need to make friends to fix processes.

Processes are the Problem

When considering challenges in large organizations, it is easy to assume that budgetary constraints or a lack of prioritization are the primary problems leading to suboptimal outcomes. For example, when I first began riding the Metro, I was continually annoyed by the countdown clocks at my station that indicated when the next train would arrive. At the time, there was no cell service in Metro subway stations (a problem that was already being fixed), so I couldn't look up real-time information on my phone. The only way to know when the next train might arrive was by looking at the countdown clocks.[17] The technology used to predict train arrival was basic, unreliable, and based on what might have been cutting-edge technology when the subway was built in the 1990s. Based on evidence[xxii] that customers highly value knowing when to expect their next train, I thought upgrading the technology should be a priority.

The lack of prioritization turned out not to be the issue. The technology in use was a hardware-based loop system, and upgrading would be significantly more challenging than simply allocating funds. It would require multiple departments (Information Technology, Operations, Communications, and Procurement at a minimum), with varying priorities and areas of expertise, to coalesce around a technology solution. Then there would have to be someone in one of those departments to lead the procurement for the upgrade, find the resources to pay for it, get time on the tracks during the limited hours of nonoperation to install it, and make sure the contractor delivered effectively.

In other words, someone with the capacity and directive from their boss would have to use *existing* processes by which upgrades to the technology could be made, which were ineffective, or else create a new process, which would take time. Both of those options are a lot to ask of anyone, and a nearly impossible task, which is probably why no one had taken it on. We would soon learn that creating real change meant that we would have to be the ones who fixed the process—or suffer the consequences of using the existing ones.

---

[17]These countdown clocks are on old, boxy TV screens from the 1990s. They often fail, but even when working they flash lots of unneeded information in between showing train arrival times.

Technology Alone Does Not Fix Processes

When our office was created there was the perception that we would have a substantial emphasis on technology. This was not due to anything Phil or I said about the office. In fact, Phil's first communication to Metro about his idea for the office mentioned technology only in passing and instead focused on bringing in new ideas, partnering with the private sector and academia, and strategic planning. Whenever I spoke about the office publicly, I would emphasize that technology was a tool, a means to an end, not the goal.

Nonetheless, whether it was the zeitgeist or the word "innovation," we were largely seen as a vehicle for harnessing new technology. Around the same time I was hired the City of Los Angeles hired a Chief Technology Officer who was seen as my counterpart at the City. The City had also hired a Transportation Technology Strategist fellow. San Francisco's transportation agency had also just recently hired a Chief Innovation Officer with—unsurprisingly—a strong emphasis on tech.

Meanwhile, technology was a constant discussion in transportation. Autonomous vehicles were all the rage, and people thought (and many still think) they would change everything. The smartphone was just becoming ubiquitous, and there were new apps for everything including transportation navigation, mapping, and vehicle arrival information. It was impossible for people to think of innovation in transportation and not think of technology.

And there were also excellent opportunities for technology to improve outcomes for LA Metro and its customers. Public agencies are notoriously slow to adopt new technology and often have outdated systems due to slow procurement processes and resistance to change. But as Jessica Grose argues in *Why Nothing Works*, simply upgrading the tech won't save us.[xxiii] The problem runs deeper: When systems are broken or nonexistent, layering on better technology only masks dysfunction. If we didn't fix the process, the tools wouldn't matter.

You Need to Make Friends to Fix Processes

If you ask most people in an organization whether they support innovation, you'll get enthusiastic agreement—especially in a public agency where outdated processes are everywhere. At Metro, we encountered things like procurement documents stored behind locked doors accessible only with an escort, mandatory desktop computers for staff, and multiple call centers for handling similar issues for different programs.

But if you walk into a room and say, "Hey this process is broken, let's fix it!" You're likely to get nowhere. Why?

1. **Pride of ownership.** The person you're talking to may have created the process, and it probably replaced an even more outdated process. Criticizing it feels personal.
2. **Implicit criticism of their performance.** Often, the person you're talking to would feel that fixing a process is their job and they are the expert—and you're an outsider. They just haven't had the time to because they have been understaffed and under budgeted for decades so how can you expect them to fix this process?
3. **They don't trust you.** If you are new to the agency, they likely don't trust you. They may feel that you're trying to make them look bad.

There is a famous joke among psychologists (as mentioned earlier, I am the child of two of them) that encapsulates this issue well.

Q: How many psychologists does it take to change a lightbulb?
A: Just one. But the light bulb must want to change.

This same concept applies to bureaucracies. Even with CEO backing and great ideas, nothing moves unless people responsible for implementation want it to move.

That's where relationships come in. Scholars call this "relational bureaucracy"—the idea that trust and informal connections are critical to getting things done in government.[xxiv] Real change happens through relationships. And relationships happen between people who actually like each other—or at least respect one another.

Fortunately, the person we assigned to work on UPs was Nolan Borgman. He'd been in the CEO's office before joining OEI, so he already had a network of contacts across the agency. But more importantly, Nolan was likable. He could talk to anyone. And he built trust fast. He was the perfect person to get new ideas going.

We sometimes played good cop/bad cop. Nolan would introduce an idea and gently disarm resistance, getting us in the door. I'd follow up and push harder for action. Afterward he'd smooth things over. People might not have agreed with everything we did—but they knew they had someone on their side, and someone who also wouldn't take no without a good reason.

And no, Nolan didn't make friends with all 12,000 Metro employees. He didn't have to. He built trust with the ones that mattered for the work at hand, and that was enough.

Making friends doesn't mean becoming best friends. It means building mutual respect, understanding people's constraints, and showing them that you're not there to make them look bad, you're there to help make things better.

MobileQubes

We ran into a process problem when we received a UP from Mobile-Qubes, a company that offered a simple product—a vending machine that sold a battery to charge phones. You pay to rent the battery, charge your phone, and then return the battery to the machine. If you fail to return the battery, you are charged a lot of money, so there is a strong incentive to return it.

When this proposal came in we thought it had merit because (1) Metro has very long train and bus lines where people could easily see their phones run out of power, (2) Metro patrons often seek out electrical outlets in stations to charge their phones, creating a potential tripping hazard for which Metro is liable, and (3) there were virtually no amenities offered in Metro stations and we thought providing customers with useful services could be a way to improve the customer experience.

This proposal also had another incentive—MobileQubes was not interested in money from Metro itself. They wanted to simply use the space in our stations to sell their product and hoped to make money from customers. So, this was a no-cost proposal to provide a benefit to customers with the potential to improve safety. It seemed like a win-win-win, and something we should have been able to do quickly.

Um, no. This project involved the following departments (and more), all of which had reason to say no to this project:

- **Security**—No because anything going into a station can be considered a security challenge.
- **Real Estate**—No because why should we give the space to them when we haven't made it available to anyone else.
- **Facilities Maintenance**—No because who is going to maintain these machines? We have no money.
- **Electrical Engineering**—No because we cannot supply power to these machines.
- **Architectural Support**—No because there is nowhere to put these machines that works in our stations.
- Also involved were Metro Art, Systemwide Design, Traction Power, and of course the usual Legal, Procurement, Risk Management and Operations.

There was no process for putting in new station amenities. Even if there was agreement that station amenities could provide value to our customers (there was not), the path to installing these things was arduous, cumbersome, and not for the faint of heart. It took Nolan Borgman two years to coordinate across departments to get these machines into three stations. He convinced security that it would be safe. He convinced Real Estate to do a lease which does not require competition. He convinced Facilities Maintenance that MobileQubes would do their own maintenance. He helped Electrical Engineering find a way to supply power safely. He found old spaces where pay phones used to be to satisfy Architectural Support. Due to his overwhelming persistence, and relationships, we were successful in this project.

And yet, in the end, MobileQubes did still not work out. The machines were popular, but also regularly vandalized. Once the pandemic hit, there were insufficient riders to support their existence. But its lack of success isn't as relevant as what we learned. We found that even when there should be obvious alignment, even seemingly easy ideas were incredibly difficult and time-consuming to test.

Understanding that this limitation would be continually problematic for OEI and other change agents, we pushed Metro to create such a process. We introduced a "test station" where new ideas could be tried out through an abbreviated process that involved preapproval for many of the key obstacles. We realized our mistake was focusing on the outcome (MobileQubes) instead of the process needed to enable new amenities in stations. The process was the problem.

Orange Line Timing

The LA Metro Orange Line (now known as the G line) is a beautiful thing. It is one of the most successful examples of Bus Rapid Transit (BRT) in the United States.[xxv] BRT is a form of urban transit famously pioneered in Curitiba, Brazil by an ambitious mayor with an urban planning background.[xxvi] The idea is to avoid some of the high construction costs and inflexibility of rail transit by running buses on exclusive rights-of-way. While rail has higher passenger capacity, faster speed, and lower operating costs, BRT has much lower capital costs, can be built in less time, and can be easily integrated with an existing bus network.[xxvii] The Orange Line was built using an old Metro-owned rail right-of-way (ROW)[18] and served as a substitute for extending the Red Line (now B Line) through the San Fernando Valley entirely within the City of LA.[xxviii] Prepandemic, the Orange Line was often packed during peak times and ran articulated (extra-long) buses at frequencies of three minutes or less.

The problem with the Orange Line is that it operates on an at-grade ROW (neither below nor above the street), which is a big reason why it costs so much less than rail. Operating at street level means dealing with cars, pedestrians, bicyclists, and anything else that happens to wander onto the BRT ROW. When the Orange Line first opened, there was a spate of crashes with other vehicles as drivers adjusted to the new line.

---

[18]The Proposition A Rail Amendment of 1980 stated that there should be an emphasis put on using existing ROW for new transit lines. In response, after Proposition C passed in 1990, in addition to State Rail Bond Measures 111, 116, and 118, LACTC procured existing rail ROW, including the ROW used for the Orange Line.

While these eventually abated, speed restrictions[xxix] were imposed on the buses, and plans were developed to put gates on vehicle crossings and eventually even convert the Orange Line to light-rail.

But those projects would take time and were far away. In the meantime, while safety had improved, the Orange Line still had to stop at stoplights. The stoplights, which were operated and coordinated by the Los Angeles Department of Transportation (LADOT),[19] were supposed to be timed so that a Metro bus operator driving the correct predetermined speed would never hit a red light. Unfortunately, in practice, this was not happening, and buses stopped at red lights all the time.

Enter Gary Spivack. Gary was a longtime LA Metro Operations guy who was obsessed with public transit in Los Angeles and saw himself as a dedicated public servant who wanted to make transit work better. For many years, Gary had an idea on how to make the Orange Line work better. If he could rig a system whereby operators could know, in real time, the correct speed to drive, then they could hit all the green lights. The idea had gone through various iterations based on the available technology at the time, but now the easiest way to do this was likely to slap an iPad onto the dash with the information the drivers would need.

Gary had proposed his idea within the Operations Department, but it had never gone anywhere. When OEI came along, Gary saw an opportunity. Despite being an employee of LA Metro, he submitted a UP to us regarding this idea. And we loved it. Nolan immediately began working with Gary on translating this idea into reality. Technically, it was not that complicated. The data needed to inform the bus operator was easily accessible, iPads were relatively cheap, and because Gary was in Operations, he knew exactly whom to talk to initiate a pilot project.

The process to get the pilot project off the ground, on the other hand, was exceedingly complicated. Largely because Nolan had to work with LADOT. The City of Los Angeles has a bureaucracy that makes LA Metro look like a nimble tech start-up. Virtually all positions at LADOT must be filled by members of the civil service, which means that hiring and firing are exceedingly challenging, resulting in very long tenures. Making change within LADOT is far more challenging than at LA Metro.

---

[19]Serving the City of Los Angeles, not the county.

When I first arrived at LA Metro, I was invited over to LADOT to visit its traffic control center—the Automated Traffic Surveillance and Control system known as "ATSAC". Those giving the tour were very proud of their system, which was in the basement of a government building. It includes hardwires at every intersection in the city to transmit information and help optimize traffic flow. What I didn't realize until later was that the system (1) had been designed for the 1984 Olympics[xxx] by the very same people giving me the tour in 2016, and (2) didn't, technically, work. The team that designed it had largely resisted upgrades from their original system and liked it just the way it was, thank you very much. Hard-wired systems were cutting-edge in 1984 but outdated in 2016. No one had been successful in moving them from that position.

Nolan and Gary had to coordinate with LADOT to make their idea work, but LADOT had little incentive to work with LA Metro. Their responsibility was moving vehicles. They were not particularly interested in whether buses had to stop at intersections, or had a smoother ride for customers, or reduced fuel consumption, or improved travel times, all of which this idea could potentially accomplish.[20]

There was no clear process or set of incentives for how LA Metro and LADOT would work together on this issue. Nolan and Gary, nonetheless, persisted. They built trust with LADOT to the point where they could do a test run at a few intersections and understand what the data was telling them. They coordinated among the various LA Metro Departments. They even procured an engineering contractor to expedite the implementation. Finally, the tests were performed.

Unfortunately, what the tests revealed was likely what LADOT feared. The intersections were not actually timed for the buses to drive at the right speed and hit every green light. LADOT had been telling LA Metro that they were, and perhaps at one point they had been set effectively. But the testing revealed that this idea was based on a false premise.

The fundamental problem here was not the technology. The problem was that two agencies, LADOT and LA Metro, were not working

---

[20]In a 2016 fact sheet titled "Los Angeles Signal Synchronization" LADOT stated that the city does not provide full preemption, because it "already prioritizes transit and full preemption would have severe negative impacts on vehicular, bicycle, and pedestrian traffic."

together effectively and there was no effective oversight process to ensure that they would or could. Cutting-edge technology could not fix the governance model that was not designed to serve customers but was instead designed to serve bureaucrats within the government. As of press time for this book, this problem still has not been solved.

Bus Lanes in Los Angeles

Los Angeles is a very American city in many respects, but perhaps the most striking is the income inequality. Like New York, the city has vast wealth on display. However, unlike in New York City, where many wealthy people find themselves interacting with the masses on a daily basis, the rich in LA can cloister themselves in posh neighborhoods that they can get to and from in their fancy cars, and use valet parking at upscale restaurants, and never have to confront anyone outside their bubble. This results in gorgeous mansions on hillsides, and a few miles away, countless homeless people on Skid Row. That is LA.

Bus lanes are the forefront of the clash between rich and poor. Buses in Los Angeles carry mostly low-income people,[21] but sometimes those buses traverse more expensive areas of the city, or at least areas where almost everyone has a car. If LA Metro and a partnering city want to add a bus lane, they must face down wealthy neighbors who have zero interest in giving away a lane, or parking, on their congested street. The fight over street space is the biggest barrier between Los Angeles and better public transportation. When buses do not have exclusive lanes in congested areas, by definition they will be much slower than cars in terms of door-to-door travel times. This is because bus riders must access the bus stop, wait for the bus, sit in traffic, stop at interim bus stops, and then travel from their exit stop to their destination.

LA Metro fought for many years to get a bus lane on Wilshire Boulevard, the densest corridor in the United States with transit demand so high that a subway is being finished underneath it as you read this book.[xxxi] After many years of effort, in 2015 Metro secured a bus lane for

---

[21] In June 2016, Metro conducted a survey of bus riders and found that the median annual household income of respondents was $15,620.

the 720—the rapid express bus on Wilshire—for most of the boulevard. Not surprisingly, one of the places where they could not secure the lane was on the part that goes through Beverly Hills.[xxxii] But still, it was a monumental achievement.

However, there was one major problem—there was no enforcement mechanism to keep other vehicles out of the bus lanes. Drivers largely ignored the bus lane designation and there were no consequences for driving in them, parking in them, or otherwise obstructing buses. This meant that the whole idea of the bus lanes—enabling buses to move faster than other traffic—was literally being obstructed by drivers.

OEI was exploring ways in which to introduce an enforcement mechanism, but the problem seemed intractable. The City of Los Angeles, and the Los Angeles Police Department (LAPD), were the only ones authorized to issue tickets for bus lane violations. They had zero interest in doing so, likely believing there were far greater priorities for city policing. They probably could have been convinced to put some resources toward this issue had LA Metro been willing to fund the effort. But that was not a financially sustainable solution due to enormous cost and manpower required to police bus routes. Moreover, with many new bus lanes planned for Los Angeles, we needed to find something that could work at scale.

Enter CarmaCam. In an age when everyone was designing a new app, some folks at the University of Southern California (USC) created an intriguing yet vengeful idea. They created an app that, when your phone was mounted on the dashboard, would record other drivers automatically on video when they did something stupid or dangerous. You could then upload the video to a site where people could comment on it and shame those captured into driving better next time.

This was a ridiculous idea, but we saw possibility. Why not use this to catch cars parked in bus lanes? If the app was able to recognize an event worth shaming, perhaps it could recognize cars that were blocking a bus lane.

We asked CarmaCam to go back to the drawing board and figure out if they could do what we wanted. They were very excited to get a response and set right to work on it, but we soon discovered another problem. The entire idea was prohibited by law. Yes, Automated Bus Lane Enforcement (ABLE) was illegal in the State of California.

As mentioned earlier, one of Phil's favorite sayings, especially when talking to County Counsel or the Inspector General, was "Just keep a brother out of jail." I always interpreted this meant that we should do whatever is necessary to achieve our mission, including bending the rules sometimes, but don't do anything that might constitute a crime. This is a very different message than "always obey the law" or "don't do anything illegal." It is also a very different perspective from "the law is always right." So, when we heard that ticketing bus lane violators with automatic cameras was against the law, our first thought was that the law was wrong and needed to be changed.

The 25th Floor

Unfortunately, this view was not necessarily shared by everyone at LA Metro, including the team known as Government Relations (GR). At that time, Government Relations was within the Communications Department but held a perch on the 25th floor. The 25th floor of 1 Gateway Plaza, also known as the Taj Mahal[22] due to its lavish design, was the penthouse of Metro headquarters.[23]

1 Gateway Plaza is a skyscraper next to Union Station, the busiest rail station west of the Mississippi,[xxxiii] near downtown Los Angeles but not actually in it. It sticks out among the low-rise and low-rent areas nearby, and the closest other tall buildings are the twin towers of the notorious County Jail (Figure 2.1).

This means that from the 25th floor, you can see sweeping views of Los Angeles including the mountains, the LA River, the Hollywood sign, Dodger Stadium, and on clear days, Long Beach and the Pacific Ocean.

---

[22]The LA Metro headquarters building was famously nicknamed the "Taj Mahal" by the agency's first CEO, Franklin E. White, during 1994 controversies over escalating costs of the Union Station Gateway project. The comment, made amid tensions with the Board over whether Metro even needed a new headquarters, was picked up widely by the press and became a shorthand for government excess. Ironically, White moved into the very building he had criticized in late 1995 and was fired by the Board just weeks later. Notably, he had insisted on a private restroom and changing room in the executive suite on the 25th floor.

[23]There is a 26th floor, but it is not easily accessible and does not have offices. It does have a yoga class.

Figure 2.1 Metro's headquarters building located at 1 Gateway Plaza is adjacent to Union Station

Source: Downtowngal, CC BY-SA 3.0. https://creativecommons.org/licenses/by-sa/3.0, via Wikimedia Commons.

Executives on this floor enjoy large offices from which they can survey the domain over which they exercise power. The 25th floor contains the Office of the CEO along with whomever the CEO deems worthy.

OEI's office was on the 25th floor (Figure 2.2).

This was one of many ways that it was communicated that we had power. It was also a way to ensure everyone resented us. Phil also chose to have Security and Communications on the floor. But unlike OEI, those larger departments could not fit everyone on one floor. Within Communications, besides the Chief Communications Officer and a handful of support people, only Government Relations was on the 25th floor.

Michael Turner was the veteran executive leading Government Relations. He was an expert at navigating politics internally, locally, and across California. He had relationships with everyone, knew where all the bodies were buried, and was incredibly effective at getting LA Metro what it needed from Sacramento.

But Michael was very careful not to step out ahead of the decision makers. He was a lobbyist and was best positioned to be effective through

Figure 2.2 View from OEI's offices on the 25th floor

Source: Photograph by Emma Huang.

serving his clients—the Board and the CEO. And thus, he knew that it wasn't in his best interest to push forward the legislative agenda of staff. If you wanted support from the Government Relations team, it was critical to first garner support from the Board.

While Michael's approach was both rational and effective toward ensuring he was well positioned to push forward Metro's legislative agenda, it was antithetical to the way in which we approached our jobs in OEI. Our view was that if something was a good idea, we should find a way to get it done. If that meant convincing the Board of it, so be it. But we weren't going to wait around for them. As defined by Phil when conceiving OEI, it was our job to get the good ideas done, not to follow orders.

I found it difficult to understand our misaligned incentives. At one point, his boss came in to serve as our translator. She sat in my office and after Michael spoke, she would explain to me what he meant. She would then do the same in reverse when I spoke. It was like we literally spoke different languages.

So, when we came to Michael and explained that we'd like to enforce bus lanes and could he do anything about that, he said no. It wasn't his job to push forward my pet project. It was his job to push forward the Board's agenda.

He was also wise enough to understand that the City of LA would not support LA Metro ticketing drivers on their streets and collecting the proceeds. If there was going to be revenue, the City would want their cut. And the City constitutes about 40 percent of the LA Metro Board, which means that the bosses Michael served would ensure that the City got its cut.

While he did not offer to help, Michael did advise Nolan on how to push our idea forward. If Nolan could successfully convince the city—including their parking enforcement arm, attorney's office, LADOT, and the LA Metro Board members from the city—that this would be a good idea, Michael would try to get the legislation done. Michael probably thought that would be the end of that conversation. But Nolan knew that it was not.

Nolan and I were not going to give up that easily. He hatched a plan to build the coalition necessary for Michael to be willing to move forward. He did the prework and built relationships with people in the city he had never met before. He collected data on how many parked cars were blocking buses. He helped build trust to the point that the City understood we were not interested in the revenues, we just wanted people out of the bus lanes. He explained that, yes, it was currently illegal, but we could change that. He worked with the OEI research staff to write a white paper on the costs and benefits of ABLE to help make the case. He talked to the Board Staff and brought them along with the idea. He brought me in when necessary to seal the deal.[24] Eventually, he got enough board members to support the idea that Michael was willing to pursue legislation. By this time, a year had passed.

Passing the legislation in Sacramento was no simple task, but if anyone could do it, it was Michael Turner. He found the right sponsors and built

---

[24]An interesting issue of hierarchy in public agencies is that staff can do all the work and find agreement on a path forward, but it won't go anywhere until the "chiefs" get together and agree. It's like when you see two world leaders shaking hands at a public appearance and you know everything was worked out in advance and this is just a show. Why we need this song and dance when no one is watching, as was the case for us, I have no idea.

a coalition of transit agencies interested in lifting the ban. The biggest obstacle turned out to be the American Civil Liberties Union (ACLU), which raised concerns about privacy from the automatic capture and storage of license plate data, which is considered personal data.[xxxiv] Michael easily dispensed with this complaint by making the point that the privacy concerns of a rich person parking their Mercedes in a bus lane clearly shouldn't take precedence over 50 low-income people on a bus. AB 917 passed. That took another year.

In the meantime, Nolan developed a pilot project. To play within the bounds of the existing laws, the pilot was designed in such a way that it could not issue tickets but would allow Metro to evaluate the efficacy of the technology. This approach enabled us to move forward with a procurement, which took another year. This effort, which began in 2019, is as of 2025, ticketing cars blocking the Wilshire bus lane.

While technology in this case was also critical, it was the easiest part. The hard part was developing a process for using technology that had widespread agreement, from the City of LA to Metro, and the California Legislature. It took more than five years and many more relationships to build that process,[25] but in this case it was worth it.

Project Delivery

Both public agencies and private businesses can be tasked with delivering large capital projects that cost billions of dollars. But the public- and private-sector risks and rewards are very different. When a private company delivers a large capital project, it is doing so to increase future profits. It is taking a financial risk, but that risk is calculated and will not be undertaken unless the risk was determined to be worth the reward.

By contrast, when a public agency delivers a large capital project, it is because voters or their representatives want that project. Future profit is irrelevant—most public investments lose money on an operating basis—what matters is delivering the project as quickly and inexpensively as possible while satisfying whatever constituencies there are that care about the outcome.

---

[25]And in the meantime, the technology got much better.

In transportation, project delivery can be even more complicated because it often involves horizontal infrastructure. Vertical infrastructure, such as a courthouse or a convention center, is relatively uncomplicated because you are dealing with limited land area and the air above it. Horizontal infrastructure in a built environment, such as a rail line, will naturally traverse property owned by numerous entities, and run adjacent to and thus have impacts on even more people and organizations. Securing the "right-of-way (ROW)" for public transit is typically the most expensive and challenging component of planning and construction.

This is one of the reasons for the high cost of public transit in the United States, a topic of much discussion in recent years.[xxxv] But whether the costs are higher than we might hope or not, in any case we are talking about very expensive projects. In recent years, the costs for building a mile of subway in the United States are around $500 million per mile even under the best of circumstances.[xxxvi] Building on the surface is less expensive but many light-rail projects also wind up costing in the billions. Due to the high cost of these projects, agencies such as LA Metro have a lot at stake.

As such, their appetite for risk is rather low and they are prone to doing things the way they have been done previously. This is a major error in assessing risk as it involves status quo bias,[xxxvii] which assumes the risk of the unknown is greater than that of the known. But if the known method has been consistently producing poor results—as it has in this country with most rail lines being delivered late, above budget, and with worse outcomes than promised—it might be time look for new strategies.

The most typical project delivery method in the United States is Design–Bid–Build (DBB). Under DBB, the public agency procures a contractor to design the project under their supervision. When that design is complete, the agency procures a new contractor to bid on the construction contract for the project. The thought is that this approach enables competition for both the design stage and the construction stage of the project, which in theory can lower costs.

One obvious drawback to this delivery method is that one contractor designs the project and a different one builds it. This means that the construction contractor may receive the plans and have a different perspective on the best approach to the project than the firm who designed it, often causing delays and cost overruns.

The solution to this problem has been the development of a newer form of contracting approach called Design–Build (DB), wherein one contractor is responsible for both phases. Even this minor change was and still can be controversial. For example, until recently many states prohibited DB.[xxxviii]

What both project delivery methods leave out, however, is far more crucial. For a project to be delivered it must be financed.[26] Financing (F) also comes with a cost, the cost of borrowing. Also, projects do not end at construction.[27] They must then be operated (O) and maintained (M), which represent additional indefinite and substantial costs. So, a full suite of project delivery involves the following costs: Design, Build, Finance, Operate, and Maintain (DBFOM). By using DB or DBB, a public agency assumes it will bear the costs of F, O, and M.

This assumption is understandable, because in the United States, the cost of public financing is typically lower than private financing as public agencies can borrow at lower rates. Operations and maintenance are typically performed in-house by transit agencies, often by a permanent unionized workforce. In part due to the entrenched politics associated with unions, using a private-sector company for O or M can often be challenging.

However, there are potentially substantial benefits of allowing the private sector to play a larger role in the project life cycle. Private sector financing is more expensive but can bring new perspective on project costs and stronger financial incentive to keep them under control. Bundling private financing with the other project delivery elements allows the private sector to have greater control over the project risks, enabling better risk management.

Private sector financing and the tangible interest in project outcomes that comes with that financial interest can also be a vehicle for innovation. In Denver, Phil saw this firsthand when he oversaw the first major transit public–private partnership (P3) in the United States, the

---

[26]Even public agencies rarely have billions in cash on hand to pay out of pocket. And if they do, they are mismanaging their money because they should have invested that cash.

[27]Though some project engineers think they do.

Eagle P3, a commuter rail line connecting the Denver airport to down-town. The private-sector consortium building that project produced an idea for single tracking that saved $300 million.[xxxix] The public agency on that project would likely never have developed that idea because they were focused on meeting technical specifications, which included double tracking. More focused on outcomes, the private sector figured out that they could achieve the same goals—in terms of service fre-quency and reliability—for $300 million less if they changed the tech-nical specifications.

LA Metro had taken a shot at P3 before. Mayor Villaraigosa, who preceded Mayor Garcetti, had pushed his 30/10 initiative intending to deliver 30 years' worth of projects in just 10 years, in part using P3.[xl] But previous attempts to work P3 through the morass of resistance in LA Metro had failed. At that point the P3 program at LA Metro was handed over to Countywide Planning, who were skeptical of P3 project delivery because they perceived that it would disrupt their ability to control the flow of money for projects. They effectively shut it down, but they still had a bench of financial advisers. When I arrived at LA Metro, it was this group that greeted me, showed me how to get coffee, took me to lunch, and then threw the bench contract in my lap. I didn't realize at the time that they were going to oppose every P3 effort we put forward, but I could tell they were happy to pass it off to me.

When Colin took over our P3 work, his only tool was this bench contract.[28] He set himself to work becoming not only best buddies with those advisors but learning their trade as he did it. We would need their support if we were ever going to make progress on P3.

The Sepulveda Transit Corridor

Innovation and cost savings were desperately needed on the Sepulveda Transit Corridor. Los Angeles is a beautiful city in part because it has majestic mountains adjacent to the ocean and desert. These contrasts

---

[28]A bench contract is a procurement mechanism by which the procuring entity preapproves a group of firms that can be hired for tasks as defined within the contract on a short turnaround time.

in topography and climate are striking and help make LA a wonderful place to live. Hang around an Angeleno long enough and they might brag about the time they went surfing and snow skiing on the same day.

The downside of this location is that while driving to the beach from the mountains one time to "say you did it" might be fun, driving every day across a mountain in the middle of the city is not. The Santa Monica Mountains cut through Los Angeles, dividing the most densely developed part of the region between downtown and the Pacific Ocean a dozen miles to the west, from the sprawling San Fernando Valley. Each area is home to about two million residents, and the West Side[29] also contains the city's largest single employer, UCLA, as well as LAX, SoFi stadium, West Hollywood, Beverly Hills, Venice, and Santa Monica. The San Fernando Valley, where the archetype of the Valley Girl originated, is a relatively less expensive and a more racially/ethnically and income diverse area.

Every morning, drivers from the Valley pour through the mountains to reach the West Side via the notorious 405 freeway, which once prompted Elon Musk to say he was sick of "soul-crushing" traffic and would be starting a new company (The Boring Company) to fix the problem.[30]

The 405 freeway is the main passage through this corridor, and it is severely congested at peak times. There are other ways to cross the Santa Monica Mountains, though these are equally "soul-crushing" winding, congested, two-lane roads including Coldwater Canyon, Beverly Glen, and Topanga Canyon. There are even some other roundabout routes through the mountains that Waze can show you during peak times. But all of them are packed with cars because demand for these routes vastly overwhelms capacity.

---

[29]In LA, everything west of Beverly Hills is colloquially referred to as the "West Side."

[30]No transportation expert believed he would succeed because, unlike him, we are familiar with the concept of "induced demand," whereby any increase in capacity along a highly congested route will quickly be filled by new traffic that was just avoiding the area previously. The Boring Company did talk to OEI about tunneling under the mountains and claimed they could do it for one-tenth the cost of currently tunneling technologies. We said we would gladly pay them for that if they could do it. We never heard from them again.

The Sepulveda Transit Corridor is intended as the antidote to this problem. Demand for travel in this corridor is so high that a subway train through it is forecast to carry over 120,000 passengers per day.[xli] The problem is that building a subway tunnel through a mountain in a major urban area is not cheap. The Sepulveda Transit Corridor is the most expensive project planned in Los Angeles, and likely will be the most expensive transit project in North America, if not the world, when constructed.

Finding a way to deliver this project more cheaply would seem like a critical priority. If there was ever a time when trying something new could generate enormous benefits it would be with a project like this one, right?

NO! You are not thinking like a bureaucrat. The last thing we would want to do is take a risk on a project as high-profile and expensive as this one! This is the time to play it safe.

That was indeed the mindset at Metro. But Colin set about changing that.

How to Make Friends and Create a Project Development Agreement

At my going-away party in DC, people came to have a drink, wish me luck, and offer parting gifts. But only one person asked to come to LA with me—Colin Peppard.

I first met Colin when he was with an environmental organization that was working on federal transportation policy. He had a knack for networking and a sharp understanding of policy—skills that would help him navigate the initially unfamiliar terrain at Metro. By the time he approached me about working for LA Metro, he was leading transportation work for Senator Tom Carper (D-DE) on the U.S. Senate Committee on Environment and Public Works (EPW) and had built a reputation for getting things done.

When Colin got to LA, he found himself in a very unfamiliar environment. As a Philadelphia-area native who had lived in New England and DC, he was competitive and skilled in blowing people away with his rigorous understanding of subject matter. These skills were far less valuable when it came to LA Metro. At Metro you had to build trust. You had to make friends. Fortunately, these were also part of Colin's unique skill set, and he quickly began employing his time-tested strategy of connecting with people one-on-one, whether over coffee, lunch, or happy hour. He made it his mission to know everyone who mattered to the work.

However, to build the relationships necessary for this endeavor, he'd need a bottomless calendar and an iron social battery. Phil was interested in selling P3s to accelerate project funding in the proposed Measure M transportation sales tax increase in 2016. The idea was that voters would be more apt to support the measure if they thought they were going to get benefits sooner. Unlike many Measure M projects, the Sepulveda Transit Corridor was a great candidate for a P3. It was a new independent transit line rather than an extension of an existing line, which meant it could be operated and maintained by the private sector with relative ease. Building a line through a mountain meant that the project included unusually high financial and technical risk, some of which the private sector would be better able to manage. And it was projected to be an extremely expensive project, so any viable way to reduce costs would be critical.

Now, while most people outside of government were not paying attention to the details of Measure M, there was one group of private-sector companies with a substantial interest—companies that had the potential to get contracts from LA Metro if Measure M were approved. Also known colloquially as the Transit-Industrial Complex. Remember how most everyone at LA Metro manages consultants? Measure M's $120 billion would buy a lot of college tuition and second homes for shareholders of engineering firms around the country.

Phil used this group to his advantage by asking them to submit UPs for major projects in Measure M even before Measure M was passed. This would show private-sector interest in financing these projects and help convince the government class that the projects could be accelerated.

Project Development Agreements

Sure enough, we received three UPs for the Sepulveda corridor. The benefit of these proposals was that not only did we get free advice from the private sector on how best to deliver this project but we also got a signal from the market that they saw an opportunity and were likely to bid on this project. Competition is critical to the success of any procurement, but especially a P3. Without competition, you are likely to pay more for your project.

What these proposals suggested, however, was that a typical[31] P3 might not be best suited to deliver this project. Instead, they collectively recommended using a more innovative approach called a Project Development Agreement (PDA). The idea of a PDA is to bring the private sector in earlier in the process, before the project is even planned. In a typical P3, the public agency would plan the project and then hand it over to the private sector to construct and operate it. In the case of a PDA, the private sector gets involved in planning the project. While the public agency must still "clear the project" environmentally, meaning go through the National Environmental Policy Act (NEPA) process, many big decisions about the project—the route, the vehicles, the frequency of service—would be led by the private sector. That same private-sector consortium would then be given the "right of first refusal" to complete the project as a P3.

The advantage of the PDA approach is that the private sector has a strong interest in planning something that they can also build, operate, and maintain because that's where the real money is for them. They will gladly just break even on planning the project if they are not going to face any competition to build it. This means they will push for a feasible project to build and operate for at least 30 years (the typical length of a P3) according to the conditions specified by the public agency. For a complex project like Sepulveda, where project costs were likely to exceed available funds, having investors behind the project with a strong desire to make it work could be a huge benefit.

The drawback is that while a PDA includes competition upfront on the planning side, it does not include competition for the building of the project itself. This means that the public agency is essentially committing to a 30+ year private consortium when it is selecting its planning firm. That is a big commitment, and a lot can go wrong. But both sides have a

---

[31]Given the overall lack of P3s in transportation, and especially transit in the United States, to say any kind of P3 is typical is something of a misnomer.

strong incentive to make it work, as both have a lot to lose if they fail. But just like a real marriage, if trust is lost the whole thing can fall apart (and there is likely to be lots of arguing either way).

The idea of a PDA on Sepulveda was not new. Previous expert consultants to the agency had suggested it and the LA Metro Board had approved the idea prior to my arrival in LA. But innovation at a public agency is usually not about new ideas. Ideas are the easy part. Getting them to become reality is the tough part, and that was Colin's job.

I am not privy to everything Colin did to get us there. I don't know how many breakfasts he had on mornings when he'd rather have been surfing, how many drinks he had when he really needed to sleep, or how many arms he gently twisted during incessant meetings about the same topics repeatedly. But I know he got us there and that it took two years.

First, he would have to befriend his primary partner, Procurement. Fortunately, Senior Executive Officer Carolina Coppolo from Procurement was assigned to work with OEI. Carolina was far from your average procurement officer. She was open to new ideas and finding solutions, even when the ideas were as crazy as those coming from OEI.

Procurement Departments really like competition. They were initially very nervous about the idea of having a right of first refusal for a multibillion-dollar project where, in theory, the private consortium could effectively extort money from Metro. They also did not have experience putting together procurement documents for a project like this one that involved, among other things, tunneling through a mountain. Colin and our advisers, along with Carolina, helped create a structure with numerous off-ramps for both LA Metro and the selected private-sector partner that reduced everyone's anxiety. If things were not going well, each side could bail on the project. The earlier the bailout, the lower the consequences for each side.

We also developed a new idea that helped assuage some of the concerns of the folks in procurement. They were concerned with competition, so rather than let the competition end when the PDA team was selected, why not select multiple PDA teams and let them duke it out?

While this idea added a level of complication, and as far as we could tell had never been done before, it seemed like a major improvement that would also satisfy Procurement staff. Some proposals had the idea of going under the mountain. Some proposals wanted to go over the mountain. Given this, why not facilitate competition to let the best proposal win?

Colin also had to befriend County Counsel. As mentioned previously, County Counsel[32] at LA Metro does not work for LA Metro. In addition, no one at LA Metro is permitted to hire outside attorneys, so only County Counsel could procure legal advisers with P3/PDA expertise. Although they allowed us to be part of that process, we could not avoid the fact that the legal experts we helped to bring on saw County Counsel as their client, not us. Indeed, they adopted the same risk-averse perspective that tended toward doing whatever had been done previously.

But another issue was that because County Counsel reports to the Board of Supervisors, rather than the LA Metro CEO, they were one step closer to political issues. In this case, they were far more aware of and sensitive to labor concerns about P3. The County Board of Supervisors was unabashedly pro-union and would never cross organized labor. County Counsel was trying to avoid a fight with the unions as much as possible and therefore found every possible reason to tell us why we, legally, could not do what we wanted to do. We got past this by agreeing that a PDA did not actually necessitate a P3. While we admitted that P3 was the intent, we wrote the contract so that it was not a requirement and in theory the project could be delivered without private-sector involvement.

---

[32]The County Counsel serves as the General Counsel for the County of Los Angeles. LA Metro contracts with the Office of County Counsel for its legal services, and the lead attorney assigned to Metro reports directly to the Board of Directors rather than the CEO. Prior to the 1993 merger with the Southern California Rapid Transit District's (SCRTD), the Los Angeles County Transportation Commission (LACTC) relied on County Counsel for legal representation. After the merger, SCRTD's in-house legal team was absorbed into the Office of County Counsel and assigned to the Metro account, despite the CEO's efforts to retain a separate in-house counsel.

Then there was befriending Countywide Planning.

The LA Metro staff in Countywide Planning wanted to say "hey, planning is our job" but they couldn't say that. Instead, they pointed out that they would still need to "environmentally clear" the project, since only a government agency, and not a private contractor, can do that—and it would obviously be challenging to clear the project without knowing what the project was. Therefore, Countywide Planning staff would need to communicate with the PDA teams. But if they were communicating with those teams, they would have information from one team that could be subject to public records act requests and thus available to the other team.

We solved this problem, and Countywide Planning staff's real objection to loss of power, through an idea called a project charter. The charter outlined everyone's responsibility on the project, and clarified how decisions would be made. It not only showed how Countywide Planning would retain control over the project but also how much more collaborative and cross-departmental this project would be compared to most previous endeavors. This made it difficult for Countywide Planning staff to object to the effort. It also solved the problem of information sharing by creating specific firewalls that protected ideas as needed.

Finally, Colin had to befriend Program Management. The Program Management group at LA Metro is responsible for building projects. But in contrast to Countywide Planning, they have a stronger incentive for those projects to be financially viable. Even though Program Management staff had some reservations about a PDA, they saw the potential value of it more than anyone else, especially because their Chief, Rick Clarke, had put together a P3 in Denver. They were thus a natural ally, and Colin leaned heavily on that relationship to build support elsewhere.

Instead of keeping your friends close and your enemies closer, Colin saw an opportunity to make (almost) everyone a friend. He started with Program Management and built that relationship as best he could. Then he leveraged that trust to bring Procurement around, since Procurement trusted Program Management having worked with them all the time.

Then he could use those friendships to deal more collectively with County Counsel and Countywide Planning.

The turning point came through the creative use of OEI's outside financial advisers. Though we were convinced that a competing PDA was the best choice, we also knew it couldn't move forward with us just proposing it. We needed outside experts to confirm this path forward, and we needed them to do it in a way that indicated openness to other ideas. So, we brought in our financial advisers to facilitate a session with representatives from all relevant LA Metro Departments. The goal of the session: Confirm the project delivery method for Sepulveda.

Facilitation by an outside party is a great way to get past individual squabbles. Even if, in this case, the outside party was technically working for us. They earned the trust of the session participants early on and beautifully guided everyone toward the answer that OEI already knew was the best option. The presence of an outside party made it difficult for department representatives to voice self-centered concerns. And the evidence presented was compelling.

Colin made many friends across LA Metro who subsequently embraced a new process for building a challenging new rail line. He leveraged those friendships to team up and build support for discussions with those who resisted. But in the end, the most critical friendship may have been with his own consultants. After the workshop we had the buy-in we needed to move forward. It wasn't always easy, but the project started down a path that made it unstoppable, using our proposed process. The Sepulveda project continues today under the process we developed. It happened because Colin invested heavily in relationship building. Buying key players a few drinks didn't hurt.

You Need to Make Friends to Fix Processes

Building relationships turned out to be one of the most powerful tools OEI had—and it's a tool that all public servants can use, regardless of where they sit in an organization's hierarchy. In fact, junior staff can often have even more benefit than senior staff when they invest in the arduous process of relationship development.

In the case of MobileQubes, Nolan had to invest two years of his life into building relationships and aligning interests. Ultimately, he was successful, even if the project wasn't. More importantly, this exercise led to the introduction of test stations, which allowed for streamlined innovation for future projects.

However, relationship building isn't a silver bullet, and the investment might not align with required timelines. For example, we couldn't improve the signal timing on the Orange Line. For that project, we had to work across multiple agencies and jurisdictions, and with a variety of people with misaligned incentive structures. While that problem at the time of press hasn't yet been solved, it will be likely be solved in the fullness of time—on a timeframe that simply didn't work for OEI.

Automated Bus Lane Enforcement (ABLE) was a huge win for Los Angeles—and a lesson for me on how to more effectively navigate colleagues with incentive structures that may differ from mine. While it may or may not have accelerated the project, if I had understood from the outset how to better collaborate with Michael Turner, I may have been able to save my staff time and approached this project with a more streamlined strategy.

But, perhaps of everyone at OEI, Colin best understood the value of building relationships to fix processes. He cut his teeth on this lesson working in advocacy in DC and ultimately in the U.S. Senate. He worked persistently to finalize a PDA, a significant step, even if the long-term payoff remains to be seen. The jury is still out on the Sepulveda project, but it is likely that the extra time spent on planning this effort will result in faster project delivery.

One thing we know is that to do something that had never been done before was a herculean task because we had to create an entirely new process for the largest transit project in the United States. That meant making a lot of friends in a short period of time and bringing them along with your vision.

That is how real change occurs.

CHAPTER 3

Recognize Impenetrable Fiefdoms

My colleagues and I just stared at one another in disbelief. "Did that really just happen?"

In business meetings in Southern California there tends to be a strong measure of civility face to face. Whereas in places I had worked previously, this was not always true. In DC things could often get contentious—I was threatened with being fired by people who were not my boss on many occasions—and in New York things were almost always contentious. In LA, people are generally friendly and nonconfrontational to your face. Aside from the occasional performance, LA Metro folks were not ones to make a scene.

So, we were more than a little surprised when our fellow Metro colleagues from the TAP (Transit Access Pass) Department yelled at us and stormed out of our meeting. This was unusual behavior, especially considering that all we were doing was asking them to consider a new technology idea before rejecting it. Apparently, their answer was no, but they were a tad adamant.

What leads to this kind of behavior in an otherwise mostly civil organization in nonconfrontational Southern California? The answer is—impenetrable fiefdoms. Many organizations contain fiefdoms where bosses tightly control their areas of responsibility, and resist outside efforts to make change. But most fiefdoms have gaps in their defenses. They have some people who really want to make change and know how to do it within the confines of their bosses. Their bosses may have some flexibility and be open to new ideas, even if they won't relinquish any control.

How to Recognize an Entrenched Fiefdom:
a Field Guide

In every large public agency, like Metro, there are leaders who establish long-term power centers, often referred to as "organizational fiefdoms."[xlii] These fiefdoms don't appear overnight and are carefully constructed, brick by brick, by people who have learned how to play the long game.

This phenomenon is well documented in business literature. It has been called "silo mentality,"[xliii] where internal departments prioritize their own agendas over the shared mission of the organization. Others have highlighted that power hoarding and fragmented structures stymie innovation.[xliv] This phenomenon is supported by the general truth that bureaucracies often reward predictability over performance, unintentionally cultivating gatekeeping behavior.[xlv]

During our time at Metro, we observed firsthand how entrenched these dynamics can become. Rather than casting judgment, it is helpful to study the architecture of these internal power centers. Here's a look at how they form—not as a how-to guide, but as a framework for those hoping to create change in similar environments.

1. ***Stick around.*** Fiefdoms are built over time. Leaders who can survive multiple CEO transitions, budget crises, and reorgs are able to gain deep, informal and formal power. They learn not just the rules but the exceptions to the rules, and they know how to deploy each strategically.

2. ***Align with the real power.*** Rather than reporting "up" through a formal hierarchy, these leaders often cultivate strong ties directly with board members, elected officials, and outside influencers. This loyalty can override accountability to their direct supervisor.

3. ***Control the flow of information.*** Control over information is a major source of bureaucratic[xlvi] power. In an age that celebrates transparency, selectively delaying, hoarding, or obfuscating information is still an extremely effective form of influence. Managers may or may not actively mislead, but they curate what is shared and when.

4. ***Cultivate just enough fear.*** When staff fear consequences for speaking to peers in other departments—or even asking the wrong

questions—collaboration breaks down. Staff need psychological safety to foster innovation and creative problem-solving—fear breaks this down.[xlvii] Managers leading a fiefdom will carefully walk this line.

These fiefdoms are not just bureaucratic quirks—they're structural features of public organizations that shape what kind of change is possible. As Jennifer Pahlka argues in *Recoding America*, real reform rarely comes from sweeping declarations at the top. It happens when people inside government understand how to redesign policy for delivery—navigating the messy reality of rules, systems, and power to serve real people more effectively.[xlviii] Her stories echo our own: progress depends not just on good ideas but on navigating the invisible architecture of loyalty, fear, and control that fiefdoms create. Understanding this terrain isn't a detour from innovation—it's the necessary map.

Trying to Open the TAP

One such impenetrable fiefdom was thoughtfully constructed by the CFO. She was in charge not only of the Office of Management and Budget (OMB) but also TAP. With substantial opportunities to improve fare payment in the region, we thought that we could help facilitate the adoption of new technology. We took on this fight without recognizing the impenetrable fiefdom that managed fare payment technology and without having any meaningful strategies to navigate it.

Most transit agencies began replacing their tokens and tickets with farecards beginning in the 1990s.[xlix] From an agency perspective, moving to a farecard represented a huge leap forward as it reduces the handling of cash (which is expensive) while also encouraging people to buy fares in advance.

Farecards are generally credited with speeding up boarding times on buses and trains, which speeds travel and reduces costs.[l] They also tend to be popular with customers, despite initial resistance that accompanies any such change, because they make it easier to pay without searching for cash and ideally can be used on any transit system within a region.

However, investing in fare payment technology represents a huge capital cost. The 66 transit operators across LA County could not, and would not, make this investment on their own. LA Metro, as the largest agency with the most resources, was willing to make the investment, but it needed the other agencies to agree to be a part of TAP.

The CFO and her team spent countless hours working with transit operators across LA County, known as the Los Angeles County Municipal Operators Association (LACMOA), to get them to agree to be a part of TAP. The municipal operators resisted for all the reasons you might expect—they didn't want Metro telling them what to do, they wanted to make sure Metro didn't take a cut of their fares, they were resistant to changing their fare media, and so on. But in the end, the CFO made it happen with 26 other transit operators in LA County.[li]

And now she was enjoying the fruits of her innovative efforts in two big ways. First, her negotiations had cemented her relationship with other transit agencies and with board members representing areas with those transit agencies in them. As if controlling the purse strings for much of the county's transportation funds were not enough,[33] now she had another lever of control.

Because those transit agencies were worried about being bullied by Metro, she had established TAP as a separate organization. While technically TAP was under the OMB, they have separate logos and branding, a separate website, and considered their customers to be 27 transit agencies across LA County.

OEI Takes a Shot

While the idea of a TAP card was cutting-edge technology in the late 1990s and early 2000s, it was already dated when we arrived at LA Metro in 2015. We were bombarded with ideas for improvement.

First, several transit agencies had begun to move beyond farecards, also known as closed loop systems, to open payment. Open payment enables you to pay using a credit or debit card to access a transit system.

---

[33]A large portion of the sales taxes the county collects for transportation are distributed back to cities by LA Metro under local return.

Second, the advent of smartphones meant that people were accustomed to purchasing everything with their phone, and technology existed to allow them to buy transit fares that way.

Meanwhile, TAP was behind the times. While there was a feature that enabled customers to purchase fares online and add them to their TAP card, those purchases were not instantly reflected when using buses.

To have the most up-to-date information about a customer's TAP account, the physical card readers on the bus would need an update by connecting to the Internet. When buses were on the street, there was no connectivity. Thus, a bus would have to return to its division to get updated. The result was that customers would have to wait up to 24 hours after buying their fares online to use them on a bus.

Then there was the bigger picture. Imagine if you landed in a new city and went to get a cup of coffee, but that city's coffee shop did not accept credit cards. Instead, they made you purchase a card that only works at their city's coffee shops and then load that with cash or credit cards. That is essentially what transit fare cards typically are—each card is only useful on specific transit systems within any given region.

Anyone trying to ride Metro for the first time would need to undertake an extra step (or two) to purchase the product. This undermined the very concept of encouraging transit use by making it harder to attract new customers.

The situation was exacerbated by the contractor for the TAP card—Cubic. Cubic's business model is built around selling agencies a fully integrated fare system including ticket vending machines (TVMs), cards, card readers, and all the back-end technology. On the surface, this may seem efficient, but in practice, it creates a kind of institutional lock-in. Once an agency makes an initial investment, it becomes prohibitively expensive to switch vendors—both operationally and financially. Further, all the hardware is incompatible with third-party solutions, and the back end is closed. This is a textbook example of path dependence, where early technology and procurement decisions create self-reinforcing feedback loops that narrow future options and entrench the status quo.[lii]

Metro fell into this path dependence dilemma. Meanwhile, Cubic had also embedded several employees within TAP and had consultants who shared clients between Cubic and Metro. They fixed errors, kept the system running, and promoted Cubic, which also discouraged switching. All of this meant that Cubic had little incentive to keep their technology up to date, much less switch to open payment, which would allow people to buy fares without a TAP card.

This was an area ripe for innovation. In retrospect, we probably should have set about in our efforts to improve fare payment in a more strategic way. But we were still new to Metro and didn't quite realize what we were up against. Instead, we just grabbed good ideas and ran—straight into a brick wall.

We started with the unsolicited proposals we were receiving. For example, one company demonstrated to us how people could walk through turnstiles and pay the fare without even removing their phone from their pocket. That seemed very customer friendly and worth pursuing, but we quickly realized the steps to get to this idea seemed insurmountable, and we were setting our sights too high.[34]

So, we focused on what we knew was possible—an app to pay by phone. Given how frequently people pay for services using their phones, this seemed like low-hanging fruit to improve customer experience. There were apps that you could use, for very little money, a proof-of-payment method on your phone. This meant that you could pay on your phone and then display an activated ticket to the bus driver. We knew it could work because LADOT, which runs local buses, was already using it (along with numerous other agencies across the country).

Yet, even when something might appear to be simple or easy, often there are still lots of reasons to say no. For one, it couldn't work on trains where there are turnstiles and no people to check your phone. Second, people could wind up fighting with bus operators about whether they had paid. Third, Cubic's contract with Metro had contemplated the potential future threat of competition, allowing Cubic to claim that they had exclusive rights to sell all Metro fares. Finally, it could be a labor issue because we'd be asking operators to do new work.

---

[34]This would have required getting rid of Cubic, getting new card readers, developing a mobile payment solution with a new vendor, and requiring that vendor to use this technology. Five years of work, minimum.

After a few of these scattershot ideas getting shut down, we decided to regroup. We'd have to play the long game. We knew the goal was open payment, which would provide customers with the most possible options and allow for integration with other private providers like Uber and micromobility providers.

We would push for open payment.

Taking on TAP and Cubic

The idea of adopting open payment seemed simple. Open payment would provide a better future for customers by allowing them to skip a step and just purchase fares with a credit or debit card. It was the future of transit fare payment that had already been adopted by leading agencies in the world such as Transport for London. We were not visionaries—we could just see the obvious, and we were not alone. So, we figured the first step was to see what TAP had planned.

The problem with our thinking was the assumption that other people were approaching this problem the same way we were. The problem, from our perspective, was that paying for transit was challenging and cumbersome. If we were running fare payment for a transit agency, we would develop a vision for the end state and how to get there. The plan would consider costs and benefits of various upgrades and make recommendations for next steps.

Having navigated and survived various leadership regimes, many Metro veterans developed an alternative approach to problem-solving. They would start from where Metro was today, rather than a vision of where Metro could be in the future. This would result in the introduction of small incremental changes that occurred slowly over time but had the benefit of ruffling fewer feathers. In this case, TAP's plan was to slowly build out functionality, leveraging the software and hardware that was already in use.

TAP's relationship with Cubic meant that TAP often struggled to get Cubic to do what it wanted because there was little to no threat of competition. TAP had no intention of rebidding their contract, as doing so would incur a substantial expense. Cubic was happy to discuss open payment, but they had little incentive to move swiftly in that direction. In fact, they had plenty of incentive *not* to move in that direction, since open payment could open the door to Metro not needing Cubic.

As we learned of Cubic's stranglehold on TAP, we decided to switch course. Instead of pushing for open payment, what if we took on Cubic? It happened that Cubic's contract was expiring soon, as they could only be contracted for five-year terms, so this was an opportune time to raise the issue.

By this point, we had developed relationships with TAP staff and a deep understanding of the intricacies of the fare payment system. Against the directive of their CFO boss, TAP staff walked us through their roadmap. Since they only felt empowered to push forward inexpensive, incremental change, they completely threw out the idea of open payments. But they did build into the roadmap the future ability to add a TAP card to mobile wallets, enabling customers to use their phone to pay for fares.[35]

From our perspective, the contract renewal was an opportunity to push TAP beyond incremental improvements. TAP staff wouldn't and likely couldn't support us. The CFO was not responding to us and was doing her best to withhold information. Left without other tools in our toolkit—we brought the issue to Phil.

Phil, having been in the industry for some time, knew of the monopolist tendencies of companies like Cubic. He too was unhappy with what he termed the "fare collection industrial complex" and was interested in taking them on.[36] We told him of our saga so far and he agreed to a meeting with TAP to discuss. While the CFO would not take meetings with us, she had to take a meeting with Phil.

The problem was that without access to the same data and information as TAP, it was challenging to make our case. Even worse, the meeting was scheduled during a time when I was trudging through JFK returning from a work trip. Not being in person was a huge drawback, but getting a meeting with Phil was not easy and I couldn't reschedule.

---

[35] This functionality was rolled out in 2020, and represents a massive improvement, but continues to be more cumbersome than open payments.

[36] This issue and Phil's terminology would arise later when the issue of free transit emerged.

I called in and made the case, but that battle was already lost—we couldn't make our case effectively and Phil wasn't going to pick this fight. His rationale was that replacing Cubic with a different company would just mean substituting one monopolist for another. We knew he had a point, but the new monopolist would be our monopolist and not TAP's.[37]

In retrospect, this was a huge battle for us to pick, and it was likely unwinnable. Phil was in a challenging position. If he ordered the CFO to do this, it would be his mess to fix if it didn't work out. He would be assigning OEI responsibility for a huge portion of the business, or at least assigning us to work with a department that did not want to do this and did not want to work with us.

The downside is that it took years for Cubic to adopt new technologies. At the time of this publishing, LA Metro still doesn't have open payment, while peer agencies in the Bay Area, Chicago, Boston, New York, and Philadelphia have all adopted it.[38] While you can use a digital TAP card to pay for fares, you cannot use any other medium. Every person still needs their own TAP card, so to pay for others in your group they need their own card. Other Metro services, for example Metro parking, do not accept TAP payment. Instead, you must download a separate Metro parking app, as this is not a service Cubic offers.

TAP was an appealing target but ultimately a fortress we could not penetrate. We would have been better off leaving it alone and saving our chips for another day.

Signal Preemption on Expo

Seleta Reynolds was trying to communicate with me, but I was missing the signal. Seleta was the General Manager (GM) of the LADOT. We were in a meeting with some of her staff, and she was looking at me while

---

[37]Realistically, there were also very few vendors who at the time were positioned to effectively take on a system of our size and scope. During this time period, Cubic was the vendor for most large systems in the English-speaking world—and continues to be at time of writing for the largest transit agencies.

[38]In May 2024, Metro Board approved the 176 contract modification to its contract with Cubic for $66M to upgrade the current system to include open payment, plus an additional $79M to support the new upgrade. It is supposed to be launched in early 2026 in time for the World Cup Games.

speaking, but the words she was saying did not comport with her facial expression. She was telling me why we couldn't do much to improve the speed of the trains on the Expo Line, but her eyes showed she was thinking something else.

The GM of LADOT is a tough job. I didn't quite understand how difficult it was until I heard Seleta speak not long after she took the gig. She recounted a conversation with her mother, wherein she had to explain that LADOT, despite the name, had control over only a small component of transportation in Los Angeles. They do not maintain the streets or street lighting—that is the Department of Public Works. They do not control aviation—that is the Los Angeles World Airports (LAWA). They do not do the planning for the city—that would be the City Planning Department. They have nothing to do with the ports—that is the Port of Los Angeles. Obviously, they are also not LA Metro.

LADOT does operate a transit system called DASH and Commuter Express buses. They are also responsible for parking enforcement. But the reason I had come to talk to her was that LADOT also operates the ATSAC.

Seleta was looking at me oddly because it was clear to her that I did not understand what was going on at LADOT. Seleta had taken this job after working on bicycle and pedestrian infrastructure for the San Francisco DOT. Mayor Garcetti had run a campaign that included the idea of making LA streets safer for bicyclists and pedestrians and moving away from total dependence on cars. Even though LADOT doesn't control the streets, Mayor Garcetti had hoped that having someone like Seleta running the place could be a way to plan for these kinds of changes.

But the City of LA is not like other big city governments such as Chicago or New York. Los Angeles has far fewer city council representatives per person than those cities, and as such, each city council person represents an inordinate number of people and wields tremendous power.[39]

City council members stick together in the sense that they typically preserve veto power for each other over any proposed change in their own

---

[39]Despite some recent efforts to expand the council, at press time any action on this is still uncertain.

district. They prioritize their constituent needs over those of the larger city, which often means prioritizing the loudest voices in their districts. This weakens the mayor's role substantially, and in turn, the power of his or her appointees such as the head of LADOT.

Not long after this meeting with Seleta, the challenges of implementing anything like a bicycle revolution in Los Angeles became apparent when the city took away a lane of traffic and put in new protected bike lanes in Playa del Rey (a neighborhood, not a city), a beachfront community just south of Venice (also not a city).[liii]

This was possible because of a city councilman named Mike Bonin, who was very pro-bike and transit and wanted to bring innovations like this to his community. So naturally the community immediately sued and attempted to recall Bonin. While Bonin survived the recall, the changes to the streets did not. Mayor Garcetti could not, or would not, stick up for LADOT and Bonin and did not fight to keep the changes.[liv]

Seleta had only been on the job for a short time when I went to this meeting. But she had been there long enough to know that I was hopelessly naive in what I was proposing.

Expo Line Opens

In May 2016, less than a year after I arrived at LA Metro, the long-awaited Expo Line extension opened. This extended the new light-rail line that ran from downtown Los Angeles to Culver City (an actual incorporated city) all the way to the beach in Santa Monica (also a city). This was a monumental achievement for LA County—finally restoring a transit line connecting downtown to the Westside beaches by rail after so many decades of living without such a link. As I rode the train with other Metro executives along the new route, I was amazed and proud. But I also thought about something else, and it wasn't because I was bored: *Gee, this sure is taking a long time.*

It is 14 miles from downtown to Santa Monica. A car trip with no traffic can take 15 to 20 minutes, but that is highly theoretical. Traffic on the 10 freeway is usually awful, and during rush hour the same trip can easily take one hour or more. A rail line would be an excellent way to avoid that traffic, and that is what I assumed it had been designed to do. But if it was designed to do that, the designer had been out to lunch or had failed miserably. On the day it opened it took 55 minutes to make that trip.

I was incredulous. Why spend so much money and time to build a rail line only to produce something that is relatively comparable to sitting in traffic in terms of time? As I rode the line, I noticed we were stopping a lot—and not just at stations. We were stopping at red lights. Why on earth would we be doing that? A train stopping at red lights? Isn't that missing the whole point?

Surely, I thought, this must be an error. LA Metro would not have spent this amount of time and money on this new rail line, only to have it fail to compete effectively with driving times. Won't the mayor, who has been touting LA's mass transit revolution, be embarrassed? Won't Phil be embarrassed? How about the Chair of the Board, Mark Ridley-Thomas, who was presiding over the opening?

OEI to the Rescue ... or Not

We were disappointed with the run-time for the Expo Line, but we felt like we could do something about it. In our still-unseasoned instinct to attack first and ask questions later, we immediately tried to figure out how to fix it.

To understand how to fix the problem, it helps to understand why the problem exists in the first place.

The first is that it was built that way to save money. This is done in part through a concept that engineers euphemistically call "value engineering." The project is defined during the planning process, and when the plans are approved, it is sent to Program Management for construction.

But the planning process is not necessarily cost-constrained, and there is a limited amount of money available to build the project. To construct the project, Program Management must find ways to cut expenses, or "value-engineer" it. This means doing things like changing an underground or elevated section to at-grade, reducing station sizes, reducing substations and eliminating supplemental pocket tracks that could speed run-times. All these things happened for the Expo Line.

Another reason Expo was built that way is that building the line at-grade is easier than trying to build underground or elevated tracks. When you build underground or elevated tracks, you create a far greater disruption for the community during construction. Many communities also oppose elevated tracks due to noise concerns during operation. Using an existing ROW in the middle of the street—which Expo Line could do in many places due to the old Red Car[40] having used that same area—was the path of least resistance.[lv]

But the line had been built already. Any major upgrades would take years and substantial investment. The place where we saw opportunity was in the intersections with trains and vehicles. This was Los Angeles, and despite the decision to build a rail line, there was no parallel decision to prioritize that rail line over cars. In the City of Los Angeles, the Expo Line had to stop at red lights so that cars could go across its path. This was not the case in Santa Monica (also a city) where a different policy decision had been made and the lights would turn green for the train as it neared the crossing. But most of the line was in Los Angeles, and that is where the slow speeds persisted. This was the jurisdiction of LADOT.

I made an appointment to see Seleta, and she brought along her engineering experts. Seleta and I had both come to Los Angeles around the same time and had been making public appearances together frequently on panels at conferences. We had in common a feeling of being outside appointees in a new administration, with the intention of solving transportation problems. What I didn't understand was that LADOT made LA Metro look like a sleek, efficient, well-functioning organization.

In Seleta's office I explained the problem: The Expo Line was too slow. It could be fixed if we added signal preemption in the City of Los Angeles. Could they work with us on this? The engineers in the room immediately pounced.

"Do you mean signal preemption or signal priority?" they asked. I really had no idea, but this was a red herring. They had no intention of doing either of them.

---

[40]Between 1901 and 1961 the Pacific Electric Railway privately operated a transit system in Los Angeles, which was often referred to as the Red Car System. The Expo Line operates on the Red Car's Santa Monica Air Line ROW.

"You are regulatorily required to have safety gates at each intersection for signal preemption, and there is no room for the gates and no money to build them."

Also they said, "If trains get priority, there won't be sufficient time to allow pedestrians to cross the street according to our latest policies."

Eventually we got to the real issue. "If we prioritize trains, we will get lots of calls from angry drivers who are waiting at these intersections." They were more concerned about motorists than transit riders or pedestrians. Whether this was because motorists are louder and wealthier, or because these guys saw their job as prioritizing cars, I do not know. But there was a fundamental disagreement here—they didn't see a problem worth solving.

Seleta had to leave the meeting early and directed her engineers to work with us. As soon as the door closed, they let us know that they did not intend to collaborate with us. They also reminded us that they will be at LADOT long after Seleta, and long after I will have left Metro.

Seleta and I later debriefed, and I began to understand. She had little power to get her employees to do anything. They were in the civil service and difficult to fire. Even if she did fire them, they could only be replaced by other civil servants based on years of experience. Bringing in new people who shared her values was almost impossible. She would have to pick her battles, and this one, started by the upstart Chief Innovation Officer at a different organization, was not one of them.

Interestingly, and not for the last time, we were just a bit early. A few years later complaints about speeds on the Expo and Blue line (which share a difficult and slow junction) grew louder. Phil set an ambitious goal for Operations to shave 20 minutes off the Blue Line run-time and settled for 10 minutes.[41] With political impetus and an order from the CEO, this could be done. But not by OEI right out of the gate.

This failure taught us several things. One is that preparation is key. We had failed to anticipate the roadblocks and educate ourselves about them, which left us at a disadvantage. We also didn't quite understand the impenetrable fiefdom of LADOT. We didn't recognize that this might have been a time to

---

[41]"Eyes on the Street: New Metro Blue/Expo Line Train Gate," *Streetsblog Los Angeles*, February 16, 2018. https://la.streetsblog.org/2018/02/16/eyes-on-the-street-new-metro-blueexpo-line-train-gate

call in the CEO that might have been worth it. When the CEO wanted this fiefdom penetrated, it turned out it was possible. But not for OEI on its own.

The Case of the West Santa Ana Branch

Metro has not one, but two budget and finance offices. Remember that Countywide Planning was a separate organization during the old RTD days and therefore at one point, had its own budget. When those organizations were merged, some duplication remained. Financial Planning within Countywide Planning, in addition to the Office of Management and Budget (OMB), was one of those lovely duplications.

Financial Planning were the folks sent to greet me on my first day at Metro. The leader of this group, David Yale, was a disheveled looking man who generally seemed harried and was often seen carrying around several binders with papers spilling out of them. He was known as a financial genius who could tell you where all the money was and where it was supposed to be spent.

David and his colleagues explained the work that had been done on P3 and how it had been a massive failure that they had to clean up. Millions had been spent on consultants[42] while the P3 program moved around the agency from one office to another. Finally, it wound up with Financial Planning, where David effectively killed it. Now Phil was here, and it was my problem.

We were not naive about taking on this task. We knew it had failed at Metro several times. However, we assumed that failure was largely due to Metro staff being pushed to do a P3 for P3s sake. They had never found the right project and were being pushed by the previous CEO and mayor to show that P3 could work and prove that it could accelerate projects. We thought if we carefully chose the right project, it was possible. David and his colleagues claimed that they had the same perspective, and over lunch on our first day they suggested four projects that could be potential P3s.

---

[42]Full disclosure, in an ironic twist I am now a partner in a later iteration of the same consulting firm that David trashed to me on that first day.

This was, in retrospect, the pinnacle of our relationship. What I did not understand at the time is that Financial Planning saw P3 as an existential threat. Financial Planning controlled the financial projections at the agency. Any use of P3 would mean giving up some element of that control to us and a private financial entity. As we would soon find out, they would go to any extreme to prevent that from happening.

WSAB Challenges

The year 2016 was a memorable election year. But the surprising presidential results were not the only major change for Los Angeles. The Measure M sales tax initiative, funding $120 billion in transportation investment, also passed. Also, the two remaining Republican county supervisors on LA Metro's Board—Mike Antonovich and Don Knabe—had been termed out and were no longer on the Board. Antonovich was replaced by Kathryn Barger, his former chief of staff. Knabe was replaced by former congresswoman and political scion Janice Hahn.

As mentioned previously, LA County Supervisor is an incredibly powerful position. Each district has approximately 2 million people and you are their sole representative in the regional government.[43] The supervisors have long been nicknamed "the five little kings."[lvi]

Not long after Measure M had passed, we were summoned to meet with Janice Hahn. The West Santa Ana Branch (WSAB—pronounced like the Japanese condiment) was her top priority as it was in her district. I had met her once before, when she was still in Congress and I testified at a Congressional hearing on autonomous vehicles after I had already moved to Los Angeles. She was very friendly to me then, as I was representing LA on a panel in DC. This time, now that she represented the Gateway Cities, she was not so friendly.

"So how are we going to build this line faster?" she asked.

---

[43]Hilda Solis served in the U.S. House of Representatives from 2001 to 2009, went on to serve as Secretary of Labor for President Obama, before deciding to run to replace Gloria Molina's seat as County Supervisor. https://www.washingtonpost.com/blogs/govbeat/wp/2014/06/04/from-white-house-cabinet-to-county-office-why-hilda-solis-is-back-home/.

I explained how we hoped that P3 could accelerate the construction of the WSAB light-rail and deliver it earlier than anticipated. She ignored most of the details and focused on the estimate I gave her for finishing the line. Whatever it was (I am sure I was being very bullish to satisfy her), it was not fast enough. She demanded I do better. I explained the funding situation again, and how we couldn't build the line faster unless funding became available sooner.

And she said, "Well, you're the Office of Extraordinary Innovation, you should be able to fix that." I considered explaining that despite the name of the office, we could not actually conjure up money. I wisely kept these thoughts to myself.

But we thought that perhaps we could use Janice Hahn's power to our advantage. We had received three UPs from the private sector proposing to deliver the project as a P3. We had done the analysis and proposed the P3 model as worth pursuing, and Phil had already agreed. If a P3 really could accelerate the project, as we believed it could, anyone standing in the way of P3 would need to answer to Janice. This line of thinking worked well in our minds, but reality was a different story.

First, while we believed P3 could accelerate the project, proving that would not be easy. The burden of proof was on us to show that this new project delivery method would be faster than traditional delivery. But there was no way to guarantee that or prove it without delivering the same project both ways and seeing which one was better, which was obviously impossible.

This is one of the main obstacles to improving project delivery—no one has to prove that the previously used method is the right one, despite ample evidence for project delays and cost overruns, but anything new must be rigorously studied. This leads to underestimating the risks of existing methods and overestimating the risks of new ones, an environment in which impenetrable fiefdoms thrive.

Second, given how difficult it would be to "prove" that P3 was better, we may have overestimated the willingness of any elected official to stand behind the idea. Without any kind of guarantee that P3 would work, Janice Hahn would have to be willing to take on an impenetrable fiefdom composed of many parts. That would turn out to be a lot to ask.

Organized Labor

The first known component of this fiefdom was organized labor. Labor proved to be a challenging obstacle. We had been trying to lay the groundwork for union acceptance of P3, but it had not been going well. LA Metro has five unions, and they had regular monthly meetings with top Metro executives. I began attending these meetings to brief them on P3 and try to reassure them that this was not an anti-labor initiative.

But the leader of the Amalgamated Transit Union (ATU)[44] was not having it. He would yell at us about all the broken promises from prior Metro bosses, how Phil had already betrayed them, and how P3 was a scam to break the union. We tried to explain that we had no plans to use anyone but his members on the project, and that the cost savings were not related to labor rates or benefits. But he had little incentive to believe us. He had every incentive to cause trouble for Phil to extract concessions later.

That might have been surmountable on its own. Eventually, the ATU would realize that in a choice between having a project completed in 10 years versus having it done in 20 years, his membership would benefit more from earlier delivery. If the decision could be reduced to that stark comparison, the outcome would favor us. But until then, labor would be part of this impenetrable fiefdom.

County Counsel

In anticipation of negotiations with labor, Phil asked me to work with the Chief Operations Officer Jim Gallagher and the head of Human Resources (and liaison to labor) to develop a strategy for working with the unions. Jim, being a veteran of labor negotiations at many transit agencies, and someone who already believed that P3 was valuable, was a very practical partner in this endeavor. HR, on the other hand, whom I had already managed to anger through the frustrations I voiced regarding HR processes, was unlikely to be an ally.

---

[44]ATU represents Metro's mechanics, service attendants, and maintenance personnel.

County Counsel, however, was HR's natural ally. As we discussed earlier, County Counsel works for the county, not Metro, even though they act as Metro counsel. This means that they have little incentive to stick their necks out to solve Metro problems, and every incentive to tell you why you cannot do something. Without consulting us, HR and County Counsel brought in outside counsel to help determine whether Metro was authorized to use P3 to build public transit. We hadn't even considered that this might be an issue, but they found some ambiguity in Metro's labor agreements. While Metro was clearly authorized to use P3 to deliver heavy rail projects, the way the agreement was written left some wiggle room about authority for light-rail projects. I am not making this up. Their conclusion: too risky. Labor could seize upon this loophole and sue and the whole project would be negated.

They advised that proceeding would be a bad idea. The unions would sue. We went back and forth between our counsel and theirs and never reached a conclusion. We collectively presented to the Board in closed session about potential challenges to P3 with labor, and it looked like the Board might still be open to P3. This obstacle might have been overcome on its own, but County Counsel was another cog in an impenetrable fiefdom.

Financial Planning

Financial Planning made it clear that they did not want Metro to use a P3. Whether they collectively believed it really was a bad idea or just wanted to ensure that their reign over the Metro financial model was preserved, we do not know. But in every meeting on P3, they successfully threw up every obstacle they could find. One of their favorite points to highlight was that P3 does not create new money. As P3 experts, we knew this. But they kept saying it so that we had to explain our way past that issue every time. This stalled for time.

They also made every other argument possible. Labor will never agree to it (see above). County Counsel isn't even sure it is legal (see above). The private sector will find a way to screw us. There are no potential savings in costs because public financing is cheaper. There are no potential savings in cost because we must use organized labor. No one is better at building and operating rail lines than Metro. All these arguments could easily be dismissed, but Financial Planning wasn't interested in the counterpoint. They were interested in delay.

One particularly effective delay tactic was refusing to give anyone else access to the information they had. Financial Planning refused to share their financial model. First, they said it wasn't updated. When the deadline for it to be updated came and went, they said it still wasn't ready. Then they couldn't share it because our consultants couldn't be trusted with it (unlike their consultants). Then they would share it, but only a piece of it. Then it had to be updated again. And so on.

Eventually, after being hammered sufficiently by Phil for the umpteenth time, Financial Planning did share the model. Now they had to switch tactics and simply argue with every cost-efficiency argument we made. We showed time and again how we projected a better value for money using P3 on WSAB than traditional project delivery.

Ultimately, Financial Planning successfully employed the time-honored bureaucrat strategy of simply waiting out the opposition. They spent enough time arguing that they were able to keep delaying until Phil announced his departure. Now we had to start over and convince the new boss, who was soon under pressure to make a final decision about the project delivery method. We kept trying, but by that time it was a lost cause. The new CEO has little incentive to take such a risk and crush this complicated fiefdom right out of the gate.

Two years after we left Metro, after 7+ years of study, millions of dollars spent on analysis, and an incredible amount of effort, Metro announced that WSAB would not be a P3.[lvii] Our efforts had gotten the agency nowhere. This fiefdom was not to be penetrated.

Recognize Impenetrable Fiefdoms

Some battles are largely unwinnable. In general, innovative concepts and new ideas are adopted through collaboration. Finding partners who are as excited as you are to incubate and implement new ideas and organizational improvements is critical to success. Sometimes, you'll identify projects that, if implemented, would add substantial value to the agency and constituents. But if the powers that be don't want to collaborate due to fiefdom syndrome, it's likely not the best battle to pick.

The concepts that we pushed forward for fare modernization with TAP, signal preemption on the Expo Line with LADOT, and P3 project delivery for WSAB were valuable. TAP ultimately pushed forward valuable fare payment modernizations, and LADOT eventually worked with LA Metro on transit signal priority and preemption. Our inability to collaborate to bring these projects to fruition sooner was in part because we weren't the right dance partner to penetrate these fiefdoms.

However, while breaking through impenetrable fiefdoms didn't align with the goals of OEI and isn't the right battle for most staff in public agencies to pick, it is worth it for leaders with the appropriate power and remit to dissolve these fiefdoms when possible. They are, and will continue to be, massive impediments to public servants improving services for their customers and constituents.

For those of us without that mandate, the best defense is identifying impenetrable fiefdoms early and finding other must-win battles to meet your goals. Here are some signs that you might need to try something else because you won't be getting through this door:

- *Refusal to share information.* If the partner you need for this project consistently delays giving you the necessary data or information you need to move forward, this is not someone who wants to work with you. Both TAP and Financial Planning consistently withheld information, but we kept pushing and hoping.
- *No interest in meeting or solving problems.* Similarly, if the partner avoids meetings, doesn't respond to e-mails, and is repeatedly unavailable to discuss the topic, they probably aren't going to help you. Both TAP and Financial Planning avoided us as much as possible, to avoid dealing with the issue we cared about.
- *Lack of agreement on the problem.* If the partner does not agree that the problem you are trying to solve is actually a problem, you are not going to get anywhere. LADOT did not agree that slow speed on rail lines was a problem they wanted to solve, even

if they purported to care, because they indicated they cared more about cars.

- ***The same questions are posed repeatedly.*** All of these cases showed people asking the same questions, largely as distractions, over and over again, like Groundhog Day. This indicates that they are not listening to or believing the answers, and are not an honest partner.

CHAPTER 4

It's a Marathon *and* a Sprint

When I first arrived in Los Angeles, I was dismayed to discover how long it took to get anywhere by public transit. In my neighborhood, Studio City, there are several buses within walking distance, and a subway station nearby. It seemed like it would theoretically be very easy to use one of these options to get where I needed to go.

My East Coast brain hadn't yet processed why these options were not going to work for me. The closest bus could connect me to another bus to go any meaningful distance, but it only ran every 20 minutes,[45] so that would mean waiting for that bus and then waiting for the next one too.

Meanwhile, the other buses were a more substantial 15-minute walk, and only one ran more than once per hour—the others were so infrequent that they rarely worked for me. The subway requires either a drive or one of those multi-bus rides.

In observing this situation, I thought of people unable to drive, or for whom car ownership was a substantial financial burden. I imagined them organizing their lives around these long (and often unpleasant) walk times, waiting times, and the need to make multiple transfers. Anyone without a car would be at a severe disadvantage when it came to doing anything. Metro had to do better if we were going to provide a service that improved our customers' lives.

Fixing this problem in Los Angeles (and most American cities) is a struggle. Those buses run at low frequencies and on certain routes for a reason—demand for transit is low in an environment where car

---

[45]In general, frequent service has headways of less than 15 minutes, or ideally less than 10 minutes. At 20 minutes, it becomes much more necessary for riders to really plan out their trips.

ownership isn't just seen as a preference, but a necessity. Research has even shown that people in Los Angeles will buy cars as soon as they can, often at the expense of other essentials, because the alternative—navigating the city without one—is often too difficult.[lviii]

This isn't just some LA cultural phenomenon—it's the result of land use policies that have prioritized the car over all other forms of mobility and accessibility. Single-use zoning, low-density development, wide arterial roadways, and minimum parking requirements have shaped a built environment where transit struggles to be efficient and competitive.[lix] The feedback loop is self-reinforcing. We design cities around cars, which encourages more driving, which depresses transit ridership, which leads agencies to reduce service, further discouraging use.

At Metro, we weren't positioned to take on land use, but we were positioned to change policies and support transit expansion. Thus, congestion pricing (see Chapter 5) was our attempt to break the cycle. But short of that, we needed to do something more feasible and immediate.

Balancing Short- and Long-Term Thinking

Before I accepted my role at Metro, I sat down with Phil and told him that, among other things, I wanted to bring on-demand transportation options to LA Metro. Two opportunities presented themselves to OEI relatively early on. First, there was a grant opportunity from the U.S. Department of Transportation (USDOT) that was aimed specifically at testing on-demand options for transit, administered through the Federal Transit Administration (FTA) under the Mobility on Demand (MOD) program. I gave my staff the green light to pursue this grant in full force. Second, one of our earliest UPs pitched the idea of on-demand transportation through microtransit.

These opportunities created two paths to push this concept and set up a useful dichotomy. We could sprint to the implementation and operation of the USDOT funded project to demonstrate success, while concurrently taking the required time to run the marathon to develop a Metro-operated on-demand service.

TNCs—Friends or Foes?

"Why would we partner with a competitor?" Our colleagues were shocked and confused when we suggested working with transportation network companies (TNCs) like Uber and Lyft. In 2016, these companies were venture capital-backed and proliferating in cities across the world. Transit agencies often saw them as the enemy, and not without reason. They tended to provide a far better service—point to point, with private rides for relatively low prices. They seemed like a way to kill off any public transit users with sufficient income.

These companies were able to pull this off because their leadership convinced themselves and their investors that the most important business metric was not revenue, but instead the number of users and their frequency of use. The idea was that once they had substantial market share, they would figure out how to turn those users into astronomical margins for their investors.

Within this logic, to expand and solidify their user bases, many of these companies made the business decision to subsidize fares. It worked. In cities across the United States and the world, riders found that they could access a comfortable, door-to-door transportation service at a lower price and in a more comfortable vehicle than traditional taxis. Ridership for these services exploded.[lx]

As Uber and Lyft grew, the transportation nerds began to analyze. The private sector was delivering a better service, and the price to the customer was in some cases not much higher than public transit.[46] If the

---

[46]During this time, the prices for TNCs were artificially low and designed to drive customer adoption. There also wasn't a simple pricing formula—these companies often used A/B testing on pricing to figure out the price point resulted in their target adoption and utilization rates. This was also paired with the introduction of UberPOOL and LyftLine, which offered shared rides for individuals who were going in the same direction. These services were priced even lower to drive adoption. For a short period of time, as measured only through our personal experiences and use of these services, we found that we could often schedule "shared" rides from origins and destinations within Downtown Los Angeles that weren't meaningfully more expensive than riding the bus ($1.75). As highlighted in our later discussion on TNCs and data sharing, there isn't any research analyzing prices that fell outside of their "standard" pricing model as none of these companies were willing to share financial data with researchers.

private sector could do that, what was the purpose of public transit? How could public transportation agencies capture the benefits of these new technologies? Were TNCs exacerbating congestion and tailpipe emissions or enabling mode shift? Should transit agencies work with TNCs (as we did with Uber-Expo), or compete against them?

Within OEI, we welcomed these conversations. While the arguments may have had varying merit, the debate helped give center stage to key challenges facing public transportation. Academics and industry associations researched some of these questions with the limited data they were able to access. A report in 2016 supported the idea that TNCs had the potential to complement transit by providing first and last mile connections to transit.[lxi] Another study found that on-demand options were expanding traveler choice, recommending that policymakers and regulators seek to integrate on-demand features into existing services.[lxii] Another study found that TNC trips were serving those who were not well served spatially or temporally by public transit services.[lxiii]

These reports and conversations were happening in real time—concurrent with pricing designed specifically to drive adoption and Silicon Valley hype that resulted in these companies having bloated valuations. But it was clear that at least in the near term, if the public sector didn't figure out how to work with these companies or regulate them, their benefits wouldn't be equitably distributed. While there were still many unknowns associated with these companies and their technologies, we felt that we owed it to our customers to test out partnerships to see if we could put forward new mobility solutions that better met their needs.

Our First Taste of Opposition

When the FTA dropped a Notice of Funding Opportunity (NOFO) for the MOD grant, we saw an opportunity. The most recent surface transportation reauthorization, the FAST (Fixing America's Surface Transportation) Act, had just passed the previous December (2015), and had authorized new funding for public transit research and innovation grants. Marla, OEI's head of research, who had worked for me in my previous life in DC, had been tracking this grant before she arrived in LA. She and Emma worked to develop a proposal with a TNC to deliver first and last mile rides to and from selected rail stations across our region. We had enough information to know this was exactly the type of grant application FTA was looking for—we thought it had to be easy enough to pull together the necessary partnerships internally and externally to make our proposal a reality.

First, we had to figure out the process for developing proposals at Metro. The Planning Department was incubating an idea, and to position Metro competitively for this grant, they intended to have only one proposal submitted from the agency. Learning this, we scheduled a meeting with the team leading the pursuit, feeling confident that we could persuade our colleagues to support our concept for this grant instead. Our proposal aligned exactly with what the Associate Administrator was asking for, which would position us well for selection. We presented our well-researched concept and referenced the various events in which the Associate Administrator directly called for such a submission.

But we found that this approach was ineffective. What we didn't appreciate walking into that meeting was that this wasn't an academic exercise. We also weren't well positioned to win them over just because we thought our idea better met the criteria of the grant. We were asking another team at Metro to forgo an opportunity to seek funding for a project that they had been working on much longer than any of us had been at Metro. Why would they throw their support behind some new idea from the innovation office?

Our colleagues let us know that they could not support OEI's proposal, suggesting it was unlikely FTA would consider such an idea. Their skepticism likely stemmed from resource constraints and differing interpretations of grant criteria. Ultimately, after enough pressure, the grants office gave us the green light to submit a second proposal in addition to the proposal the Planning Department pushed forward.

Developing a Winning Proposal

The FTA's MOD grant laid out an ambitious vision of delivering seamless, multimodal transportation through "enabling technologies and innovative partnerships." The program's guiding principles included (1) a requirement to be partnership driven and demonstrate teaming efforts from the public and private sectors, (2) a requirement for partners to share sufficient data, and (3) a requirement to demonstrate and promote equitable mobility service for all travelers, "including communities such as low income, the aging populations, and persons with disabilities."

We saw an opportunity and quickly set out gathering an array of partners, including academics, and partner transit agencies like Foothill Transit and LADOT. But we knew the big whale to catch would be one of the two major TNCs, Uber or Lyft.

At the time, TNCs were notorious for largely operating without permits or regulatory structures. Companies like Uber and Lyft positioned themselves as technology companies, rather than transportation companies. Their party line was that they merely provided a mobile application to connect riders to drivers. Why should a technology company be subject to regulations that were designed for transportation companies, such as having background checks for drivers or carrying a certain level of insurance coverage? When they started feeling the threat of potential regulations at the local levels in California, they lobbied the state to preempt localities from regulating. In 2014, they won this battle in California and TNCs became officially regulated by the California Public Utilities Commission (CPUC).[47]

CPUC's regulations were business friendly and allowed the TNCs to operate with limited oversight. The TNCs heavily invested in lobbying campaigns in states across the country to drive for state level regulation. As TNC ridership increased, cities felt steamrolled. Not only could they not define the framework by which these new services would operate in their jurisdictions, but they also didn't have the data necessary to measure the impact that these services were having on their streets and transportation systems more broadly.

Uber and Lyft refused to come to the table and share useful data with cities or transit agencies. They were afraid that any data that was made available to cities or transit agencies would be used against them,

---

[47]Determining and implementing new regulations on a new industry takes time, and even though the CPUC became the regulator in 2014, they still had to do extensive work to determine what the regulations would be and how they would regulate them. This took time, and meant that in 2016, it was still a "new frontier" relatively speaking.

either leaking to their competitors through public sector open data requirements, which could reduce their competitive advantage, or used
by governments to figure out how to more meaningfully regulate their
businesses.[48]

Uber and Lyft's core business model was to provide service directly to
the end customer, not to work with governments. FTA hypothesized that
perhaps these companies would share data if given the proper incentive.
To that end, data capture was written in as a specific requirement in the
NOFO, requiring private-sector project partners to share data with the
lead implementing agency and ultimately the federal government.

We liked this requirement. Government is like any other business
where investors (the public) demand data driven metrics and insights to
better understand their return on investment (ROI). If we were going to
subsidize TNC rides, we needed data to be able to independently measure
and evaluate the pilot's success and to better understand how to operationally coordinate. Data would also allow us to continually evaluate and
iterate on our approach, yielding better outcomes in the long term.

It was going to be challenging to get a TNC to agree to sufficient data
sharing terms. But TNCs were even less prepared to navigate equitable
service requirements. While, it may have been technically "compliant"[49]
to secure another service provider to ensure that there were options for

---

[48]While these were their actual concerns, as Marla can attest to from her time
working at Bird, the public-facing arguments that TNCs were promulgating were
about "privacy issues," a concern that could better resonate with the public.

[49]The ADA has an equivalent service requirement that says transit agencies
must provide passengers with disabilities services that are as good as the service
provided to passengers without disabilities. There is also a "stand in shoes" requirement that says that if a transit agency procures service from a private-sector
company that the private-sector company is beholden to all the same requirements as the transit agency. There is some space for interpretation, and at the
time, the Chief Civil Rights Officer at Metro's interpretation was that if we were
going to use public dollars to pay for TNC service, then the TNC operator had to
provide the same service to people with disabilities. As of writing this, these rules
still don't have a consistent interpretation. For example, publicly subsidized bike
share doesn't offer a fully equivalent option for people with disabilities. While the
ADA is critical landmark legislation that has played an important role in building a more equitable society, creating space for the provision of services such as
publicly subsidized bike share or on-demand transportation also contributes to
building a more equitable society.

people in wheelchairs or people who needed other support, as required by FTA and the ADA of 1990, we wanted our TNC partner to innovate and come up with solutions for providing equitable service within their standard operating model. This would prove to be a huge challenge.

Nonetheless, with all the arrogance and naivete in the world, we called up the policy folks at Lyft and asked if they wanted to pursue this opportunity with us. Emily Warren, then the Head of Transportation Policy at Lyft, had made a name for herself in the industry. She had been on the conference circuit for a handful of years preaching Lyft's desire to align the needs of the public and private sectors in delivering high quality transportation. She had a background in public policy and had previously worked on Capitol Hill. Her team supported the idea that TNCs complemented transit rather than cannibalized it, and had heavily invested in a marketing campaign spreading the good word in the hope that partnerships with transit agencies would give their brand a competitive edge against the competition.

Uber, on the other hand, had cultivated a bad-boy, anti-regulatory image. A few months prior, in February 2016, Uber and Pinellas Suncoast Transit Agency (PSTA) in Florida announced a first and last mile partnership.[lxiv] As a part of this partnership, PSTA subsidized Uber rides that originated or ended at designated transit stops. PSTA, however, did not receive what we believed to be sufficient data, nor did they provide solutions to meet FTA and ADA regulatory requirements. Our vision exceeded what Uber was willing to provide at the time, leading us to believe they weren't the right fit for this partnership.

After an initial conversation, Emily and her team visited Metro headquarters. We walked through our vision and expectations of what the Lyft team would be responsible for when the time came for project implementation. To our surprise and excitement, they agreed to all our requests without negotiation. We officially had a partner for our MOD proposal, and not just any old partner, a service provider with a meaningful user base in Southern California. From our perspective, we thought this would help position our project for success, allowing Metro to leverage the marketing and customer acquisition expertise of Lyft, thereby easily driving adoption of our program. It seemed almost too good to be true. It was.

We submitted our proposal in July and eagerly waited to hear back. It was an election year and the end of President Obama's two-term presidency. As Hillary Clinton and Donald Trump waged challenging campaigns, the Executive Branch tried to support Secretary Clinton by announcing as many grant awards as possible prior to voters going to the polls on November 8. The MOD grant was among a tranche of grant awards announced in October of that year, pushed through in record time.

We were thrilled to learn that FTA selected our proposal for an award, granting us and our vast array of partners $1.3 million, the largest grant of the cycle. This was a huge win for OEI. Our office had been staffed for less than a year, and we had already brought in meaningful federal funding to test our ideas. We had alignment from our external partners and a defined funding source. We thought we were well positioned for success.

Doing the Work Up Front

I have this crazy and sometimes anachronistic idea that thoughtful public interest policy is informed by rigorous research. One of my favorite examples of this can be found in the U.S. history of deregulating the air, rail, and trucking industries. Supported by extensive analysis, economist Alfred Kahn argued that deregulation of these industries would increase competition, lower fares, and benefit the public. His research and leadership ultimately led to the Airline Deregulation Act of 1978, and the subsequent Staggers Act and Motor Carrier Act.[lxv] Kahn's research and advocacy resulted in reduced rates for these services across the board and enhanced competition. Most importantly, it demonstrated that there is inherent value to research-informed policy making.

Informed by this belief, prior to winning the grant, we studied the partnerships that had been executed between transit agencies and on-demand service providers. We had conducted initial research on this topic even before we arrived at Metro. We had read the relevant literature and interviewed a variety of folks who had been on the vanguard of partnership with on-demand providers. But we felt there was value in conducting a more thorough analysis to better understand the partnerships our peer transit agencies had developed and the barriers they had encountered in contracting and implementing these programs.

We found that while these partnerships were at the time being touted at every industry conference, they had largely been marketing partnerships in which no money exchanged hands, like the Uber-Expo Metro partnership Colin Peppard had facilitated a few months earlier. While Colin was able to impressively pull off that partnership in just six weeks, we wanted to do more. The fact that most agencies hadn't tried to move beyond marketing suggested that many of our peers faced similar bureaucratic challenges and lacked an institutional structure like OEI with the capacity to push their agencies to the next step of partnership.

There were, however, two projects that included service delivery and the exchange of real money. PSTA was subsidizing TNC rides that originated and ended at transit stops. Similarly, the Kansas City Area Transportation Authority (KCATA) was operating the first of its kind microtransit service. We conducted extensive interviews with stakeholders working on both projects to learn from the challenges and successes that each project encountered.[50]

This exercise informed the design of our program and our approach to working with both internal stakeholders and private-sector vendors, creating a roadmap for potential challenges to anticipate and manage early in the process. We even published a paper on our findings through the Transportation Research Board.[lxvi]

Taking on Silicon Valley

After the initial enthusiasm over winning the grant opportunity wore off, it was time to figure out how to implement the concept. This meant figuring out how to define a new business model with Lyft, which at the time was a unicorn valued at multiple billions.[lxvii] But working with Lyft would turn out to be just part of the battle. We would also have to figure out how to move this concept within Metro and FTA.

We got to work designing the project with Lyft. We were excited—going into this project, Emily and her team had enthusiastically agreed to all our asks. We were going to build a first of its kind partnership with a

---

[50]Both agencies faced challenges and have since refined their programs but still operate some version of on-demand transit today.

major TNC that would be the blueprint for transit agency partnerships with TNCs for years to come.

But we were quickly disillusioned. Lyft was a start-up, and Emily was a start-up executive. Start-ups teach their staff to move fast, break things, and ask for forgiveness later. This can be a useful strategy for getting things done quickly and makes a lot of sense for businesses whose value is built on speed and hype. Emily was able to say yes to us without running it up the food chain because that's what she and everyone else who has been mentored by Silicon Valley had been taught. The first job is to win the project—the second job is to figure out what to do once you win.

Emily had, to her credit, anticipated that the biggest internal hurdle to implementing our MOD project, and similar projects they were working on with other agencies, was going to be data sharing. While FTA was reviewing our proposal, the Lyft team was trying to get internal buy-in on what they were comfortable sharing with transit agencies. They weren't, however, trying to figure out how to deliver on the other commitments they made to us, such as providing equitable service (read—operating vehicles that are accessible to people in wheelchairs).

As we attempted to finalize the project details with Lyft, it became apparent that they had selective amnesia regarding the commitments they had made to us during the proposal development phase—even those commitments that were made in writing. Whether or not they truly forgot what they committed to (which is entirely plausible for a person working a job with an early-stage start-up culture) or it was a negotiation tactic, we found ourselves in a confusing and frustrating position.

Unfortunately, we didn't have a Memorandum of Understanding (MOU) or anything official—we just had a few e-mails. But perhaps more problematically, we really wanted to work with Lyft. We knew that without one of the two major TNCs, our vision would have to take a different shape, as it would mean that rider acquisition would be much more challenging. And Lyft was the easier TNC to work with at this time.

Lyft suggested that we shift our project to better align with the "partnership" approach that Emily's team had been developing internally. The idea was that they would generate a promo code that was valid within specific geofences around whatever stations we selected, and then some discount could be given to riders who used that promo. They agreed that they could still share data with us, but not the data that we had initially agreed to—it would be aggregated in a way that rendered it meaningless for our intended analysis. Further, they took our equity and accessibility requirements off the table and suggested that we work with a third party to deliver on those components of the project.

Emily genuinely wanted to work with us. A partnership with LA Metro—the third largest transit agency in the country by ridership—would be a huge win for her personally and her vision for the opportunity of collaboration between TNCs and transit agencies. A vision and potential that we shared with her. But public policy teams at start-ups are often treated, in practice or in organizational design, as an arm of their marketing team. The vision the OEI and Emily's team shared did not align with the vision of Lyft's investors, making it impossible for Emily's team to follow through on their initial commitments.

In retrospect, this made a lot of sense. Lyft's financial backers were investing in a direct-to-consumer business model. As a pre-IPO company, Lyft's job was to position itself favorably for a high valuation for its next round of venture capital. This meant giving the investors what they wanted. For our project, we were asking Lyft to shift its business model toward business-to-government, which was a much less appealing business model to their investors. After working to negotiate with Lyft for more than six months, we saw the situation with increasing clarity. It eventually became obvious that we had to break up with Lyft.

This wasn't news OEI wanted to acknowledge. We had already invested a significant amount of time in the partnership with Lyft. And we were still really focused on the idea of leveraging the "network effect" of a company that already had a large user base in Los Angeles. We worked tirelessly to drive our vision into reality, and for better or for worse, we weren't ones to wave the white flag unless we really had to.

I decided to bring the dilemma to our Advisory Board[51]—our group of outside academics, thought leaders, and advocates—for advice. After I explained all the machinations that had gone on in our negotiations with Lyft, it was obvious to our advisers that we needed to pull the plug and move on. To these outsiders, it was clear that we should in fact have

---

[51]Additional explanation on our Advisory Board is included in Chapter 5.

pulled the plug long before, which was a huge advantage to having an Advisory Board. We had been so committed to making it work with this one service provider that we missed the larger picture that we just needed to implement a project and start iterating. Inertia is powerful stuff.

Emily and I found time for a call while I was sitting eating a bland fish taco at the Las Vegas airport (we were both a bit busy). She was not surprised, and the breakup was far easier than I had anticipated. While OEI had burned a lot of valuable time, we learned some critical lessons. We were sitting in the innovation office of the most well-funded transit agency in the United States. While that gave us a lot of external power to throw around, it wasn't going to give us the power to change the business model of a multibillion-dollar company from Silicon Valley.

Sole-Source Justification

One of the many forward-looking components of the MOD grant was that named partners written into the initial proposal could be included on the project without going through a competitive procurement. While in theory competitive procurements play a valuable role in giving vendors a fair shot at winning contracts, they are also extremely time-consuming, and don't necessarily always yield the best outcomes. FTA wanted selected demonstration projects to be deployed and iterated on quickly, with a written expectation of projects being implemented within 12 months of project award. By allowing recipients to bypass competitive procurement, they could support recipients in accelerating projects.

We knew that we wanted to use this flexibility, which was in part why we did the upfront work during the proposal phase to assemble our team of partners. We also knew both from the experience we had in launching the Uber-Expo marketing partnership and from our research that procurement and contracting were likely to be a challenge. Any added flexibility to make this process easier was welcomed with open arms.

Within this context, we opened conversations with Metro's Procurement office as soon as possible. We started by educating our procurement partners on the project and its goals. Because this project was very different from much of Metro's work, this took time. Remember, when working in a public sector innovation office, you'll quickly discover that "no" becomes a familiar response from both internal and external partners. At first, those rejections will sting or feel insurmountable. But eventually, you'll hear them enough times that it becomes background noise. They are actually a sign you're headed in the right direction!

Procurement offices are not exactly known for being innovative. But sometimes you can find an individual who wants to break new ground. As mentioned in Chapter 2, Senior Executive Officer Carolina Coppolo was assigned to support OEI in navigating vendor/contracts management. While she was extremely vigilant to ensure that we followed all laws and regulations, she was unburdened by the idea that things had to be done the way that they had always been done. This worldview is not common throughout Metro's Vendor/Contracts Management Department, and it is also not common across similar Procurement offices at peer agencies. Working with Carolina was a gift. Yet, when we asked her how to sole source (directly award without competition) the contract we had previously been working on with Lyft, even she told us it wasn't possible. Naturally.

But since we didn't know how to facilitate this type of sole-source procurement, we called up our point of contact at FTA to get a better understanding of their envisioned process. While language was directly written into the grant opportunity noting that key partners were "eligible for noncompetitive awards," it turned out that the other grant recipients had not called up FTA to discuss how to facilitate this in practice. Sometimes, just asking the question is key to innovation.

A classic policy tool for innovation is to remove barriers and create flexibility within a regulation or policy. The idea is that after a barrier is removed, decision makers will have an opportunity to create a new and better solution to the problem. In practice, it often doesn't work that way. Decision makers are subject to the rules of (1) inertia (i.e., our delayed decision to break up with Lyft), and (2) fear. When they are given the opportunity to do something new the easiest thing for them to do is just to continue to do what they were already doing (inertia). And when they want to take a new approach, they often won't because of the fear of retribution.

These rules applied to many of the winners of the MOD grant. Most project managers simply used their standard procurement rules and did not leverage the procurement flexibility, termed a "sandbox" to indicate experimentation, that FTA had created for us.

Our point of contact at FTA didn't have an immediate answer. Was FTA really giving us the flexibility to sole source? After months of bureaucratic back and forth, we got the written interpretation that, yes, we could use a noncompetitive procurement for key partners within the grant.

By the time FTA was able to give us a written interpretation on sole sourcing, six months of working with procurement had already elapsed. This meant we had six months of nearly weekly meetings with our lead, checking in, and developing a trusting relationship. Thus, by the time we received the written confirmation from FTA, Procurement became comfortable using the e-mail from FTA as a sole-source justification for a noncompetitive procurement.

Finding a New Dance Partner

After discontinuing negotiations with Lyft, we were 12 months post notice of award, and we didn't have a service provider. Although very few, if any, other recipients in our cohort were much further along in their project implementation, we were anxious to not only show value to FTA but to the powers that be in Los Angeles more broadly. We no longer had our named partner at the table, but we didn't want to delay project deployment any further.

While we felt we were falling behind FTA's expectations in implementing our project, we had spent the previous 12 months doing something that many transit folks working with FTA are hesitant to do: overcommunicating. Historically, the role of FTA is to distribute funding and provide "guidance" to transit agencies. The funding has a suite of strings attached to it, and because transit agencies heavily rely on funding from FTA, those strings, or guidance, ultimately act like the rule of law. As such, FTA is perceived to be "Big Brother" breathing down the neck of transit agencies. The human response is often to tell them as little as possible and retain as much local flexibility as possible.

One of the key findings from our research was that FTA had demonstrated a unique willingness to provide support and flexibility in developing new mobility pilot programs. Informed by this finding, paired with our complete naivete, we decided early in the process to be a complete open book with FTA. This proved to be extremely valuable. This grant program was facilitated by FTA's Office of Research, Demonstration and Innovation and was designed to support transit agencies in trying new things; they didn't expect us to have everything figured out from day one.

When we came to FTA to discuss whether we could name a new key partner and continue to be exempt from competitive procurement, the conversation was shockingly easy. We had built trust with our federal partners, and they were excited to help us figure out how to move forward. They let us know that we could define it however we wanted and whoever our selection was would be our new key partner.

Metro's Procurement team eventually gave us the green light to define our own process. We knew that whoever we selected as our new partner needed to commit upfront, in writing, to the key terms of the program that Lyft was ultimately unable to commit to. We pulled together a term sheet, MOU, and developed the scope of our project—and then solicited proposals from all the vendors in the industry that we thought could have a shot at delivering on our scope, ultimately facilitating an extremely expedient informal procurement.

We received five proposals and selected Via as our service provider. While Via was not one of the two major TNCs, it had the advantage of having a business model that specifically called for working with the public sector. In retrospect, this was probably a more critical success factor than size or brand recognition. With our new partner at the table and a signed term sheet, it was time to do the internal heavy lifting of implementation. By this time, we thought we had overcome many of the key challenges of delivering this project. But despite all that work, we were still just at the beginning of project implementation.

Zone Selection

As part of the pilot, we had to select not only the three Metro stations but also the surrounding areas that would form the "catchment area," within which customers could access rideshare for travel to and from the station. Emma analyzed all of Metro's stations based on a series of criteria—including equity and access for civil rights and Environmental Justice populations, geographic diversity, and current first and last mile access and feasibility—and also considered where Via determined they could provide the greatest value (they looked at indicators like high daily rider activity, high employment density, high population density, and limited access to other public transit connections). One criterion that we did not initially consider, and which was left out of our FTA reports, was the political one.

Figure 4.1 is the boundary of the North Hollywood zone in May 2019, after we expanded the zone from 6 to 13 square miles. If you think this zone looks funky, it's because it is. From a customer service perspective, it is important to have intuitive boundaries for a zone, so that people can easily determine whether they are in the zone, and thus eligible to use the service. When you see extreme carve-outs like this, there is almost always a political rather than technical reason. In this case, Operations did not want the service to extend north of Burbank Boulevard or west of Tujunga Avenue because this is where some of the most robust Metro

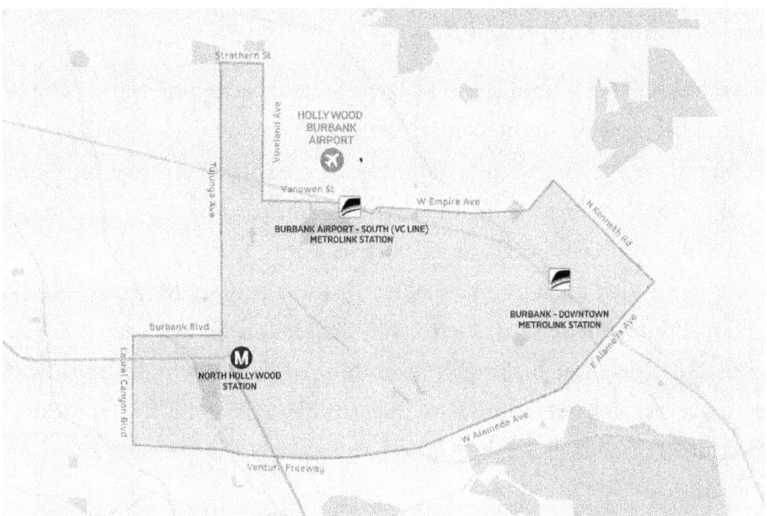

Figure 4.1 Map of the North Hollywood Mobility on Demand zone after expansion

Source: Los Angeles County Metropolitan Transportation Authority, "Metro's Partnership with Via: Quarter 1 Report," May 28, 2019, Fig. 2.

bus lines run. Operations' justifications for these limits vacillated between the claim that we would be cannibalizing our own service, and that we would piss off the unions who saw MOD as a threat to their future. OEI's perspective was that the point of this pilot was to learn from the technology and new service, and to test whether we could improve the mobility and access of our current and new customers. We were also concerned that this carve-out made it difficult for riders to understand the zone boundaries.

We did not win this fight. Jim Gallagher and I presented our cases to Phil regarding this service area like two lawyers advocating for their clients. Jim argued that we could not put in a private service where there was already a robust bus service because it would reduce ridership on the buses. I found this to be a confusing argument. If we provided customers with a better service (a first/last mile TNC ride) and they chose to use it instead of the bus, wouldn't that be because we were providing a better service? Wasn't that the whole idea? Phil liked this line of thinking, but in the end did not want to anger the unions any more than we already had. He ruled in Jim's favor.

Unlikely Allies: Legal and Risk

A typical planner within a transit agency who is designing transit service is not likely to have to interact regularly with the Legal and Risk Departments. However, the inherent nature of the type of projects that OEI pursued meant that most of the team was very familiar with County Counsel and Risk. For MOD, this was an asset we leaned into.

County Counsel's primary objective is to protect Metro from litigation. Unfortunately, at Metro, the distinction between legal advice and actual decision making is often blurred. What should be treated as input for consideration is frequently treated as the final decision. "Legal says no" is generally viewed as an acceptable reason not to do something.

It isn't completely unreasonable for staff to behave this way. Metro has extremely deep pockets. Metro's FY26 budget is around $9.5 billion. That means, depending on the size and scope of a lawsuit, the opposing side's legal team could theoretically go after insane sums of money.

From our research, we knew that contracting and working with Legal had been a challenge for peer agencies. So, like our approach with Procurement, we engaged with County Counsel as early as possible. Greg Levine was assigned to work on our project, and he patiently worked with us as we educated him on our crazy project, and he educated us on contracting at Metro. We met with him regularly and created a rapport that extended beyond red lines and strikeouts. Perhaps a benefit to the failed overextended courting phase with Lyft was that while we were Metro newbies coming into this project, by the time we really got to a contract, we had developed a strong, trusting relationship with Legal.

Similarly, when you are an agency that employs over 12,000 people, with a fleet of over 2,000 buses that cross 1,447 square miles of service area, and 107 stations with 109 miles of rail service, you have a very large risk profile. You probably also have a Chief of Risk, Safety, and Asset Management. Ours was Greg Kildare, and he became a frequent collaborator with OEI. At the time that we were pursuing this type of service partnership with Via, we were navigating uncharted territory. Actuaries did not know how to quantify risk and determine the appropriate coverage levels for insurance. Additionally, given that a signature feature of the TNC model was to leverage the personal auto coverage of their independent contractor drivers, there was concern that a service partnership would leave Metro vulnerable to gaps in coverage. To solve this, we had to negotiate for Via to purchase additional insurance coverage and also indemnify Metro. Given that we were in uncharted territory, Greg's initial instinct was to demand very expensive additional insurance policies and very high levels of indemnity, which in turn, would drive up the price and then make each individual ride that much more expensive.

However, throughout the four months of our project focusing almost exclusively on insurance and indemnification terms, Greg negotiated in good faith on our behalf, even when it would have been easier for him to demand that Via meet our stringent requirements or walk away. We deferred to him as the expert and kept him engaged in all our communications throughout, but we also were persistent in our message that we had to find a solution to make it work, and walking away was not an option.

In the end, when we had finalized all of the terms and conditions of our contract with Via and were only waiting on reaching an agreement on the level of insurance and indemnification with Via before signing the dotted line, Greg wrote a memo to Phil where he acknowledged that while we were moving forward without some risk, he was in agreement that a contract could be finalized.

The two Gregs and Carolina emerged as our strongest advocates. They supported us in educating our colleagues in other departments, allowing OEI to build extremely positive relationships across the agency through this process. After the contract was finally inked with Via, we felt like we had already run a marathon. But now we had to launch and operate our service, while concurrently pushing forward our second on-demand initiative, microtransit.

Metro Micro

In parallel to incubating and implementing MOD, we were also working on developing a microtransit project to bring on-demand transit service with a wider reach than MOD.[52] At the core of our hypothesis was that on-demand technology would add value to our customers, and we still had a lot to learn about the trade-offs of applying the varying business models, form factors, and use cases.

Early into my tenure at Metro, I called my friend at Via (the same company we ended up working with for MOD), whom I had known from my prior job, and suggested that their concept might make for an exciting pilot program. He flew to Los Angeles, and we walked around several Los Angeles neighborhoods, until we had blisters on our feet, observing where the service might make sense. When he returned to New York, he developed a UP and submitted it to Metro. It was one of the first that we received.

The initial reaction within Metro (outside OEI) to this proposal was, to put it mildly, negative. At its core, Metro is a bus agency, second only to New York's in size. The primary service it provides is by bus, and the entire agency is set up to provide those services in accordance with many

---

[52]Remember, MOD was testing the use case of independent contractor drivers using their own vehicles providing first-and-last mile shared rides to/from Metro stations.

rules, including federal, state, and local regulations, union contracts, and internal procedures. It was one thing for the agency, in 1990, to launch rail services, though I am sure that was a challenge as well. Paratransit is operated by Access Services, an entirely different organization that works closely with Metro, but is not the same organization. But launching an entirely new kind of vehicle service that was on demand and in partnership with a technology company was anathema in 2016.

The business model we were proposing was meaningfully different from MOD. This on-demand service would be operating using Metro-owned vehicles and operated by Metro staff. For all the challenges that we had launching MOD, it was in many ways a much easier concept for Metro to accept because it didn't require anyone except OEI to adopt a new job or new responsibilities.

In response to the concept of microtransit, many people within the agency were quick to bring forward reasons why it could never work. We had good answers to these questions, but that wasn't relevant to the people at Metro, who were more interested in presenting problems than developing solutions. That part was up to us. For example:

Point: The unions will never accept nonunion drivers operating Metro services.

Counterpoint: We are going to ask the unions to operate the service.

Point: Who will maintain the vehicles? That is also a union issue.

Counterpoint: The contract does not require vehicles to be maintained by the union unless they are on Metro property.

Point: Then, where will you store the vehicles?

Counterpoint: That is up to the private provider to figure out.

Point: Not everyone has a smartphone.

Counterpoint: We will provide a way to call for a ride without a smartphone.

Point: Not everyone has a credit or debit card.

Counterpoint: We will provide a way to pay with cash.

Point: How will you serve disabled people?

Counterpoint: All vehicles will be ADA compliant.

Point: It isn't safe to pick up and drop off just anywhere.

Counterpoint: We will provide specific pickup and drop-off areas that we know are safe.

Point: Funding microtransit will take away from funding operations.

Counterpoint: Microtransit will be a tiny fraction of the entire agency's annual budget.

And on and on. There were many obstacles, and we were mostly alone in trying to overcome them. It was also very difficult for staff to identify the potential benefits that offering such a service could provide. We had to methodically work through each of these challenges ourselves, finding solutions to problems we hadn't envisioned and, in many cases, that we didn't know existed.

Surprisingly, in the case of microtransit, we found ourselves facing opposition from outside the agency as well. In most cases, OEI was cheered and supported by the transit industry because we were trying to implement the ideas that everyone in the industry knew were worthwhile but faced serious bureaucratic internal challenges. In this case, the industry itself was resistant to the idea, and some of that resistance remains today, even though agencies around the country have now adopted some version of microtransit.

Several thought leaders, including Jarrett Walker, a consultant, expressed the belief that microtransit was nothing new. In his view, technology companies were trying to sell transit agencies on what was essentially a new version of "dial-a-ride"—a transit concept from the 1970s whereby people called for a ride that was then provided in a shared vehicle that pooled people together. Dial-a-ride was once hailed as a potential transit solution for sprawled suburban neighborhoods, but it largely failed to meet its promise. According to Walker, the tech companies had taken this failed idea, adorned it with the latest technology, and then sleekly packaged it to sell to naive transit agencies—but it still wouldn't work.

Admittedly, Walker had good reason to view the tech companies working in transportation skeptically. Uber's approach had been to storm into cities, ignore or thwart existing regulations, and hope that its service would be so popular that it couldn't be stopped. It prioritized growth at all costs, with little regard for how its actions might increase congestion and pollution, put taxis out of business, or hurt public safety. Lyft was in many ways worse, as it purported to be saving the world, and it was even founded by a transportation planner, but was doing the same thing as Uber. I attended a conference where the cofounder and president of Lyft said they were going to save the world from climate change by increasing the number of people in each vehicle. All of this came to a head when they (like Uber) hubristically invented the bus.[lxviii]

Jarrett was rightly concerned that transit agencies could be drawn toward shiny new objects like microtransit, instead of focusing on getting the basics right. At OEI, we had also developed a healthy skepticism toward technology companies with solutions in search of a problem. We were approached by people with flying cars, bike tires that didn't need air, light-up plug-in safety vests, autonomous buses that didn't actually exist, and many other ridiculous concepts. But we also knew that the transit industry needed to test new ideas.

While microtransit might just be an upgraded dial-a-ride, it is a major upgrade. Instead of calling and then waiting an uncertain amount of time for a ride, microtransit on a smartphone functions like Uber and gives you real-time information about your travel from start to finish. It guides you to where you need to be, counts down to pickup, presents estimated arrival times, and even shows where the vehicle is on a map. The reduction of friction is drastic and improves customer experience tremendously.

Some industry advocates were more stuck on the idea that the job of a transit agency is to run large vehicles as frequently as possible, period. They did not believe there was room for any other kind of service, because no other service could be as cost-effective on a large scale and solve the age-old coverage versus frequency dilemma.[lxix] And they are correct in the sense that microtransit is inherently more expensive than buses on a per-passenger basis. This is a simple numbers issue—buses have more capacity and therefore, if successful in attracting riders, will have far more riders per vehicle than microtransit. Since their operational costs are relatively similar—you must pay for a driver and fuel either way—the bus blows a smaller vehicle out of the water on a cost per passenger basis.

These advocates argue that because of this cost differential, and because transit agency budgets are limited, it is not worth investing in or even experimenting with microtransit. Why not even experiment?

Because when agencies experiment with microtransit, it tends to be popular and tough to eliminate, thus sucking up precious budget dollars that could be used to run more buses.

And therein lies the rub. Microtransit tends to be popular because it provides better customer experience than buses in many cases. For the person who now has a far shorter commute, it may not be relevant that it costs more to provide the service. It is possible that providing a service like microtransit can ultimately result in more funding for public transit because it will increase customer satisfaction and constituents will demand more of it. Even if the budget is fixed, is the idea to serve as many people as possible with existing funds, even if the service provided is terrible, or to provide the best service possible to fewer people? This question is at least worth considering, which is why we determined that an experiment in microtransit was worth it.

That said, we did have our fair share of naysayers from outside. We had a heated call with Jarrett in our naive attempt to see if we could find common ground with someone who shared values and goals but perhaps disagreed about how to achieve them. While the call was enlightening, it did not change Jarrett's opinion. However, he did clarify that he was more concerned for agencies with fewer resources than Metro adopting microtransit and eliminating bus services.

Joe Linton ran LA Streetsblog, an online publication generally favoring increased walking, biking, and transit, and he was the only reporter who live-tweeted from every Metro Board meeting. He even wrote a positive article about our office when we first arrived. But Joe made the editorial decision that microtransit was a terrible waste of money that could otherwise be used for the things he cared about. As is typical, the most vitriolic opposition to microtransit came from within the transit community.[53] Just last year, he wrote about how it cost too much and should be cut,[lxx] and previously criticized the program, calling it a "waste."[lxxi] Thankfully, while the outside opposition didn't help things, it was manageable.

---

[53]This is best thought of as the Judean People's Front effect: https://www.youtube.com/watch?v=WboggjN_G-4.

Learning from Bike Share

The internal opposition, however, was quite strong. Thankfully, we had one key ally—Jim Gallagher himself. From the beginning, Jim was open to the idea of experimenting with microtransit. Jim was an old-school guy, but he also recognized that new technology could bring improved services for customers. In an early meeting in his office, the two of us did some back of the envelope calculations about running a microtransit service and determined it could be done without negatively impacting bus operations.

With Jim on board, we had the juice internally. Now we could focus on the longer-term issue—we would need this approved by the Board. We had seen what had happened to bike share, another experimental Metro pilot, and wanted to avoid their fate. Bike share, also seen as a costly innovative pilot program, but somehow one that Joe Linton was fine with, had been caught in the politics of the Metro Board. We were fortunate enough to have Avital Shavit, who developed that pilot program, in our office and available to help us avoid a similar fate. Here are the ways bike share struggled:

- **Location**. Instead of beginning downtown and expanding outward as it gained riders, the service faced political pressure to expand to different areas of the county so that more board members would be able to claim that their constituents were benefiting from the program. The service area selections for MOD experienced some of this gerrymandering. This meant that it failed to attract sufficient riders in many places, and a network was created that was separate and disjointed.

  Proposed solution: Use the PDA concept that we were planning for Sepulveda for microtransit. By having private firms compete to design the program, we would avoid pressure from the Board to put it in their preferred area. "Hey, what can we do—this is where the private sector said it would work."
- **Funding**. Instead of just funding the program, Metro decided to only partially fund bike share and require the cities where it was located to pony up a portion of the funds. This meant that they often had to expand to where they could get funding, instead of

where they might attract riders. It led to expansions in Pasadena and in Venice, for example, both of which are too far from the original program downtown.

Proposed Solution: Use funding from existing operations. Microtransit was incorporated into the existing bus network as part of the NextGen bus reorganization plan. This meant funding for bus and microtransit operations would be one and the same.

- **Incompatibility**. Metro bike share used a different operator than bike share systems in Santa Monica and Culver City. This meant that you could not get a bike in neighboring Los Angeles and ride it to one of these cities to drop it off. Bike share also was designed without the ability to use a TAP card to pay for it, and even when TAP cards were accepted, they had to be from a separate account associated with the same card.

   Proposed Solution: Work with TAP from the very beginning to integrate paying for microtransit. Unfortunately, this one was a challenge, due to the nature of TAP. See Chapter 3, "Recognize Impenetrable Fiefdoms."

- **Fares**. Bike share was priced in line with how other bike share systems in the nation were priced. It seemed like a good idea at the time, but other bike share systems were operating in cities where owning a car could be very expensive, and where plenty of people with means would choose to use transit or bikes to get around. In LA, where lower income people tended to be the market for any transportation that was not a car, the price was too high.

   Proposed Solution: Charge an introductory $1 fare. Even though we knew this would make the service more costly, we hoped we could raise the fare if the service proved popular.[54]

- **Labor**. Bike share was operated by a private company without Metro labor. This meant that bike share could not be placed in Metro property, as that would violate the union contract that gave them exclusive rights to maintain transportation on Metro property. This reduced the ability of Metro riders to use bike share as a method of accessing Metro stations.

---

[54]Metro has, in fact, now raised the fare to $2.50.

Proposed Solution: Negotiate with the labor union to operate the service. We would still use the technology and vehicles from a private provider, but this way we could avoid a labor fight and perhaps create an ally.

Most of these solutions worked rather well. We proceeded with a procurement for a microtransit provider that was arduous and challenging. As OEI, we insisted on an unorthodox procurement process that helped us work more closely with the private sector before selecting a provider. It was not easy, but it ultimately yielded a contract with RideCo to provide the technology for the service. Via, who had submitted the UP, was furious. They called me and yelled and then demanded a meeting with Phil. But we held fast to Metro's decision.

Selecting the provider was the easy part, however. Union negotiations would prove to be much more challenging.

SMART Negotiations

The tension was undeniable. We had just started our first day of negotiations with leaders of the SMART union, which represented the operators of Metro's buses and trains, and within the first five minutes, they were threatening to walk out. We had asked them to sign an NDA that would protect any corporate information we would be sharing with them regarding the technology firms that might provide microtransit software and dispatch.

How did we get here? We had worked so hard to bring the union along. We had invited them to join the OEI Advisory Board, where we discussed microtransit and other issues monthly, so that they would feel like a part of the office. We had brought them along with the idea to the point that they had appeared in front of our Board of Directors to speak in favor of microtransit, despite the opposition of other unions to the idea. When we began negotiations, we figured it might be challenging, but we didn't think it would fall apart within the first five minutes.

Perhaps what we hadn't anticipated—and within "we" I include the heads of Operations and HR respectively—was that the level of trust would be so low in the first place. I underestimated the deeply entrenched labor–management divide at Metro, a relationship shaped by decades of complex institutional history that could not be overcome by sound logic and reasoning alone. I failed to understand that the union would not believe what we were saying, would assume we were out to screw them over, and would believe that they were negotiating from a place of weakness.

In my mind, none of these things were true. While we wanted to make microtransit service affordable for Metro, we had no interest in doing that by paying lower wages. We also felt that they held all the cards, because we would never be able to move forward with microtransit without them. And we had no reason not to trust them, and because they had never met me before, I didn't understand why they wouldn't trust me.

The answer was that they didn't trust me because to them I was a foreign entity. I was an executive who wore a suit and had gone to graduate school and made lots of money. I had driven a long way from my fancy office downtown to the far reaches of the San Gabriel Valley to this meeting at their modest offices. These things made us seem very powerful and very likely not to care about them.

So perhaps beginning the meeting, as we would have begun any meeting on microtransit,[55] by asking them to sign an NDA, was not the best move. They took this as a sign that we did not trust them. While signing NDAs is a normal course of business for corporate professionals in the technology space, and was recommended in this case by our attorneys, it was a foreign concept to the leader of SMART. When we presented the NDA for their signature, not only did they not sign it, but they moved to caucus, which means they left the room to discuss their response in private. When they returned, they told us that not only were they not signing the NDA, but they wanted to end negotiations. We had to beg them to reconsider, and discard the idea of the NDA completely, for them to continue. While they did agree, the relationship remained tense.

Eventually, after many meetings, we started to make progress. As they got to know us, they started to realize that our intentions were not to

---

[55] As we were going to be dealing with private companies and their data, we thought an NDA was important to retain the confidence of our private-sector partners. But as it turns out, we didn't really need it.

overpower them. They did have one holdout who was convinced that our MOD pilot was a stalking horse, and that we were not serious about having them operate microtransit. This negotiation, in his mind, was a way to keep them occupied while we moved toward our real goal of privatizing transit by outsourcing to Lyft or Via.

In our mind this was a preposterous idea. First, we would never be able to get away with that even if we wanted to, as the Board would have stopped us and probably gotten us fired for even trying. Second, from a transportation perspective this would have been problematic. We needed buses and we needed operators. Even if we could have crushed the union, it would have not made a substantial difference in the bottom line for the agency. But we couldn't crush them and had no desire to do so. It took some convincing for them to see this, and for me to recognize my own bias.

A turning point came via an unusual encounter. The Communications Department had a smart idea to conduct interviews with all the chiefs at Metro and broadcast them across the intranet (Metro's internal server). In my case, they opted for my former deputy Nadine Lee and me to interview one another (she had been promoted to LA Metro Chief of Staff). The interviews were widely viewed by Metro's 12,000 employees, and many people attended in person.

One question Nadine asked me was "What skill do you wish you had that you do not have?" I've been playing basketball for a long time, but despite being told quite often that I look like Manu Ginobili (Figure 4.2),[56] I am only 5 ft. 11 in. and cannot jump all that high. I love playing and always wished I had more actual skill. I quickly answered, "Dunking a basketball" and explained that I played in a regular game at Metro and had played most of my life.

Right afterwards, one of the union guys who had been part of the negotiations approached me enthusiastically. "I didn't know you played basketball!" he said. He also played, but that wasn't even the point. It seemed my passion for basketball had revealed a connection point neither of us had anticipated during our more formal interactions.

---

[56]Manu Ginobili was a star Argentinian basketball player for the San Antonio Spurs in the NBA. He and I are roughly the same age, and yes, people ask if I am him all the time. Ginobili is 6 feet 6 inches. I am not.

Figure 4.2 Manu Ginobili

Source: Mike, CC BY-SA 2.0. https://creativecommons.org
/licenses/by-sa/2.0, via Wikimedia Commons.

It is easy to forget that everyone approaches the world from their own perspective. Activities I consider ordinary parts of my life, like shooting hoops, might challenge others' perceptions of me in my professional role. Those who primarily saw me as a fancy suit in a corner office naturally formed certain impressions that I needed to contend with. People construct their own realities, and only time spent with them can bring them back to yours.

We wrapped up the negotiations with the union within a year. In the end, we had a side letter signed by SMART and Metro that provided microtransit drivers with the same benefits as part-time Metro drivers. This compromise meant that the union could add members that could eventually become full-time drivers if desired, and it meant we could afford the service.

Not long after negotiations were concluded, Jim Gallagher unexpectedly called a meeting with Phil and me about microtransit. I had no idea what the meeting was about, and Jim didn't feel the need to tell me in advance. When I showed up, I was shocked. Jim was requesting that microtransit be moved into Operations before it launched.

My initial reaction, like many other Metro chiefs, was to object. But unlike other chiefs, I couldn't come up with a good reason to object, and I wasn't going to say I wanted to protect my fiefdom (even if part of me wanted to). After my initial shock I realized that not only was this desirable, but it marked a significant turning point for OEI. We had designed a new program with new technology that was successful enough, and popular enough, that another department wanted it. And they had the operations expertise, not us, so it made sense. In retrospect, nothing else would have worked.

Microtransit was launched in December 2020. This probably was not the ideal time to launch a new service, but it proved very popular. In fact, it proved so popular that people were requesting more rides than Metro could provide, leading to high wait times. It was very challenging to recruit new drivers during this time, and the program struggled for a while. But, eventually, it became a mainstay of Metro's service offerings, to the point that they rebid the contract and awarded it to Via, the original unsolicited proposer, instead of RideCo. Persistence can pay off for the private sector too!

It's a Marathon and a Sprint

Leaders across both the public and private sectors struggle with defining an optimal balance of short- and long-term thinking and objectives. Our experience with on-demand transit at Metro was emblematic of this and taught us several critical lessons about driving innovation through bureaucracy.

In the short term, we had to sprint toward early wins to build credibility and momentum. Winning the MOD grant was that initial sprint, giving us the initial cover to continue pushing forward when faced with opposition. But the subsequent process of implementation, requiring patience through negotiations, procurement processes, and organizational politics, demanded marathonlike endurance.

We discovered that finding unlikely allies is essential, as first discussed in Chapter 2. The bureaucratic landscape at Metro wasn't divided neatly between supporters and opponents. Some of our strongest advocates emerged from departments we initially feared would block us: Legal, Risk Management, and Procurement. Meanwhile, we faced unexpected resistance from transit advocates outside the organization who shared our values but disagreed with our methods.

We learned that you must be willing to let go of ownership and control to be successful. When Jim Gallagher requested to move microtransit into Operations' purview, my initial instinct was to object—to protect my fiefdom. But real success isn't measured by how long an innovation remains "yours." It's measured by how thoroughly it becomes integrated into the organization's core operations.

We saw firsthand that trust can't be manufactured through logic alone. Our negotiations with SMART revealed that institutional mistrust runs deeper than rational arguments. Sometimes a shared love of basketball can build more goodwill than months of formal negotiations.

And finally, we see now that meaningful innovation in public transit requires both vision and pragmatism. We had to simultaneously envision the future of transit while navigating the realities of union contracts, political expectations, and organizational constraints. It was tiring but worth it!

CHAPTER 5

Both Naivete and Experience Are Required

Whenever I mention congestion pricing in Los Angeles to someone outside the transportation world, they think I'm out of my mind.

The idea that drivers might pay to use the roads, especially in a city so deeply shaped by the car, feels outlandish to most. But as Derek Thompson and Ezra Klein argue in *Abundance*, real progress doesn't begin with a perfect policy—it begins with belief: belief that the future can be better and that public institutions can help make it so.

At OEI, we didn't see congestion pricing as just another technical intervention. We saw it as a bet on institutional imagination: the idea that even here, in the land of the freeway, something so ambitious could take root.

For those unfamiliar, congestion pricing means charging drivers a toll to use the road, typically with higher fees during peak hours. It's widely recognized as the only reliable way to reduce traffic, because it tackles demand directly.[lxxiii] But in Los Angeles, for the uninitiated, it can sound like heresy.

"You want to charge people to drive … on a freeway?"

Yes, exactly. And for your information, the term "freeway" has nothing to do with the cost. Its etymology can be traced to the idea of free-flowing traffic, meaning freeways need congestion pricing to be true to their name.[lxxiv] Check mate.

"That will never happen in Los Angeles."

We shall see. It already happened in Los Angeles on the 10 and 110 freeways, where Metro constructed High-Occupancy-Toll (HOT) lanes and uses congestion pricing to ensure throughput. When that program was conceived, despite federal funding[57] being made available specifically for that project, it was widely dismissed as impossible, and Metro assigned only one person to the project. The person they assigned, however, was singularly determined not to fail and worked against all odds to make it happen. The project was a huge success, and she is now the CEO of LA Metro.

Admittedly, tolling new lanes when federal money is being provided to build them is very different from placing a new toll on, say, the 101.[58] But we felt that our job was to improve traffic in Los Angeles. That is the reason 71 percent of Los Angeles voters supported Measure M—it was sold as a way to ease congestion even though the transit plan behind the sales tax had little chance of doing so. But traffic congestion was a plague in Los Angeles, the biggest transportation problem, and congestion pricing is widely known in the literature as the only way to tackle the problem effectively. How could we not take a shot at solving it?

We were naive enough to think that congestion pricing in Los Angeles might be possible. We weren't blind to the challenges, but we saw a window where the improbable might become probable and we had little to lose. As a Chicago native, our boss Phil Washington was fond of the

---

[57]This funding was made available through the Urban Partnership Agreements, where USDOT partnered with six cities to test congestion management strategies. The funds Metro received were initially slated for New York City, which had proposed a concept like the congestion pricing program that is in operation today. For New York to receive funding, the State Assembly had to approve the plan by a certain date, but the Democratic Conference of the State Assembly decided not to vote at all on the proposal due to the political opposition. Due to this decision, those funds were reallocated and granted to LA Metro and to Chicago.

[58]Per the law on Federal Aid Highways (Title 23, USC), introducing a toll on existing capacity paid for by Federal Aid grants is prohibited. The surface transportation reauthorization of 1991, ISTEA, introduced the Value Pricing Pilot Program (VPPP), creating flexibility of this prohibition, allowing the implementation and evaluation of value pricing pilot concepts to manage congestion on interstate highways through tolling and other pricing mechanisms. The NYC congestion pricing program was approved by the Biden Administration under the VPPP, which is now under fire by the Trump Administration as we write.

Daniel Burnham quote "Make no little plans."[59] This is exactly what we endeavored to do. However, had it just been OEI running around with our grandiose ideas, we would have failed miserably. What made success possible was a unique combination of wondrous naivete and hard-earned experience.

The Value of Not Knowing the Rules

Coming to LA Metro from DC, I was the epitome of an outsider. Thinking that this was a good thing, I was quick to hire three other outsiders. In many ways, this ended up being wise on my part. None of us knew the rules, and that turned out to be one of our greatest advantages. Because we didn't know what was allowed, we didn't hesitate to question everything. We didn't know where the lines were, so we colored all over the page. We moved fast, we asked questions, and we found we often had to beg for forgiveness.

It's a well-documented organizational phenomenon that outsiders can be powerful agents of change because they are not yet fully socialized into norms, power structures, or constraints of an institution.[lxxv] They aren't yet weighed down by the invisible boundaries internalized by insiders. Innovation scholars call this "cognitive distance"—the idea that those furthest removed from entrenched systems are more likely to see new paths forward.[lxxvi] But fresh eyes come at a cost. It also meant that we had to learn everything from scratch. It was time-consuming, sometimes mind bending, and usually humbling.

Perhaps from years of military leadership training, perhaps from instinct, perhaps on the advice of some very wise consultants,[60] Phil understood this tension and built in a counterbalance—the internal fellowship

---

[59]Daniel Burnham is an esteemed American urban planner and architect, credited with developing the master plans for both Chicago and Washington, DC. At a town planning conference in London in 1910, Burnham said, "Make no little plans; they have no magic to stir men's blood and probably themselves will not be realized. Make big plans; aim high in hope and work, remembering that a noble, logical diagram once recorded will never die." This quotation is now a rallying cry for urban planners.

[60]Namely Mike Schneider of InfraStrategies.

program. Later we applied the same logic when we created the Advisory Board, pairing internal veterans with external visionaries.

The mix of naivete and deep organizational fluency turned out to be a winning formula. It gave us the momentum and knowledge to tackle two of the most consequential projects we took on: the Strategic Plan and Congestion Pricing. It also taught us that the real magic happens not by breaking all the rules, but by knowing just enough of them to know which ones can be bent.

OEI's Fellowship Program

When Phil first told me about the OEI fellowship program, I liked it, but I didn't understand it. His idea was that OEI would not just be a team of people we hired. It would also include "Fellows" from other departments within Metro.[lxxvii] These fellows would apply to come to work in OEI for a year and then return to their original department.

I liked this idea for two reasons. One, since we were going to be a small office trying to do big things, we could use all the help we could get. But second, I loved the idea of bringing the smartest people from within the agency to work with us, indoctrinating them about making change, and releasing them back into the wild.

What I hadn't anticipated was how much our office would learn from them. This was the greater wisdom of the fellowship program that Phil understood. OEI was intentionally filled with passionate disruptors, unburdened by convention, with big plans in a region they were not from and composed mostly of people who hadn't worked in public agencies. We needed someone to temper us and show us how to get things done.

We also had not anticipated the feelings that the rest of the agency might have about our office. The best way to describe the feelings the rest of the agency had about OEI, even before we started, was that they either wanted to be a part of it, or they hated it, or both. When I took the job, I didn't realize the extent to which it was seen by people in Los Angeles, and particularly at LA Metro, as a highly coveted position. In fact, I had been talking to Phil about being his Deputy CEO and was slightly disappointed to be offered this job instead. But within Metro, this job was seen as someone who had the CEO's ear on everything, who got to do all the fun stuff, and who had a very fancy title. This helps explain why one of my colleagues within the agency, when I complained about the high expectations of the job and how challenging it was, began rubbing her fingers together to play the world's smallest violin.[61]

The hatred of OEI was frustrating but understandable. If you were a Metro veteran, working there for years to try to move things forward and slowly working your way up the chain, it had to be difficult to see some new folks from out of town brought into very powerful positions. If you applied for the fellowship and were denied (it was very competitive), you might feel even more embittered about it. But I suspect many folks didn't even apply based on fear that they might be denied and feel even worse about our existence.

This arrangement was also a burden on other departments, giving them more reasons to hate us. When we accepted a fellow from, say, Planning, that department was not given an FTE[62] to fill the missing slot. They had to make do without that individual for the year, figure out how to get that person's job done with existing resources, and then prepare to bring that person back and reassign duties again. Or if that person didn't return, they simply lost one of their best people.[63]

Once the fellows came to work in OEI, they did not tend to leave. The excitement and energy of working to make change and being near the power center of this large organization were unbeatable, and no one wanted to go back to their old department. The fact that Nadine Lee and I ran the department like people who didn't understand or believe in hierarchy also made people want to stay. Of our first six fellowships, only one person returned to their previous department, and that only happened in the third year of the program. We made sure to trumpet this event, trying to reassure the rest of the agency that we were not just stealing all their best people.[64]

---

[61]Again, the current CEO, Stephanie Wiggins.

[62]An FTE means full time equivalent and is a tool for calculating staff.

[63]If someone didn't return, we found a way to make sure that they at least got their FTE back so they could hire someone new.

[64]But alas, that person would also wind up returning to OEI a couple of years later and still works there today. We did, eventually, send someone back to their department who—we promise—never returned to OEI.

The Fellows

The power of the OEI fellowship was remarkable. Our first two fellows, plucked from dozens of applicants and selected after several interviews, were great examples. We have already discussed Nolan Borgman, who came to OEI from the CEO's office. Having been with the CEO's office, he already had the perspective of someone who thought about the big picture. But this also meant he had the experience of working with people throughout the agency. Also, Nolan was a young guy recently out of college, and was very social at work, including playing in Metro's pickup basketball team[65] and organizing other Metro activities. He was the perfect person to run the UP Program, which required cooperating with people throughout the agency.

It was Nolan who connected us with the right people, and knew what every department did and who might be someone we could work with there. Nolan never shied away from big challenges, and people in the agency trusted him enough to give him candid feedback and help OEI navigate difficult situations. He also understood how the Board process worked, and how the CEO's office worked. He was a natural fit to lead our "Ride-Along" program where he brought Metro employees out on the system once per month to observe and suggest improvements.

Our other fellow from the inaugural class was Tham Nguyen. Tham was an agency veteran and part of a stream of smart and talented planners who flowed from grad school at UCLA to Metro. Tham told me that her mother alternated carrying her across a river on her back and shoulders (depending on the water level) when she was a child so that they could escape Vietnam and emigrate to the United States. This story exemplified her work ethic, which was born of someone who never took anything for granted and wanted to get every detail right. But she also had the experience of working at Metro and trying to get plans adopted, which made her the perfect person to lead our strategic planning effort.

---

[65] As mentioned earlier I also played in that run and felt like it was a great way to find potential allies by seeing who was a team player and a leader, and who was a ball hog.

Where we would have plunged ahead like maniacs, Tham was able to tell us to slow down. She understood that power within a public agency is built through trust and collaboration, not by force. We had to talk to people, ask them what they wanted, and give them what we could. We had to do the work upfront to save time later in the process. She saved us from ourselves on many occasions.

The fellowship program also brought us people whose perspectives we might otherwise never have heard. From the beginning we wanted to include frontline workers, such as operators and mechanics, in the program. But labor contracts made that difficult to implement. Union workers were reluctant to leave their post for a year if they would lose status when they returned. Through some creative efforts, we did wind up bringing on unionized fellows three times—a bus operator, a customer service representative, and a division supervisor.

These cases are also instructive. Darrell Carter, a bus operator, joined OEI in the early years. The head of bus operations,[66] fought to prevent him from joining us. In examining his record, Operations saw that he had some blemishes. But we weren't concerned about whether he followed all the rules; he was eager to make changes. He had one thing he cared about—bus stop locations—that he articulated in his application. We got Operations overruled and we brought Darrell on.

Darrell was as naive about making change at a public agency as we were about driving a bus. His idea was simple—all bus stops should be after traffic lights instead of before traffic lights. That way, an operator and customers would not have to stop prior to the light to pick up and drop off passengers, and then get stuck behind that light again when it turned red. If Metro moved all their stops to the far side of traffic lights it would speed up operations, improve customer experience, and increase consistency. Made sense—simple, easy, and a win for everyone.

Not exactly. He hadn't anticipated several critical issues:

1. Metro does not own most of its bus stops. They are typically owned and controlled by the local municipalities.

---

[66]Who played basketball like he ran operations—he was in charge, so watch out!

2. In some cases, there may not be room to safely locate a bus stop on the far side without major infrastructure changes that can take years, if even approved.
3. Many people in Metro Operations did not even agree with his assessment that far side stops were better in the first place.

Darrell went from pushing wholesale reform, to trying to get a pilot in place, to finally writing a paper about why it was so difficult to make this change. It was a disheartening experience for him, but as a magnetic personality and a stand-up comedian on the side, he took it in stride.

Our customer service agent, Dennis Arnold, had a different experience. Not surprisingly for someone from customer service, he was one of the friendliest, most likable people I've ever met. He always had a smile, loved playing saxophone in the Metro band (The Metro Express), and told great stories about all the jobs he had enjoyed in his decades at Metro. We gave Dennis a task that seemed ideal for a Metro veteran—to create an employee rewards program. We had seen people at Metro come up with great ideas and yet reap no rewards. For example, one group of mechanics developed a streamlined way to rebuild a bus engine. Their strategy saved millions of dollars, but all they got was an innovation award. Imagine if Metro offered cash for good ideas from employees. How many more ideas like this might emerge?

Of course, people at Metro immediately threw up roadblocks. Isn't this just a glorified suggestion box? "If we don't respond to and implement people's ideas, they will become angrier at Metro." Also, "it is illegal for a public agency to give bonuses to employees." And even if we found a way to do that legally, "we are exposing ourselves to legal fights" over that money. And the classic "we already tried that, and it didn't work."

Dennis was undaunted. Guided by Nolan, he researched each one of these issues and laid out a program that was workable. We presented it to the Senior Leadership Team (SLT). Phil loved it and approved it. He told HR to move forward. Unfortunately, this was one of several times when a memo approved by Phil was necessary but not sufficient to get new programs going. First, HR ignored it for a while. Then they said they didn't have the budget or resources. We offered them both budget and resources. Then they slow-walked it for a bit until we had to get Phil to remind them to do it. Then, eventually, they were saved by the pandemic, which became a great excuse not to do anything (see Chapter 6).

The one fellow from the front lines who was very successful provides a critical lesson learned. We brought in Andrew Carrasco, a supervisor on the Orange Line (now the G-line busway), specifically to help with our Metro Micro program. Given that none of us had operations experience, and Andrew was interested in being a part of this new microtransit service, we got Phil and Jim Gallagher to approve a six-month fellowship for Andrew on top of our other two fellows that year. Andrew was tremendously helpful, was a key staff member in launching Metro Micro, and still works on that project today.

Unlike Daryl or Dennis, Andrew was not coming in with ideas. He was coming in to support an existing idea about which he had specific expertise. This was a far better model, and in fact, was what characterized our most successful fellows in the program. For example, Tamar Fuhrer also came from Operations and was able to help us move our Unsolicited Proposals forward. Avital Shavit, who launched Metro Bike Share, was also able to help launch MOD and subsequently launched pilot programs to pay people not to drive, and to create a mobility wallet. Eileen Hsu, who was a design specialist, was the designer behind our Vision 2028 Strategic Plan.[67]

The fellows who worked in our office were quickly taken aback by our tendency toward radical transparency. In their home departments, they were rarely given information about the high-level discussions among executives or asked their opinion on big policy problems. They had been firmly embedded in a hierarchy. Here at OEI, they received regular briefings on what was happening in SLT meetings, and they were asked for their perspective on all issues that arose, which kind of blew their minds. And once they had a taste of it, it was tough for them to go back.

---

[67]Eileen is the first Fellow who returned to her department after working in OEI. She was then rehired by OEI a few years later and still works in that office today. Avital also continues to work in the Innovation Office at Metro, now called the humbler Office of Strategic Innovation (OSI), and led by Seleta Reynolds, formerly of LADOT (see Chapter 3).

OEI Advisory Board

Phil had always intended for OEI to be a liaison between the research community and the practitioners of transit. Unlike many transit CEOs, Phil was interested in research, and not just when it backed up what he was already planning to do. He would often invite researchers on relevant topics to brief him or the SLT, and he would digest their findings and memorize the critical components to work into his speeches. He would bring up the research findings in internal meetings to make his points. And even though he sometimes called me an "egghead" he still listened when I told him what the research indicated.[68]

So, when I approached Phil about the idea of an Advisory Board for OEI composed of top researchers, advocates, and nonprofits, it was an easy yes from him. In fact, he asked to have all the meetings put on his calendar. Emma, Marla, and I set out to create this Advisory Board immediately. However, while Marla and I had assembled similar boards in the past, we had done so at nonprofits rather than public agencies. We were not prepared for the cynical way that the rest of the agency would look at this new entity. Several objections were raised:

- Will this Board be given inside information on procurements? Even if not, if members intend to do any business with Metro, this could be perceived as a conflict.
- We already have several other Advisory Boards at this agency. Do we need another one?
- What is the process for choosing board members? It needs to be approved.
- You want to bring people in from out of state? Who will pay for their travel?

---

[68]Phil used lots of great old-school expressions including calling people "Jack" who were not, technically, named "Jack" (as in "I don't think so, Jack"), and "drug deal" (meaning backroom deal but making everyone slightly uneasy as illegal drugs are not often discussed in government transportation meetings). But "egghead" was my favorite.

Creating the Advisory Board was one of the first things OEI did, and thus we were able to just ignore some of these objections. We agreed that all advisory board members would need to be people who were not under contract with Metro, and had no plans to be. We also agreed the board would be largely confined to local people or at least California, for the time being. To support the inclusion of out-of-state folks who had important perspectives, we worked out a deal with Transit Center—a national civic foundation based in New York—to fund travel for those out-of-state public sector participants. Other than that, we just proceeded as we wished and created the new Board in a way that we thought would be most helpful to us and Metro.

OEI treated the Advisory Board the same way we treated the private sector in general. With rampant and radical transparency. This group was composed of many people with strong expertise who had wanted to help inform Metro policy for decades. For example, the group included legendary UCLA professors Marty Wachs and Brian Taylor, both of whom had dedicated much of their careers to studying public transit in the United States, and public transit in Los Angeles in particular. While they had certainly been consulted for their expertise before, they had never been presented with an inside look at what was happening at LA Metro on a regular basis. Now they were hearing once a quarter from what was essentially an arm of the CEO. They could not have been more excited.

At every meeting we would present the Board with our progress on our projects and ask for their feedback. While some members were more vocal than others, all of them pitched-in in various ways. Some brought their expertise to bear in the meetings, while others could be consulted privately. Sometimes they had relationships that could help us move things forward, or they had done research critical to what we were trying to do.

The Advisory Board trended a bit academic and could veer into unhelpful territory. There was one time that the head of the Institute for Innovation in Large Organizations (ILO) got into a heated dispute with the former Chief Technology Officer at the City of Los Angeles about the future of autonomous vehicles. This argument, while entertaining, was largely irrelevant to what OEI was doing.[69]

But more often the Board provided us with critical advice and perspective that would have been difficult to find elsewhere. In Chapter 4 we discussed how they saved us from ourselves by convincing us to break up with Lyft. In another case, when we were struggling to get Metro to adopt some smaller innovations, such as station-based amenities, these minor improvements took too much effort to get through and were getting lost. Jeremy Dann—a USC Professor on our Board—suggested that a "test kitchen" model might be useful, wherein we would have one station on the system where we could test things quickly. We took this idea and moved it forward, and it proved to be a far better approach.

Perhaps most useful was how the Board brought together different perspectives who were rarely in the room together. We had academics and nonprofits—people with big ideas and broad perspectives—together with labor representatives and transit agency executives—who had a much narrower lens. They were forced to see things through one another's eyes. For example, an academic who might be in favor of a policy that could benefit thousands of people would be confronted with the fact that if the union or an elected official didn't like it, that benefit could not be realized. Alternatively, labor unions and transit executives were pushed to look at ideas they opposed more broadly.

One example was our pursuit of microtransit (see Chapter 4), which most academics and technologists favored. We brought the transit operators' union (SMART) onto the Advisory Board specifically because we wanted them to be part of the process of adopting microtransit. As the idea grew from conception to reality, SMART was regularly informed about the process. We managed to earn their trust enough to convince them that we genuinely believed this was the future and that we genuinely

---

[69]From the beginning of OEI in 2015, people were always asking us about autonomous vehicles. We believed that autonomy of vehicles was not all that relevant to Metro, but we were also open to testing the technology on our buses as soon as it was available. In 2025 this conversation is still in a similar phase. While the technology has progressed, it hasn't produced the promised revolution. I was told autonomous buses would be ready any day. We are still waiting.

wanted them to be a part of it. They wound up going from being against the idea to one of its biggest supporters and eventually operating the program.

Overall, the Advisory Board was a huge benefit for OEI and Metro. The Board, like our staff, brought both naivete and experience to the problems at hand. On the naivete side, the academics brought years of research and data analysis to the table, but now had to be confronted with the reality of what it was like to implement the ideas that they knew would work. On the experience side, those in the nonprofit and advocacy space knew the challenges of moving forward with big ideas, but were now being presented with ideas they may not have considered. This combination was highly productive.

Metro Strategic Plan

It might seem odd that strategic planning would be housed in OEI. When Phil mentioned this upon OEI's creation, I didn't think of it as something I would care about and was far more excited about the other OEI functions of working with the private sector. It turned out that strategic planning was the most powerful tool we had been given to change the course of transportation in Los Angeles.

An effective strategic plan articulates the mission, vision, goals, and objectives for an organization. Using this framework, the plan then lays out the specific actions that the agency will take over the course of the plan. These actions should, ideally, accomplish the goals and objectives for the agency, which in turn will achieve the larger vision the agency seeks. The mission of the agency articulates the broader goal that everyone should be thinking about as they do their jobs every day.

This means that a strategic plan has the potential power to change the course of an agency, and in LA Metro's case, of a region. But it also means that if the agency is to do anything new or innovative, the strategic plan offers the opportunity to articulate those new actions and put the weight of the CEO, Board of Directors, and the rest of the agency behind them. A strategic plan is therefore directly linked to innovation. It had the potential to be our most effective tool.

The People

When taking the job, I realized that I would need some help with the strategic plan. This is one of the primary reasons that I hired Nadine Lee. Nadine had been working with Phil in Denver as a project manager, not an executive. At RTD, she led the development and implementation of the Flatiron Flyer Bus Rapid Transit, which produced a 40 percent increase in corridor ridership just in its first few months of service. She was a nascent talent and had written to Phil making the case to him for why she should be considered for Chief Innovation Officer in LA. He forwarded me her e-mail and suggested I consider her, along with a few other candidates he recommended. But when the two of us met, it was obvious that she was the perfect fit.

Nadine was an engineer, which initially gave me pause. In my field, I'd encountered engineers whose training emphasized technical solutions over human-centered approaches. But Nadine was more of a recovering engineer. She had both an exceptional engineering perspective on problem-solving and the emotional intelligence needed to navigate Metro's complex social dynamics.

Like me she wanted to start the revolution and change the world,[70] but unlike me, she had years of experience working at a public sector agency. Most critically, she was interested in, and capable of, leading our strategic planning work.

Our other key ingredients were the OEI fellows already mentioned above. There was Tham Nguyen, who had put together strategic plans within LA Metro before. In fact, before she could join us, she had to finish up her work on the Metro Countywide Active Transportation Strategic Plan. Given that neither Nadine nor I had ever technically completed a strategic plan of any kind for a public agency, Tham was a critical addition.

We had a saying in our office we called the "Tham Doctrine" because Tham would often bring it up and it was incredibly useful. The Tham Doctrine asked, "What, exactly, are you trying to achieve?" followed by,

---

[70]Nadine and I would occasionally rub our hands together like villains and cackle as we plotted world domination. This was a joke … mostly.

"Are your strategies and actions aligned to help you achieve those desired outcomes?" It was a motto we would live by, as so often people in public agencies get distracted by so many other things, that they forget why they were doing what they were doing in the first place. A strategic plan is the ultimate answer to the Tham Doctrine.

Tham knew that any strategic plan worth doing had to have buy-in from the rest of the agency. While Nadine and I thought we could just write down whatever we thought was best for Metro and somehow everyone would do it, Tham brought us back to reality. We could push the envelope and get Metro to go in a better direction, but we couldn't do it by ourselves.

Tham taught us how to bring people along with our harebrained plans. Instead of just writing the plan, we went and asked people across the county what they wanted. We conducted a countywide survey that asked everyone about their transportation preferences, what they thought of Metro, and what we could do to make their lives better. We also went to each department and had extensive discussions with employees about their ideas for what Metro should be doing and what it should be trying to achieve. We conducted multiple four-hour workshops with the Metro SLT where we discussed what the organization should be doing and even delved into the specific goals we should be achieving.

Perhaps the most important thing we did was conduct an internal employee survey. While LA Metro has over 12,000 employees, only about 1,500 of them were connected to e-mail. Most of the employees are unionized, frontline employees such as maintenance workers, bus operators, mechanics, and security personnel. These folks are not easy to reach for several reasons. First, at the time they did not have Metro e-mail addresses. Second, even if we could e-mail them the survey, they were unlikely to take it. For one, they were suspicious that anything they said might be used against them. For another, they were hourly employees and not particularly interested in giving their time away for this purpose.

But if we didn't reach this huge swath of employees, we would be missing a tremendous amount of critical data. Solving this problem was a multipronged operation. OEI's role was to get the Chief Operations Officer, Jim Gallagher, to agree to pay the hourly employees for taking the survey. Jim said that an employee survey, done right, would be the most important thing we could collectively accomplish. He recognized how important it is for management to be responsive to employees and ask them what they need. If we followed up to ensure we solved the challenges the employees identified, it would be a legacy for the organization.

Tham's role was to get out to the divisions[71] with her team and get employees to answer a survey. She came up with an intensive but effective strategy. We bought dozens of iPads for the project, which was a challenge because procurement probably would have preferred to issue an RFP.[72] Then Tham organized teams of people to go out to the divisions and find times when workers might be hanging around and be available to participate. This meant early morning, midday, or late night. It was an exhausting but effective strategy, and we managed to get the highest participation levels for any employee survey at Metro.

The Plan

The vision we developed for the future of Los Angeles was simple— everyone should be able to get where they want to go when they want to get there. Building additional roadways in a region already overwhelmed with pavement was highly unrealistic and would not accomplish this goal. Even building more transit on a grand scale, as planned in Measure M, would not get us there by itself because we expected the number of cars and drivers to continue to increase. We suggested the goal should be to increase—in fact, double—the number of people using any mode other than driving alone in LA County within 10 years. We would do this in large part by dramatically improving bus service, the core of what Metro provides.

We knew this would be a drastic change. We knew it was highly ambitious. But the purpose of a strategic plan is, in part, to set high expectations and motivate the workforce. If even some of that vision could be fulfilled, it would represent great progress. The Los Angeles we came to was, as we put it in an early draft of the strategic plan, a

---

[71]The "divisions" refer to bus divisions—where buses are stored and maintained. This is where most frontline workers can be found.
[72]Seriously.

"traffic-choked-smog-burger." Traffic was getting worse, pollution was increasing, public transit was insufficient, and no one was happy with their transportation options. We were leaders at an agency funded with local tax dollars to fix these problems. To propose small incremental changes in this case seemed to us to be malpractice.

Tham's strategy of bringing people along was critical. But given the scale of change we were after, it also had to be balanced with a willingness to push back when people proved unwilling to change or moderate their perspectives. Of course, people will rarely tell you that they do not want to change and prefer just doing what they are doing, they have a good thing going, and they don't particularly care whether they accomplish any greater outcome. They also are unlikely to say that they are afraid of change or scared to take risks, or that if you could just leave them alone, they will soon vest their pension at a crazy high level and get out of here. Instead, they will say things such as the following:

1. **That is unrealistic**. We often heard this reaction when we pushed for more ambitious timelines. For example, the head of the Express Lanes program—which builds HOT lanes on freeways—told us that our timeline for completing more lanes was unrealistic, which it probably was. HOT lanes are a powerful way to enable people to avoid traffic, either with buses or if they are willing to carpool or pay, and a HOT lane network lined up well with the vision of the strategic plan. But the person leading this program—and responsible for implementation of these lanes—did not want to be held accountable for getting them done faster. We could understand why, since from her perspective, she could not control the reasons they were being delayed. But on the other hand, someone needed to be held accountable for getting this done, or else it would never get done.

2. **That won't solve the problem**. Sometimes, what sounds like a policy disagreement is really something else—personal, professional, or political. Take the person in charge of highway building at Metro. Naturally, he wasn't thrilled with our suggestion that maybe we should stop building highways. And while decades of research show that expanding highway capacity doesn't reduce

congestion or improve long-term transportation outcomes, he had little reason to embrace that conclusion. He may have disagreed with the data, but he also had a strong incentive to ignore it—because accepting it would mean questioning the very premise of his job. As Upton Sinclair famously put it, "It is difficult to get a man to understand something, when his salary depends upon his not understanding it."[lxxviii]

3. **The Board will never approve it**. Rather than accept the fact that they don't want to do something, people will often prefer to blame "the Board" or "politics." They will predict failure to avoid trying. This is called "negotiating with yourself" and it is something we often had to fight against because there is a tendency to assume that whatever has failed politically in the past will fail again in the future. We ran into this with the issue of congestion pricing, which is a solution to traffic congestion that has been demonstrably effective wherever it has been implemented. Metro staff could not disagree with the idea, but they could predict it would never happen. They argued for keeping it out of the strategic plan because otherwise, the Board would reject the entire plan. What they really meant was that they were afraid the Board would approve it, and then they would have to be responsible for implementing it. The Board approved the strategic plan, with congestion pricing in it, unanimously.

4. **We don't have budget**. Yes, in many cases we do not have the budget. This is a great excuse for not even trying to make the case for funding. We ran into this with Operations. They didn't like the fact that we were calling for a massive boost in bus service because they barely had enough money to run the existing bus service. How could the plan call for an increase when we didn't even have enough now? This misses the entire point of the plan, which is to set priorities and change the budget. Rather than accept the status quo and work within it, a strategic plan sets a course for a new status quo that better accomplishes our goals. Some people genuinely don't see the distinction. Others simply don't want to stick their neck out for a bigger budget.

When faced with this kind of opposition, even Tham had to bring in the big guns. Within Metro's strict hierarchy, most chiefs will only talk to another chief. Otherwise, a chief could wind up talking to some lowly plebeian, such as a deputy executive officer or—heaven forbid—a lowly manager. This might result in a damaged ego or worse. Tham was not even an executive, so she could not speak to an executive without one of us present.

Therefore, it was up to Nadine and me to attend all meetings with other executives and play bad cop to Tham's good cop. Woody Allen once said that 80 percent of life is just showing up—this adage held true for these meetings. The life of an executive at Metro can often include just attending a meeting to show that you are supporting whatever the people who work for you are saying. As a new department with a small headcount, we had staff at the senior planner or principal planner levels that would often ask me or Nadine to just sit in critical meetings with them so that the other department would take them seriously. We might have to speak up on occasion to make a point but just being there was most of the battle.

The Plan Meets Planning

The Strategic Plan set up an inherent conflict with Countywide Planning for obvious reasons—we were both "planning" for the future of the agency, so whose plan would rule the day? Countywide Planning is responsible for the Long-Range Transportation Plan (LRTP) for LA Metro, a 30-year plan for everything LA Metro plans to do. The LRTP is part of a long federally mandated bureaucratic process that few people are aware of, but it determines what is eligible for federal funding and therefore has a major impact on what gets built. Not surprisingly, Countywide Planning considers it to be a rather important process, and now our strategic plan was coming along and messing with it.

So, the first thing we had to do was agree on how the two plans would relate to one another. This became an issue as soon as we started talking about our planned strategic planning process with Board Staff. LA Metro had not done a strategic plan in 10 years, so there was little to no understanding of what it was. Board Staff were confused about how to explain it to their bosses, who only understood the LRTP and the Measure M expenditure plan. These were precious political documents they had skillfully negotiated to extract maximum value for their bosses—they wanted clarity.

When clarity is needed in a bureaucracy, one way to fix it is with a graphic. A graphic can be approved and then presented to everyone to show how the plans relate to one another. If we could agree on a graphic, perhaps we can move forward. So, we spent months negotiating what the graphic would look like.[73] Eventually we agreed that the strategic plan would be the "umbrella" under which all the other plans would sit. Planning reluctantly agreed to this when Phil made it clear that this was what he wanted. But that wasn't the end of it.

One day, I was summoned to the Deputy CEO's office. The Chief Planning Officer, Therese McMillan, was in there—and she was mad. A fight with Planning was probably inevitable from the moment I came to work. When I met Therese's predecessor, Martha Welborne—she told me that she was glad my office had been created because we would get to do all the fun stuff that she wished she had time to do. I took that as a not-so-subtle hint.

Therese was mad because of one word—"implement." We had said in a proposed communication to the Board of Directors that our office would "Implement the Strategic Plan" after it was completed. There was real concern that our office's language could suggest a shift in authority.

In our naivete, we had not imagined that this was how that sentence would be perceived. Our thought was that once the plan was complete, someone had to be responsible for *making sure* it was implemented, following and tracking the progress for all the initiatives, and that should probably be us. We never conceived of the idea that we would have the staff or resources to lead the implementation of every initiative in the plan, nor did we desire to do so. In hindsight, the wording lacked nuance and created unintentional tension.

This problem had a very easy solution, which we eventually got to after some gratuitous yelling. Instead of "implement" we would say "monitor strategic plan implementation." Problem solved! Another fine day at the office.

---

[73]Your hard-earned tax dollars at work.

The takeaway from this series of events is clear—it is probably safe to assume that people will often look at others in positions of power as trying to accumulate more of it. We also experienced this during our labor negotiations for microtransit, our development of a podcast, and our discussion with TAP, among other projects. Even if that is your intention (and it shouldn't be) you need to go out of your way to explain that it isn't. Or if it is, why it is beneficial for the organization.

Nonetheless, Vision 2028, Metro's 10-year strategic plan, was passed unanimously by the Board. It included our plan for "World Class Bus" that would shift the focus of the agency toward bus improvements.[74] It included ambitious plans for changing the culture of the agency. It also included our favorite component—congestion pricing.

Congestion Pricing

When Phil Washington asked me to be the Chief Innovation Officer for LA Metro, everything happened very fast. He needed an answer from me right away, and I was making a big decision that affected my entire family, so I needed to fly out to Los Angeles ASAP to talk to him and others at Metro so I could decide. Unfortunately, the timeline for this decision coincided with my family's annual summer trip to the beach. During our vacation I arose in Rehoboth, DE, put on a suit and tie, drove the family Subaru two hours to Philadelphia, and got on a plane to Los Angeles. As I flew across the country, I considered how I would fix transportation in Los Angeles if I got the job. I decided to present these ideas to Phil and see how he felt about them. If he agreed that we should do them, I would have to take the job. The four things[75] were as follows:

1. Build a network of bus lanes across Los Angeles with frequent services.
2. Create an on-demand, publicly provided microtransit service.

---

[74]This was later watered down to "Better Bus" once Communications got ahold of it. No need to be too ambitious.

[75]Notably, all four of these ideas are for tangible transportation improvements. As I would learn, it would have made sense to also include improving at least one internal process (HR, Procurement, etc.). Keep this in mind as you think about your priorities for public policy change.

3. Develop public–private partnerships (P3) that would become a model for project delivery in transportation.
4. Bring congestion pricing to Los Angeles.

When I arrived in Los Angeles, my brother-in-law met me at a steak restaurant where we had martinis while looking at famous celebrities on the wall, and he gave me the pitch on everything he loved about the city. He was a transplanted East Coast guy too and said he could not envision ever going back. I stayed at my in-laws' house in the hills overnight and looked out on the mountains and stars and contemplated whether I was crazy enough to do this.

The next morning my in-laws dropped me at the North Hollywood Red Line station, and I took the train to Union Station to LA Metro. Unfortunately, when I arrived from my cross-country journey, there was a slight problem. Phil was sick. He wasn't in and wasn't sure if he would be in at all.

What could I do? They had set up meetings for me with existing metro staff. I met with many executives who had no clue about the future I had with them, and many others who would be replaced before I arrived or soon thereafter. I even attended a SLT meeting where Phil's eventual successor Stephanie Wiggins had to lead the meeting in Phil's absence. I worked in a cubicle between meetings, waiting and hoping that Phil might show up.

Finally, he did. Phil is not the kind of guy who takes sick days or misses work. He looked and sounded terrible. But in these pre-COVID-19 days of 2015 I didn't think twice about meeting with him (though he did thoughtfully fist-bump me instead of shaking my hand). I don't remember much about the meeting, other than when I told him my four ideas, he said yes to every single one.

All these ideas came to fruition to some degree. Phil wasn't crazy, and neither was I, apparently. Everything took longer than we thought it would, and none of these ideas have been built out as extensively, 11 years later in 2026, as I might have hoped. But of all these ideas, only one is still being studied and has not been enacted. This is the one idea that is the most powerful, most controversial, and if enacted, I am certain it would immediately become the most popular—Congestion Pricing.

Congestion Pricing—a Primer

Ever since Nobel Prize winning economist William Vickrey first popularized the idea in the academic literature in the 1950s, congestion pricing has been the fantasy policy of every urban planner and economist who got excited reading Jane Jacobs, angry at Robert Moses, and captivated by Jose Gomez-Ibanez.[76] Planners around the world swooned when Singapore, then London, then Stockholm, and even Milan introduced congestion pricing as a mechanism in their urban cores. And on January 5, 2025, New York became the first U.S. city to employ congestion pricing across its central area, after a journey that took at least five decades.

There is a reason it took that long. Congestion pricing is one of those policies that people tend to dislike before implementation, but once implemented, they want to keep it in place. It is a classic example of "status quo bias" wherein people are more inclined to support an existing policy instead of a new one. Even if they know that an existing policy isn't working well, e.g., there is a lot of traffic, people will be reluctant to embrace a new policy that will fix it, especially when that policy sounds a lot like "pay us and there will be less traffic" and most people do not have sufficient faith in their government to believe that to be true.

But when properly implemented, congestion pricing works because people respond to price signals. Right now, most roads in urban areas are "free" in the sense that drivers do not need to pay out of their pockets to drive on them. True, most drivers are paying for their vehicles, insurance, maintenance, gas or electricity, as well as taxes that go toward roadway maintenance and repair. But none of these fees account for the cost of so many people using the same roads at the same time, also known as traffic.

---

[76]William Vickrey was a Nobel Prize-winning economist at Columbia and is considered the father of congestion pricing, introducing the concept decades ago. Robert Moses was an urban planner and public official in New York, credited for building much of New York's highway network. His accomplishments and shortcomings are detailed in Robert Caro's *Power Broker*, required reading for all aspiring urban planners. Jane Jacobs fought against Robert Moses, arguing against both urban renewal and slum clearance, and writing *The Life and Death of Great American Cities*, also required reading. Jose Gomez-Ibanez is a professor at the Harvard Kennedy School of Government, and a thought leader in transportation economics and policy.

When fees for road usage based on demand are introduced, traffic congestion decreases. It is simple economics—people will buy more of something when the price is lower, and less when the price is higher. When the price of a road is effectively zero, people will "buy" more of it compared to if the price is higher than zero, so that "shortages" of expensive-to-provide free roads inevitably occur. Congestion pricing just means charging people to drive on roads at certain times when the demand for free roads exceeds the supply. When introduced, it causes some people to forgo their trip, or seek an alternate route, at the busiest time, thus freeing up the roads for those who are willing to pay to use it at that time. If priced correctly, the total number of users on the road at the peak time will be just below the capacity of the road, allowing it to flow without traffic and maximizing throughput.

I am guessing that many people flinched at the words "those who are willing to pay" in the last paragraph. While economists use this term all the time, to the layperson it may sound like "rich people." The fear for elected officials and their constituents is that when pricing is introduced, only wealthy people will be able to afford to use the roads at peak times. The policy of congestion pricing sounds, especially to liberals, like a way to make a public good into something that only rich people can use.

Meanwhile, more conservative electeds and their constituents are less likely to trust the government to collect these funds and use them in a fair manner. Their objections to congestion pricing tend to be that it is like yet another "tax" that the government will then waste, and that it simply won't work. It can also raise privacy concerns if the fee is collected through transponders or apps that give the government information on your location. The upshot is that both the left and right sides of the political spectrum tend to dislike this policy before it is implemented.

However, the flip side is also true. Those in favor of congestion pricing can come from both sides of the political spectrum. Liberals tend to like it because it reduces emissions from cars by discouraging driving and making traffic move instead of idling, and because it produces funding that can go toward public transit and other equity improvements. Conservatives like it because it is an efficient, market-based economic policy for allocating a scarce resource that mimics the private sector and helps drivers move faster.

Moreover, such fears do not hold water in theory or practice. For virtually all goods in society, including many public services, we use pricing to allocate resources. For example, everyone needs water and electricity. We do not give those essential things away for free because if we did, there would be water and electricity shortages constantly (just as there is regular traffic in major cities because we give away road space for free). Instead, we might offer government programs that aid those who struggle to afford water and electricity, to ensure they are not left without an essential service. In practice, congestion pricing does shift people off the roads at peak times, but those who choose to use other modes or forgo their trip are not necessarily low-income. It turns out there are high earners who also prefer not to spend money at peak times if they can go at another time, and there are low-income people for whom the cost of paying a peak fee may be less than the cost of sitting in traffic or showing up late to work.[lxxix]

This gets to another key point about congestion pricing. Whether it exists or not, people are paying. When there is no pricing, they pay with time. When there is pricing, they pay with money. It is true that some people may prefer a policy of paying with their time instead of money. Witness people who wait in line for Black Friday deals, or Ben & Jerry's free ice cream cone day. But as a society, we can recognize these behaviors are irrational, and that it is far more efficient for people to pay with money instead of time.

OEI Plants the Seed

Urban Planning is not an exact science. We often get things wrong, as evidenced by past urban planning ideas that are largely discredited such as urban renewal, plowing freeways through neighborhoods, and segregation of land uses. However, to the extent that we can trust the consensus on an issue in urban planning, there does appear to be strong evidence that you cannot reduce traffic in any meaningful way without congestion pricing.

Transit, bike lanes, wider sidewalks and other alternatives to driving do not alleviate traffic, though they can provide a better means of getting around. Building more roadway capacity does not reduce traffic, and in fact exacerbates it.[lxxx] Waze and other mapping software did not fix traffic, nor did better street signal timing. Los Angeles has struggled with traffic congestion for decades, and urban planning research has largely concluded that this struggle will not end until the roads are priced.[lxxxi] Pricing alone may not be sufficient, but it is necessary if the goal is to fix traffic.

I had come to LA to work on this very issue. Voters had given LA Metro billions of dollars, not because they wanted a better mass transit system (though surely many did) but because they were sick of sitting in traffic.[lxxxii] We wanted to take a shot at congestion pricing. If we didn't at least try to improve traffic—as the CFO said—why were we even there?

Fortunately, Phil agreed with this perspective, and we were able to override the reservations of some other executives at LA Metro and include the idea of a congestion pricing study in Vision 2028. While there were some moderate objections that this issue could derail the entire strategic plan, the Board either didn't notice or didn't care that this study was included in Vision 2028. Nor did the press pick up on it when Vision 2028 passed unanimously in the summer of 2018.

While OEI quietly jumped for joy and began to prepare to do the study, we knew we had to be cautious. Our friends at the Southern California Association of Governments (SCAG) had recently completed their own study of congestion pricing for Los Angeles, only to have it go up in flames.[lxxxiii] SCAG is the Metropolitan Planning Organization for Los Angeles and five other surrounding counties. They have an enormous footprint and board, but largely lack any implementation power and function more as a planning think-tank.

At the time they were led by Hasan Ikhrata, a visionary planner and leader who was unafraid to take on big issues such as congestion pricing.[77] He had proceeded with a study without any substantial political buy-in. When the study was released, it recommended a pilot program for congestion pricing on the West Side of Los Angeles. While this made great logical sense, SCAG apparently failed to secure political support from the

---

[77]Hasan later went on to lead the San Diego Association of Governments (SANDAG), which does have implementation power and where he came in proposing pricing and fought for it the entire time he was there. Unfortunately, he lost and left the organization in 2023.

city councilman[78] in that area before they released their study. His immediate reaction, along with the way it was portrayed in the press, made their pricing idea dead on arrival.

Determined to avoid this fate, we took our time and approached the issue carefully. This is where Tham and her expertise at building support for new ideas would be fully tested. Tham laid out a plan wherein we would work to study the issue and build support for it simultaneously. Rather than going into communities and presenting our idea for pricing, we would work with communities on their ideas for improving traffic and be sure to put pricing on the table. The idea was to make sure that these communities would tell us what they needed, and we could show them how pricing could deliver those benefits. For example, communities might want more frequent bus service, or a bike lane, or wider sidewalks, or bus shelters. Funding from congestion pricing could bring those benefits, plus it would improve traffic.

We also prepared a plan for building political support. Before going public with anything, we would ensure that our board members were fully engaged and able to support, or at least not oppose, any plan we put forward. We would also work with the press to ensure that the issue was covered fairly. OEI had cultivated a very positive relationship with news organizations in LA by being one of the few departments at Metro that was willing and able to talk to them quickly and candidly.

But despite this plan, we didn't have an angle by which we could start this study. We needed more than tacit support from the Board if this was to move forward, and it wasn't clear how we were going to get there. If we just went out and hired a consultant to assist with the study, the Board would need to approve the contract publicly and this could kill the study before it even began.

Fortunately, the Board unwittingly presented us with an opportunity.

Metro Board Meetings

Metro Board meetings are a combination of drudgery and spectacle. They occur monthly and LA Metro's executive staff spends lots of time preparing for them (and Board Staff Briefing that precedes them). When I first

---

[78]Mike Bonin, who was also a Metro Board member at the time.

arrived, I failed to grasp their importance or my role with respect to board meetings. It was an unwritten rule that executives, especially the chiefs, would attend all board meetings and committee meetings. We had a "squawk box" in our offices that would transmit audio from the meetings if we needed to be at our desks, but if you were needed in the boardroom, you'd have 25 flights to get down if your presence was requested, so better to be there in person.

Full board meetings begin at 10 a.m. on the last Thursday of the month[79] and tend to last several hours. This is the big show, and everyone has a role to play:

- **CEO**—Board management is the biggest and most challenging role for the CEO. Phil did plenty of work behind the scenes before the meeting to get things to flow smoothly, but he would also need to be prepared to react in real time to unanticipated events. The CEO gives remarks at every Board meeting that are intended to update the Board and the public on the latest goings on at Metro.

- **Board Chair**—The board chair runs the meeting and must handle the agenda, other board members, staff presentations, and most challenging of all, public comment. The chair must try to keep the meeting moving along despite all these other folks trying to get their time to speak. And of course, the chair is an elected official who will use their pulpit at the meeting to advance their own agenda.

- **Board Staff**—Board Staff treat each meeting like a congressional hearing where they are behind the scenes pulling the strings. They prepare remarks, comments, and amendments for their bosses, and sit in a room behind the Board meeting where they have lunch while the meeting drags on. During the meeting you can see Board Staff hustling behind the board members and sometimes conferring with metro staff.

---

[79]Approximately once each quarter, the calendar yields a "fifth Thursday," an extra week of breathing room before the next cycle begins. For those who live within this cadence year after year, that additional week becomes a quietly cherished reprieve.

- **Metro Staff**—Metro staff, mostly the executives, sit in the audience and await their items. If their item or items are on consent and they are not a chief, they will typically leave after the consent agenda is passed. But the chiefs and others expecting to make presentations will stay until anything they might be involved with comes up.

- **Consultants and Lobbyists**—There are many consultants and lobbyists who hang around Metro meetings either because there is an item on the agenda that might be a contract for them, or one they are involved with, or because they are looking for face time with metro staff.

- **Journalists**—There is a surprising dearth of journalists at these meetings given the amount of money involved and the enormous policy decisions being made there. The LA Times had a transportation reporter who would show up occasionally. Streetsblog had a reporter (the aforementioned Joe Linton) who would live-tweet the meetings and was often the only source of (very biased) information regarding what was happening at the meeting for the outside world.

- **General Public**—This was the most entertaining crew. There were regulars who would show up at every meeting and comment. Some of these folks were from nonprofits and advocacy organizations and would comment on items to make their positions known. Others functioned more as performance artists, showing up just to have their moment in the sun and comment on every item. Some of these folks were hopelessly trying to influence the Board, but most were just trying to get attention and be as outrageous as possible. Then there were the nonregulars—people who would mobilize to show up on a specific item and overwhelm the public comment period. When these folks were in the house, you knew you were in for a long meeting.

The destiny of most items on the agenda is known before the meeting. Because of the early mentioned Brown Act, even if an item is not on consent, Board Staff are unlikely to allow it on the agenda unless they think they have the votes to pass it.

However, there are several ways things can go awry:

1. **Amendments.** Board members can put forward amendments to an item either in advance or in real time. This can just be a case of a board member using their platform to make a stink about a specific issue, in which case the amendment doesn't usually change anything. However, sometimes amendments are put forward because there is disagreement among board members.

2. **Unforeseen issues.** Sometimes a board member will have an issue with a contract and intentionally not bring it up before the meeting, or they won't be paying enough attention to an issue before a meeting, or they might have inadequate staffing. These surprises can be very challenging as everyone is reacting in real time to satisfy a board member concern. Board members are reluctant to criticize each other in public and will allow the other members the opportunity to speak and disrupt a meeting to their heart's content.

3. **Public comment.** Board members are elected officials, and they generally seek public approval. When masses of people (nonregulars) show up to speak in a specific direction against an item, it has an impact. This can be the case even if there are millions of people who would benefit from the item but have not shown up to support it because they have jobs and families and other responsibilities on Thursday mornings.

Public comment period is by far the most entertaining and disturbing part of any board meeting. Members of the public are entitled to one-minute comments each on every item, plus there is a general public comment period at the end of the meeting for additional one-minute statements (one per person). Regular performance artists included:

- **Puppet guy.** This man would speak on every item and use puppetry to make his points that sounded occasionally coherent. He had a pig and a goat on his hands and would use them to articulate his general disdain for board members, often using animal noises.
- **Disheveled yelling guy.** This man would begin every speech by announcing his website and then proceed to yell about whatever

issue was on the table and how it showed that board members were corrupt or incompetent. He did not appear to enjoy bathing, and he regularly used the n-word in his speeches as a way of indicating that *others* were racist.

- **Dog guy.** This man would show up with his little dog, perhaps a service animal, and give f-bomb-laden speeches citing specific provisions in law that may or may not have had any relevance to the subject matter at hand.

Board chairs varied in how they dealt with the challenges of public comment. Most would try to keep commenters on topic, threatening to prevent them from speaking if they did not address the matter at hand. Some would threaten and then remove people using offensive language, though some did not. Most board members and the CEO took the tack of using a gentle smile and trying to look like they were listening without engaging, no matter how outrageous what was being said. For example, one commenter often repeated a conspiracy theory about the mayor, who was the board chair, having a secret gay lover, with graphic details about sex acts that were being performed. Another commenter (who was White) called Phil and Board Chair Mark Ridley-Thomas (who are Black) racists for using the acronym APE (Annual Project Evaluation) as shorthand. These produced no reaction.

Sometimes board members couldn't help themselves. During a discussion about the Crenshaw Line, a new light-rail line through a Black neighborhood, one board member finally had it. The new line was being built aboveground to save costs, and members of the community wanted it below ground and they showed up en masse to protest. They argued that they would focus on the possibility that the aboveground line would wind up running over pedestrians, and that since these pedestrians were likely to be Black, this project amounted to a "Black genocide." They even had t-shirts made with the claim of Black genocide. They were led by an attorney who made a speech where he noted that he himself was Jewish, and therefore an authority on what was or was not a genocide, and that there was no doubt that this—yes, this construction of an aboveground light-rail line—was genocide.

Board Member Najarian asked the chair for a chance to respond and let out his wrath. His grandmother and other family had been killed in the

Armenian genocide, and being accused of genocide for building a rail line pushed him over the edge. His retort likely didn't change anyone's position, but it may have made it a little more difficult for other board members to consider backing the protesters. The item passed and that line has now been built.

Congestion Pricing—the Board Opens the Door

The chaos and insanity of Metro Board meetings also provided opportunities for change. In 2017, Los Angeles was awarded the 2028 Olympic and Paralympic games.[lxxxiv] Mayor Garcetti, who was considering running for higher office, saw this as an opportunity to build his legacy and national profile. While he knew he wouldn't be mayor in 2028 due to term limits, he was the chair of the Metro Board and could use that pulpit to draw attention to all the things Los Angeles was doing to prepare for the games as he considered a run for president.

His proposal was called "Twenty-Eight by '28."[lxxxv] It was a list of 28 projects (what a coincidence!) that Metro would complete by 2028. When he initially came to Metro with this idea, we tried to dissuade him from doing it. We knew that promising any major project by a specific date is a recipe for disaster, as projects almost always take longer than expected. But worse, the projects on the mayor's initial list included new rail lines that had no hope of being completed anywhere near 2028. The list would become an unkept promise from day one.

After much negotiation, we reached a compromise. The list was recalibrated to include numerous smaller projects that could be completed by 2028, including microtransit and other OEI initiatives, as well as larger projects that could realistically be completed by 2028. But there were still three signature projects that remained on the list that had little hope for completion within that timeframe—Sepulveda, West Santa Ana, and the Torrance extension. For these projects, Metro staff reluctantly agreed to keep them on the list as "aspirational," meaning they were on there, but it would take a miracle for them to be completed by 2028. This wasn't ideal since it was setting Metro up to never be able to accomplish "Twenty-Eight by 2028," but it was better than the original list the mayor had proposed. The Board adopted the mayor's list as a policy statement but without any actual changes to the agency budget.

Staff were optimistic that this issue had been resolved. What they hadn't anticipated was that the Board, despite hearing directly and clearly from professionals that these big projects could not be completed by 2028, had no interest in dealing with reality. They wanted to fight for their projects. The ink wasn't dry for long on Twenty-Eight by '28 when the board asked staff to provide a plan for how they would complete these aspirational projects by 2028. They were critical of staff and Phil for not doing more. Unfortunately, reminding the Board that these projects were aspirational for a reason was not an acceptable answer.

Another unacceptable answer would have been to point to the Board as the reason these projects take a long time. Projects are delayed for many reasons, but in Los Angeles one reason is that outside of LA Metro, most government officials have little interest in getting the projects done quickly or at all. In fact, they have an opposing interest, which is to wring as much money from LA Metro as possible when they are planning a project through their area. Metro has money, so City X sees Metro's new rail line, for which they need permits from City X, as an opportunity to get funding for other needs in the corridor such as utilities, sidewalks, trees, lightbulbs, or anything else that catches their fancy. LA Metro board members will typically let Metro fight these battles on their own, as they would rather not get involved.

Phil, unlike his Board, was a chess player. He felt attacked and blind-sided by the Board for pushing these projects on an unrealistic timeline after he had already made it clear that the timeline was unrealistic. He felt they were trying to blame him for a problem that was the Board's creation. But instead of reacting negatively in real time, Phil turned this attack into an opportunity.

He began by directing staff to develop a cost estimate for what it would take to get these projects done by 2028 compared to expected revenues. The way Measure M works is that projects are spread along a 50-year timeline so that sales tax receipts can come in and fund projects along the way. All projects cannot be built at once because the funds won't be there yet. The Board was asking to move multibillion-dollar projects up in the timeline. This money had to come from somewhere, so Phil wanted to see what it would take, and he wanted to show the Board a big number. They needed to appreciate the scale of what they were asking.

The report back to the Board had to happen quickly. Phil assigned his top person—Deputy CEO Stephanie Wiggins—to directly oversee its production. She had to perform miracles just to get the report done. One of the biggest challenges was Metro's aforementioned two finance teams, each of which had different numbers. Stephanie had to wrangle these two groups and get them to agree on a common set of facts to present to the Board.

More importantly, Stephanie needed solutions. It wasn't sufficient to give the Board a price tag—we had to propose ideas for how we would fill the gap in funding. This was where OEI came in. We were asked to provide an estimate of how much revenue congestion pricing could bring in. We were also asked about another one of our ideas—a fee for rideshare—that we had also discussed in the strategic plan.

Providing estimates for revenue from plans that are barely a kernel of an idea, especially with a very short turnaround time, is exactly the kind of thing that gives academic researchers heartburn. So naturally we decided to ask researchers at UCLA for their opinions. They agreed it was an exercise that could not possibly produce accurate results, but they were so excited about the possibility of congestion pricing being considered in Los Angeles that they agreed to do what they could, and quickly. They came back to us with numbers that were shockingly high. Congestion pricing, under assumptions that discarded politics but considered raw numbers of vehicles and demand, could bring in sufficient revenue to fund everything the Board wanted.[lxxxvi] We were armed with what we needed to make our case.

Confronting the Board

At the Board meeting where staff were to respond to the Board, Phil chose to give the presentation personally from the podium where staff or the public would typically speak. This was highly unusual, as the CEO usually sat with the Board at meetings and let staff handle the presentations. Also, this presentation was going to be rather provocative. CEOs do not like to take on their Boards. It is likely to be a losing battle, with the possible result of the CEO being ousted. They especially eschew taking on their Board publicly. But Phil Washington was ready to do both. What were the circumstances that made such a confrontation a good decision for Phil? They were as follows:

1. **The Board started it.** Phil was being asked to respond to a request from the Board to come up with revenue sources for the projects they wanted completed. This was not his initiative; he was just being responsive to their needs (albeit with something slightly different from what they likely expected).

2. **Phil was still a relatively recent hire and would be tough to fire.** To fire Phil at this point, the Board would have to admit they made a mistake in hiring him. He was beloved by staff and had performed well as CEO, showing unmistakable leadership skills. He also had a contract.

3. **Phil wasn't just giving them a challenge.** He was giving them something they wanted. They wanted projects and they wanted them done faster. He was honestly providing them with a solution, even if it was a controversial one.

But Phil had one more sweetener to add to the pot. Proposing congestion pricing to accelerate projects was one thing, but to actually get it done Phil would need to make the Board an offer they couldn't refuse. He found that in the idea of free fares.

The idea had been percolating for some time. A few years prior at an SLT meeting, I suggested introducing free fares and everyone immediately said I was insane. Even Phil couldn't believe I was serious. But I was and the reason was simple. LA Metro's budget was approximately $8 billion annually. Fare collections, in a good year, were $300 million. The median household income on the system was approximately $20,000 per year.[lxxxvii] So effectively we were charging the people in our society who could least afford it a fee that had almost no impact on our budget (about 3 percent) but likely made a big difference in their lives. Raising fares to a rate that would be meaningful was not only politically impossible but would likely reduce ridership substantially.

Eliminating fares would likely increase ridership without meaningfully impacting the budget. In fact, it could potentially even save money given the substantial number of resources dedicated to fare collection. LA

Metro had a vast network of fare box readers, ticket vending machines, and turnstiles, all of which needed maintenance. Plus, we had to pay cash counters, fare checkers, and vendors for fare collection under a huge contract. Then there was a whole team of customer service agents dedicated exclusively to helping people with TAP, the fare collection media, plus a whole team of people who work for TAP itself.

When I first suggested it, the idea went nowhere. But Phil made a mental note of it in his brain. Then, sometime later, a planner named doreen[80] Morrissey took the project on as part of an internal leadership class. When she presented her results to Phil and the other executives, he looked over at me and told her we should work together on this idea. Not long after that, doreen applied to be a fellow in our office, and we brought her on to develop the idea further.

Phil saw something in free fares that we did not. He saw that if he offered the Board the combined solution of congestion pricing and free fares together, they would be hard pressed to say no. They had asked us to come up with revenue, and we proposed something that would raise revenue and reduce traffic. And while board members at transit agencies hate to raise fares, they love lowering them. How could they publicly oppose—in Los Angeles—raising revenue from drivers and using it to provide free public transit for all?

They couldn't. When Phil made his presentation, the Board agreed that we should proceed and study congestion pricing for implementation in Los Angeles.[lxxxviii] They only had one caveat—this was not to be studied for the purpose of raising revenue for projects.[81,lxxxix] It was

---

[80]Not a typo. She does not capitalize her first name.

[81]From a policy perspective, focusing on reducing and managing congestion rather than generating funds results in a focused policy that efficiently achieves the intended goal. In addition, most congestion pricing programs have some interface with Federal-aid highways, and per Federal law, you can't tax preexisting capacity. The Federal Value Pricing Pilot Program (VPPP) offers a pathway for Federal approval for congestion pricing exclusively for the purposes of managing congestion (and not generating revenue). The New York City congestion pricing fell under fire from the Trump Administration in 2025 because the political campaign for the program built support in part through committing to reinvesting revenues back into the system, and thereby in theory not enabled by the VPPP. At the time of publishing, this lawsuit is ongoing.

only for reducing traffic and providing free fares. In other words, the Board completely reversed their original position of wanting to raise more revenue for projects. They had to because once confronted with the idea of charging drivers to pay for projects that were supposed to have already been funded by Measure M, they realized it was untenable. But they also wanted free fares and were willing to explore congestion pricing to do so. That moment represented the first time in Metro history that the Board formally endorsed road pricing—not as a revenue tool but as a policy lever to deliver free fares and reduce traffic. It fundamentally shifted the Overton Window[82] on what was politically possible.

Both Naivete and Experience Are Required

Innovation is fundamentally about challenging the status quo. It requires people with fresh eyes—those who aren't steeped in the "way things are done"—to identify broken processes and systems and imagine better ones. But outsiders can't go it alone. They need insiders who understand how the system works and how to actually move new ideas through. At OEI we learned firsthand that it's a combination of these two forces that makes change possible.

Organizational scholars call this "ambidexterity"—the ability to balance exploration of new ideas with the exploitation of existing knowledge and capabilities.[xc] Phil understood this better than anyone. He built OEI to include both Metro veterans and bold outsiders. Phil himself also had experience as a CEO that he brought to bear on our most controversial ideas. That staffing model was essential to nearly every OEI win—but nowhere was it more important than in our work on the agency's strategic plan and our ambitious efforts to pursue congestion pricing.

---

[82]The Overton Window is a model that describes the range of policies that a politician can support without being considered extreme or unelectable. It represents the spectrum of public opinion on any given issue, and as public attitudes shift, so too does the Overton Window, making previously radical ideas more mainstream over time.

Despite OEI's efforts, Los Angeles still does not have congestion pricing, but not for lack of a clear, actionable strategy.[83] We developed one of the most plausible and politically calibrated congestion pricing proposals the city had ever seen, grounded in technical feasibility and community input. But timing matters. When the pandemic hit, congestion temporarily disappeared, and with it, the urgency to act. Leadership transitions soon followed: Phil left Metro; Stephanie Wiggins took over as CEO; Mayor Garcetti departed for India; and Mayor Bass, facing a crisis of homelessness, set different priorities. Though the project technically remains in motion, it has been deprioritized. Still, the groundwork we laid endures, ready to be picked up when the next window opens.

Vision 2028 and congestion pricing represented major policy shifts that emerged during a narrow policy window. What made that progress possible wasn't just good strategy—it was the unique makeup of OEI. We were naive enough to believe that big change was possible in Los Angeles, and experienced enough to navigate the machinery required to try. That's not magic. That's structure. And it's replicable—if leaders are willing to build teams that intentionally balance disruption with durability.

---

[83]At the time of writing, the Traffic Reduction Study is still up on Metro's website with a status report that Metro is refining the concept design for potential pricing areas based on modeling results and public feedback. https://www.metro.net/projects/trafficreduction/.

CHAPTER 6

Beware Your Expiration Date

A little over a year after we arrived, Phil decided that OEI should have its own office suite. Until that time, we had been given a few offices and cubicles in a prominent position on the 25th floor, but it was ad hoc. We had now grown to the point where we would be given our own area right next to the CEO's office. To do this, we had to work with General Services to design our space.

A kind but nervous gentleman from building management was assigned to support our team in designing our new digs. He was used to dealing with people across the agency who wanted a space designed just for them. He had been at Metro for a long time and was a survivor. He knew that one of the keys to longevity at Metro was keeping your head down and not sticking out your neck, but he also wanted to do the right thing.

So, when we started asking for unusual design elements—such as open coworking spaces to foster collaboration—he gently pushed back. He explained the policies and why providing exceptions was possible, but not desirable. But then he said something very blunt:

> You know, Joshua, one day there will be a new CEO at Metro. And that CEO might not want an innovation office and might have their own special initiatives. That is when I will have to reverse all the work you want me to do.

His honesty was refreshing. He eventually conceded to most of what we wanted, but his prophecy was telling. He had seen CEOs come and go. He had seen new ideas come and go. He was planning to be there long after we had left, and our "eccentric" design ideas were going to be his problem to restore back to standard Metro policy. He knew something that I didn't fully understand at the time—that our time to act was limited.

Policy windows are moments of time when there is alignment between problems, politics, and proposals that allow bold change to happen.[xci] These windows don't last long. We found that there were both windows that applied to specific projects, as well as a window that applied to OEI as a whole and our ability to advance our vision for change. In this chapter, we explore some of the big changes we tried to make as these windows closed.

Monorails, Hyperloops, and Personal Rapid Transit

Getting people where they want to go when they need to get there is challenging. There are spatial considerations—how a city is designed, the relationship between where people live and where people work, and physical geography like mountains or hills. There are also financial considerations—how to pay for capital investments and ongoing operations and maintenance. These issues are overlaid with implications of how transportation is governed and who makes decisions. For the most part, these are policy challenges.

It can be convenient to believe that policy challenges can be solved through the introduction of new technologies. Navigating the challenge of human nature and policy is often more challenging than approaching problems scientifically. Technology can solve many challenges, but when it comes to building and operating a transportation system, technology is usually not the answer.

The concept of the hyperloop is a great example. In 2013, Elon Musk published a white paper "introducing" the idea to use elevated pneumatic tubes to move people at faster speeds than a typical train or plane. This paper garnered substantial hype.[xcii] At the time, Musk's SpaceX and Tesla were both viewed as successful companies and Elon was thought of as a genius. (This was well before Elon became meaningfully engaged in U.S. politics!) The public sentiment was that if Elon was championing the idea, it must be a worthwhile investment.[84] Several hyperloop companies were introduced and subsequently failed, leaving in their wake moribund hyperloop agreements with various governments and a few underground tunnels with Teslas that bear no resemblance to the hyperloop concept.

Hyperloop failed in part because it solved the wrong problem. A hyperloop might be a useful technology for facilitating faster transportation, but there are many technologies that might accomplish that goal. Magnetic levitation (Maglev) technology can levitate rolling stock using electromagnets and can go up to 375 miles per hour. Maglev has been promoted as a new technology for over 100 years. Electric-propulsion high-speed rail technology can go up to 220 miles per hour. Theoretically, a hyperloop can go faster than any of these technologies, but no train reaching any of these speeds is in operation in the United States as of 2025 and that is not because of a lack of technological options.

High-speed ground transportation requires substantial dedicated space where vehicles won't run into people and kill them. Securing dedicated space for transportation, called a right-of-way, is extremely challenging. It requires purchasing land from property owners, which can result in lengthy and expensive negotiations. Where negotiation doesn't yield the desired outcomes, the government can try to use eminent domain, which is politically difficult and historically ugly, and can also be expensive, litigious, and potentially ineffective. Thus, most high-speed transportation projects are slow and expensive due to the challenge of identifying a project alignment where ROW can be secured.

Take the case of the California High-Speed Rail (CAHSR) project to efficiently link 670 miles of major cities across the state. When California voters approved Prop 1A in 2008, the 520-mile route between San Francisco and Los Angeles was estimated to cost $33 billion (in 2008 $) and be completed around 2020. As of 2025, that same segment is estimated to cost about $130 billion, and funding has yet to be fully identified.[xciii]

---

[84]Musk did not, in fact, introduce the concept of using pneumatic tubes for moving people—the idea dates to the nineteenth century. Pneumatic tubes were proposed and tested for transportation but ultimately the idea stalled.

CAHSR continues to work toward acquiring sufficient ROW. While CAHSR is facing an uphill battle, none of its challenges are a function of identifying a technology that can move people quickly.

Hyperloop joins the long list of technologies that demonstrate why technology cannot solve policy challenges. Monorail is another great example. In 1959, Walt Disney introduced the Disneyland monorail, making it the first monorail in the western hemisphere, and branding it as the technology of the future.[xciv] Indeed, monorail technology does provide some advantages. For example, it reduces the width of the required ROW by only using one rail and it can reduce costs associated with tunneling, as monorails are necessarily elevated rail. Monorail is even one of the technologies that is being considered for Metro's Sepulveda Pass.[xcv] It's another technology that can be useful when applied to the right use case, but it doesn't magically solve policy problems.

A 1993 episode of *The Simpsons* contemplated the exact challenge public officials face when a new transportation technology hyped. *Marge vs. the Monorail* paints a picture of the stereotyped monorail as a technology being sold to foolish people and governments by a con man. The episode ends with Marge lamenting that the monorail was the last folly that the people of Springfield embarked upon, except for "the popsicle stick skyscraper, and the 50-foot magnifying glass, and that escalator to nowhere." New technologies can sometimes be game-changers, but they can also just be the latest thing someone is trying to sell you.

Perhaps the most infamous "transportation of the future" is Personal Rapid Transit (PRT). PRT is like a horizontal elevator. It runs around on tracks and stops for you when you summon it. PRT in theory provides a small vehicle for you and your companions, isolating you from "other people," a common concern people have about mass transit. In theory it runs automatically and so frequently that it becomes both cost-effective and convenient. The only PRT that exists in the United States was built in 1975 in West Virginia, connecting the three Morgantown campuses of the West Virginia University.[xcvi]

While PRT may "solve" for people not wanting to share space with strangers, it still requires substantial amounts of ROW to be acquired for public transit usage in a built environment. Once that ROW is acquired, which is expensive, it often makes more sense to use a higher capacity, less frequent service like trains. The premise of PRT is that acquiring ROW is cheap, which it most definitely is not, but PRT continues to be promoted by entrepreneurs in the United States as a potential transportation game-changer.

Going Gondola

As discussed in Chapter 2, OEI received numerous UPs and those that were successful took substantial internal effort and collaboration. Many of these proposals were for new technologies, such as PRT and other technology solutions that were, from our perspective, likely unworkable and not in response to a problem Metro needed to solve.[85] These proposals did not come with any proposed funding source but were proposed by companies that had developed or owned the rights to a specific technology.

Investors of these technologies believed their solution was so amazing, so cost-effective, that we should fight to replace all planned rail and bus projects in the county with it. They were continuously frustrated when we said that, no, we would not be trying to build a completely new mode of mass transit that was unfunded, unproven, and had been rejected most everywhere.

But one proposal came in for a new technology that was different. First, it was for a form of mass transit that exists and is in use in many places. Second, and more critically, it came with its own funding. The proposal was for a gondola between Union Station and Dodger Stadium, connecting two iconic Los Angeles landmarks.

For many veteran transportation planners, gondolas fall into the same category as PRT, Hyperloop, and Monorail. From their perspective, they might work for ski resorts, but as urban transportation they are often inadequate. First, they require elevated structures (towers) to be placed in an urban environment, which means that someone must agree to relinquish a portion of their ROW. (Remember, securing ROW is hard.) And, importantly, they have lower capacity compared to buses or trains because they are smaller vehicles, making them a less efficient tool for moving

---

[85]One of our favorites was called "Tubular Rail" was a train that couldn't turn. Instead, the cars were on rigid tracks that were moved through a series of hoops. This was a serious proposal.

large numbers of people. This means most planners would see them as too expensive and time-consuming to meet basic transit needs.

OEI, however, was not most planners. When we were approached with this idea, we were intrigued for several reasons that directly countered those concerns:

1. **Funding.** The proposed gondola was to be funded entirely with private money. The funder, Frank McCourt, who owns an interest in parking and other land near Dodger Stadium, even offered to pay for any Metro staff time devoted to this project, and to hire additional Metro staff if needed.

2. **Use case.** The reason the private sector could fund this project was that, unlike most public transit, a gondola is more than a means of getting from one place to another. It is a destination itself. There are only 81 home Dodger games per year (plus the playoffs), which leaves at least 260 days during which the gondola could be used as a tourist attraction. It promised beautiful views and would connect Chinatown and Union Station, two other tourist sites.

3. **Private development.** The private sector also stood to make money by developing the sites near the stadium that it owned. This meant the potential for more housing in LA's housing-starved market, but it also meant creating a new transit-oriented community within walking distance of the stadium, and with easy access to Union Station.

4. **Appropriate application of technology.** The topography of Dodger Stadium—it being up on a hill—made a gondola a more suitable mode of transportation. Gondolas—not buses or trains—are used to get people up mountains all over the world for a reason. Where buses and trains may struggle to climb or descend steep hills, potentially causing safety concerns, gondolas work very efficiently in these conditions.

The proposal was also put forward by a group that was well informed and politically savvy. The group knew that OEI would be open to the idea and could potentially help it navigate through Metro and thus came to us via our UP process. My introduction to the idea came from the former

Chief of Planning at Metro, Martha Welborne, who had left shortly after I arrived. She took me out to lunch and previewed the idea, which was a savvy way to ensure that I would trust they were serious when it arrived.

But the folks proposing the idea also knew that the game ultimately would be won or lost politically and began building support for the project among elected officials even before submitting it to Metro. By the time it reached my desk, Mayor Garcetti, the county supervisors, and even some champions in the state legislature had already been briefed on it. Critically, Garcetti was excited to champion the project.

Other Metro staff were less excited. Planning saw it as a project that no one asked for and that was not in any plan. Remember, Planning oversaw the LRTP and likely perceived that its "power" came from its role in creating and managing that plan. The idea of another department moving a project forward that was not included in the LRTP may have been perceived as a threat to its fiefdom.

While from our perspective the idea that the private sector was not only proposing the project to us but offering to pay for it was extremely compelling, for Planning this presented a concern. Ingrained in Metro's culture is a deep suspicion of the private sector, likely informed by a history of entering contracts that were more favorable to the private-sector vendor than they were for Metro. They applied this suspicion to the gondola project, asserting that the planning and investment of infrastructure should be facilitated through a democratic process and public dollars, and not supported by a capitalist investment.

This was a problem that Nolan Borgman was uniquely positioned to solve. By the time this proposal came in, he was a veteran of the UP process and was expert in running the playbook to build the required internal support for testing new concepts. Immediately, Nolan knew that to get this project through the UP process, he would need to build support within the Planning Department.

He worked the process carefully, documenting it every step of the way. He facilitated the proposal through Phase 1 (agreement that the idea merited further consideration) easily, and the Phase 2 proposal, a more thorough and detailed version in response to our questions, included everything we needed to move forward.[xcvii] He carefully brought the Planning Department leadership along with the process. While they still hated the idea, their concerns were heard and documented, and Nolan assured them that no final decision would be made without them.

Nolan also foresaw some of the potential issues that could derail the project. He knew that the gondola would need to go through Chinatown, and if the residents and businesses in that community objected, it would be challenging to move forward. So, he worked with our Community Engagement personnel to talk to some people in that community,[86] asking them for their perspective on the project even before it was approved. We were somewhat surprised to learn there was some strong positive sentiment for the idea if there was a station in Chinatown. The proposers agreed to add such a station. Nolan also found that residents wanted to be sure it would be affordable to them as mass transit. To ensure that it was accessible to the local community, the proposers agreed to a discount for residents. Nolan also worked with the proposers on possible alignment ideas to develop a project that was less intrusive, did not require an easement or any taking of ROW, and still carried people effectively from one place to another.

While Nolan was knocking down barriers left and right to move this project forward, Planning would still have to agree to take it on. The ask from the proposer was for Metro to lead the environmental process for the project, a statutorily required evaluation of a project's potential impacts on the environment and community, with all costs covered by the proposer. Planning was the only department with the ability to conduct such a process. If they refused, the proposer would likely ask the City of Los Angeles to do it, but they knew that this was suboptimal and would probably take even longer given that they had bureaucratic challenges even worse than Metro's, and no clear path for UPs.

Procurement and Legal presented another issue. The proposers were asking for an exclusive negotiating agreement (ENA) with Metro. This is different from a traditional procurement for a construction project. The proposers suggested that, since they were the ones paying and the only people able to build this project, Metro should work with them exclusively rather than put out competitive tender. This would be a sole-source

---

[86]This included a tour of the neighborhood from the Chinatown Historical Society.

project. The words "sole source" set off alarm bells for Procurement and Legal. As we knew from our other projects, Metro's Procurement and Legal Departments were conservative and many project managers allowed them to make decisions on the best way to manage risk. OEI, on the other hand, did not. We took the issue to Phil.

Phil got Procurement and Legal to agree that if there was a letter from the Dodgers stating that they supported this project's proposers and were therefore tied to it, this could be used as a sole-source justification as it would indicate that no other proposer could hope to build anything similar. The proposers got the letter, and the legal team signed off on a sole-source project. While to our team this whole process felt like a long negotiation with ourselves, it wound up being important later. Read on.

The time came for the big meeting where we would collectively decide on whether the project would proceed. For most unsolicited proposals, this final decision was made with me, Nolan, and a few people from other departments. But this one was a big deal, so it involved chiefs and high-level executives and took place in Phil's conference room with Phil present. Therese from Planning was still upset and refusing to sign on. How could she support this project when there were so many other projects that we were supposed to be building based on a democratic voter mandate? What if the proposers didn't follow through with the money and Metro ultimately did have to foot the bill? Could they compensate us for staff time, realistically?

Phil respected Therese and listened to her concerns. We postponed the decision, and Nolan and I left somewhat dejected. We knew Phil supported the project, and he had asked us only to do some more work to alleviate Therese's concerns. But we felt like it was unlikely we would get there.

Fortunately, the project's proposers grew impatient and were not planning to wait around anymore and *they* brought in the big guns. Phil started to get calls from the mayor and other supporters asking why the project hadn't moved forward yet. Within hours, he overruled planning and the project was approved. As often is the case, political work was the most crucial element of moving the gondola forward. Planning came around to that reality, and the proposed ENA moved to the Board, where it was approved.

We didn't know it at the time, but we got that project approved just in time, and the work we had done proved critical in keeping it moving after we left. The California Endowment (CE), a nonprofit organization with a campus underneath the proposed project, began to mobilize opposition after it was announced. They complained that the project was moving forward without public input, and that the concerns of the community had not been heard.[87]

We found this to be a disingenuous complaint because the project wasn't even designed yet. All Metro had done was agree to an ENA. A UP process does not include public input as it is internal to the agency and is not a determination of project design. It is the next step in the process, the environmental review, which includes a formal process to gather public input required by law. The approval of the environmental document was the point at which the project would begin construction, and we were years away from that. CE was essentially complaining that we hadn't talked to the community when we were at a point when it was not yet possible to give the community any meaningful information. This was reminiscent of internal opposition we had often faced within Metro. If we came to people too early in the process, they wouldn't want to talk to us. If we came to them too late in the process, they would be upset we hadn't included them earlier. Finding the exact right goldilocks time to talk to people about a project was a constant dilemma.

The opposition decided that their best legal option was to therefore claim that this project had been an inappropriate sole-source procurement and a flawed application of the Unsolicited Proposal Policy and filed a lawsuit. By this time Phil had left. The opposition demanded a meeting. Stephanie Wiggins, Phil's successor, and I explained to them that the UP process—including the need to meet criteria for sole sourcing—had been followed to the letter, and they had no basis for the suit. They were in no mood to hear this and threatened to proceed anyway.

In the end, they dropped their lawsuit when they realized it had no chance. Despite our frustration with Legal and Procurement, in the end they had saved us. A letter from the Dodgers and the County Counsel

---

[87]Their actual problem with the project was that it would use land that they might have wanted to acquire for themselves in the future.

going on the record concurring with a sole-source procurement approach was sufficient to keep the project going.

The California Endowment decided to try another route and build greater opposition by getting the city council to oppose the project. They argued that the project would drive up housing costs and increase gentrification and that more/better buses would be a better solution. Eventually they got the local council person in that district to insist on a study of traffic problems in the area before the gondola could proceed.[xcviii] These arguments seemed empty. If a new transportation project is bad because it brings gentrification, then how can new transportation projects ever be built in low-income areas? Which means that low-income neighborhoods will continue to suffer from poor infrastructure and bad traffic, and that new projects could only be built in wealthy areas. This would seem to be the opposite of the goal of those opposing the project. Also, while more or better buses might be useful, who exactly was offering to pay for them?

But the proposers—now named Los Angeles Aerial Rapid Transit—also had tricks up their sleeves. They transferred the project to an environmental nonprofit group, Climate Resolve, and they continued to use their strategic political power to keep the project going. While it may take more time than planned, and the city council continues to oppose it, the project lives on and LA Metro environmentally cleared it in December, 2025. Our efforts just under the wire ensured that the project had sufficient momentum to survive and would not be quickly discarded by a new administration under political pressure. The opportunity presented itself, and we seized it and devoted significant time and resources to it. It was a battle we were glad we picked, and it could provide a long-lasting legacy for Metro and Los Angeles.

The Pandemic

Phil was fond of quoting Rahm Emanuel,[88] who often said, "Never let a crisis go to waste." This meant that while the pandemic was terrible, it also created a policy window that presented an opportunity to make change. Overnight, we had political alignment for public agencies willing

---

[88]And Rahm Emmanuel was quoting Winston Churchill.

to make the decisions necessary to help everyone survive. Phil saw the potential for our crazy ideas to become a reality during the pandemic, even if the other departments did not. He created an internal Recovery Task Force (RTF) and appointed me to chair it. This was our shot. As it turned out, it would be our last shot.

The Recovery Task Force

Metro's new planning chief at the time was angry. Fuming. Unfortunately, I couldn't see how mad he was because it was the pandemic, and we were not in the same location. Normally for this kind of meeting, we would have been in person and not on a conference call. But he made it clear even if I couldn't see his face—"I'm pulling my people off!" he said. "We're not going to participate if our opinions aren't listened to."

He was talking about the RTF. The RTF was an internal committee responsible for providing advice and recommendations to the Metro Senior Leadership Team, CEO, and Board of Directors. Phil created it in April 2020 with the idea that it would issue a report in September 2020 as we emerged from the lockdown and things went back to normal. It didn't quite work out that way.

Phil also created the RTF because he saw an opportunity. He was right—and if the pandemic had ended sooner or Phil had stayed at Metro longer, we probably would have been able to seize this crisis. But our ability to make change was only within a window of time, and sometimes you cannot know exactly when that window is going to close. But knowing that it will close, and keeping watch on when that might happen, is critical.

"We are better equipped than anyone to emerge stronger from the pandemic because we have the Office of Extraordinary Innovation." Phil made this statement during the onset of the COVID-19 pandemic. Los Angeles and Metro were hit hard by the pandemic. Within Metro's own workforce, there were 17 deaths and 7,001 confirmed cases up until 2024. The mortality of those living in the poorest areas of LA County was four times higher than affluent areas. LA had the nation's highest unemployment rate in June 2021. We had our work cut out for us.

Phil's desire to make change during this crisis juxtaposed with another of his strongly held principles. Phil always believed in bringing people up from within the workforce. Despite his military background and being CEO of Metro, he did not stand on hierarchy and enjoyed cultivating leadership pipelines. So, when he created the RTF, he decided that it should be composed of people who were not the chiefs or even deputy chiefs in their departments. He wanted cross-departmental staff who were middle managers and emerging leaders, unencumbered by leadership of their departments during the crisis. Members of the task force were nominated by the SLT and chosen to represent a diversity of experiences and perspectives, with a preference for graduates of, or participants in, Metro Leadership Academy, Eno Multi-Agency Exchange Program, and/or the Metro Women & Girls Governing Council.

While this made sense in theory, in practice, it proved challenging. Metro is a very hierarchical organization, and what the RTF was doing threatened that hierarchy. We were charged with providing specific advice and recommendations for Metro leadership to decide on how best to recover from the pandemic, and Phil made it clear that the goal was not to just recover, but to come back stronger. The RTF was generating ideas for the organization without the leaders of the organization involved. These were leaders who typically kept tight control over their departments, and who were typically risk averse. Unfortunately, contrary to our desires, the pandemic made those leaders even more risk averse.

As the leader of the RTF, I began facilitating conversations with the representatives from various departments, including Planning. The goal of these conversations was to incubate and eventually implement bold and ambitious ideas. The RTF representatives, however, were reporting back to their supervisors, who in turn reported to their chiefs about these ideas. They would then come back with all the reasons why their department did not support the idea, even if they themselves had generated it. Instead of accepting their rejection, I continued to move the ideas forward. I didn't see the problem in considering new ideas; if they needed to be changed or discarded later that would be fine—but they should be put on the table.

The planning chief did not agree. He oversaw anything Planning related, and he wasn't going to have his people participate in the discussion of ideas that he didn't like. He barred his people from attending our (virtual) meetings. Phil was upset, but not enough to fight him on it. It was a setback, but something from which we could—no pun intended—recover. That would not be true for what came next.

The Leak

The RTF was an opportunity to consider big, bold, and radical ideas. Keep in mind that this was the summer of 2020. The pandemic was raging, there was no vaccine, George Floyd was murdered, a presidential election was underway, and protesters were out in force.[89] It was a tumultuous time for everyone, including public transit.

One night as protests and fires raged across the city, Phil made the tough decision to shut down parts of our system for the safety of the operators.[xcix] Unfortunately, this led to customers being stranded all over Los Angeles. The innovation team is rarely turned to in a crisis, but I found myself on the phone with Phil late into the night as we tried to see if our private partners—Via, Lyft, or Uber, could help us pick people up. It was a nerve-racking, but exhilarating time.

It was in this zeitgeist that we conducted our regular RTF meetings. As we wrote in our final report, many of the problems highlighted by the pandemic had their roots in LA County's prepandemic "normal." Long-standing and well-documented inequities—in transportation, education and housing policies—grew starker during the pandemic and put the most vulnerable at highest risk. In this context, Metro had a responsibility to put forward ideas that could help prevent a return to vast disparities in access to opportunity, to gridlocked and dangerous streets and to run-away climate change.[c]

I often say that part of our job was to "brainwash" new arrivals[90] to OEI from other departments. They would arrive with all kinds of rules

---

[89]On May 25, 2020, George Floyd, an unarmed Black man in Minneapolis, was murdered by the police. In response to this murder and in the context of growing unrest regarding police brutality and racism, protests and riots broke out in cities across the United States, including Los Angeles.

[90]Not literally. But Nadine and I often joked that we were brainwashing our staff to be open minded and to challenge everything. I've taken a similar approach with my children, to my own detriment.

and protocols and narrow thinking, and we would open their minds to the idea of transparency, lack of hierarchy, and big-picture thinking. Ordinarily, this took time. Now I had to do it very quickly with a task force composed of people who were not my employees. Over Zoom. This was a challenge.

One day I was growing frustrated as I was facilitating an RTF brainstorm to solve the challenges of the pandemic such as diminished ridership, security challenges, and general unease. People were throwing out ideas like using technology to clean our vehicles, which is great but not exactly revolutionary. I pushed people and asked them to think bigger. What was something that would really change things? What would upend the way things were?

"Defund the police," someone said. That was a start. It may have been reductive and just a repetition of what they were hearing from their political circles, but at least it wasn't "disinfect the elevators." From there, we were exploring. Many of the members of the RTF started to understand that this was not just another Metro committee putting out run-of-the-mill recommendations. We were here to change the world—there was no opportunity like the present.

While we came up with some fantastic ideas, what we didn't anticipate was that even if most of the group is ready for revolution, this is no guarantee of success. All it takes is one person determined to stop change for major change to be halted in its tracks. And that is what happened.

One of our most controversial ideas was about funding. With the pandemic-era behavior changes, people were riding transit less and our already low farebox revenue was nearly nonexistent. Sales tax revenue, a major funding source for Metro, had also taken a big hit. We felt that if our role was to help to facilitate Metro's recovery, we should be exploring how to generate new revenue. And, in considering a revenue source, we also had to consider ways to lessen income inequality.

During the summer of 2020, the previously nascent conversations about equity were gaining momentum. In addition to the George Floyd murder and exposure of racial inequities, there was also growing recognition of the growing gap between rich and poor, especially in Los Angeles. While most white-collar workers stayed safe at home making money during the pandemic, many service workers found themselves risking their lives, and often, riding public transit. Those who could afford cars, always a group with greater advantages, were now even more privileged.

Therefore, we proposed the idea of a vehicle registration tax to help low-income people with transportation. This seemed an elegant solution. The tax would be based on the value of the vehicle, ensuring that people who bought luxury vehicles would pay more. The revenue would be used to give money directly to low-income people through a "mobility wallet" for the purposes of accessibility—getting around town however worked best for them.

Technology to allocate funds that can only be used on transportation services is relatively easy to implement, and has now been tested in several places, including Los Angeles.[91] However, at the time, it was still a radical idea. Even more radical, though, was the idea of increasing vehicle registration fees.

Another idea we put on the table was about the Metro Board. We observed that the Metro Board does not have anyone on it who represents the riders of the system. Most board members rarely rode the system, if at all, and were typically removed from it and unaware of what it was like. This was true prepandemic but had been exacerbated given the perceived danger of riding transit.

We also knew that even aside from this issue, the Board was composed almost entirely of elected officials. They were understandably more focused on the constituents who elected them than the greater good of the county transportation network. This led to many challenges including difficulties building projects, building new rail lines with questionable value, and board members siding with auto interests (richer people) over transit interests (poorer people).

So, within the confines of the RTF, we discussed studying how to reorganize the Metro Board. Perhaps adding a rider representative, or considering different methods of representation, could be valuable. Other transit Boards have rider representatives, and many other regions periodically reconsider board structures, so this didn't seem to us to be a particularly crazy idea.

---

[91] This is Metro's mobility wallet, mentioned earlier, and led by Avital Shavit.

These two ideas were listed, among dozens of others we were tossing around, in a spreadsheet that kept track of all the ideas. They were being researched and discussed, with the thought that we would eventually propose the best of them in our final report. But before we could get there, someone leaked the spreadsheet to Board Staff, leading to an immediate uproar.

I found out quickly when Phil called me into his office. While he was not upset with me, he made it clear that he was in an impossible position. He wanted to support the RTF and OEI, both of which he had created, but he couldn't allow us to consider the idea of rearranging the Metro Board. There were already bills in Sacramento on this topic and he didn't want us to wade into that fight. Plus, board members tend to get persnickety when you try to find a way to fire them. He also couldn't have us proposing to tax drivers in Los Angeles for Metro so soon after Measure M had passed. Congestion pricing was hard enough.

We dropped the idea of board reorganization and modified the vehicle registration fee idea to be about finding new sources of revenue based on studying the issue, rather than the specific tax. But it wasn't the watering down of ideas that was problematic. It was that someone within Metro thought to leak these ideas to Board Staff. Most likely that individual knew that leaking the ideas would successfully kill them.

If this had happened early in Phil's tenure, he might have tried to find out who did it or made it clear that this behavior was not acceptable. But Phil, while we didn't know it yet, was already planning to leave Metro, and he was not picking this battle. A few months later he announced his departure. The leaker had accurately guessed that the window of change was closing.

Beware of Your Expiration Date

The RTF eventually released a report filled with bold and pragmatic ideas, many of which led to real action and tangible improvements.[ci] But our ability to pursue the biggest, most transformative ideas was fading. Once Phil announced his departure, the decline accelerated. For all intents and purposes, OEI had functioned as an extension of the CEO's office. The influence that we wielded across Metro came directly from Phil's authority and the Board's trust in him. His departure marked the end of the OEI as we knew it and signaled a chance for the next CEO to determine her priorities and strategies.

For example, while work continued on the West Santa Ana Branch (later rebranded the Southeast Gateway Line or SGL) P3 project, the Planning Department stopped sharing data with us and quietly stalled the process, opting to wait for the leadership transition. Eventually, Metro's new CEO, Stephanie Wiggins, formally chose a different project delivery model for SGL. She also paused the Traffic Reduction Study (TRS) to avoid it becoming a political liability during the 2022 mayoral election, though it has since been revived. OEI was renamed the Office of Strategic Innovation (OSI) and shifted its focus from P3s and pilots toward the upcoming Olympics and Paralympic games.

I left Metro in January 2022, and most other OEI employees left around the same time. It was clear that our role as instigators of bold, future-facing change had ended. I was no longer in the inner circle of trust, and it was time to go.

OEI was part of a fleeting moment when big, bold change didn't just feel possible, it felt inevitable. We pushed ideas that once sounded outrageous and watched as many of them took root either in LA or elsewhere. Congestion pricing is now a reality in New York City. Programs that pay people not to drive exist. Transit agencies across the country are piloting fare-free service and on-demand models. The Sepulveda PDA and Dodger Stadium Gondola, once long shots, still move forward. We didn't win every battle, but we shifted the terrain.

Today, Metro's Office of Strategic Innovation continues, but it operates in a different political moment. Some seeds we planted are still growing, like the Mobility Wallet and the One Car Challenge, led by Avital Shavit. Vision 2028 is still in effect. The Traffic Reduction Study is still moving forward. The spirit of OEI hasn't vanished, it's just scattered, carried forward by those still willing to push.

Policy windows close. That's the hard truth. But they also open again. They always do. And even when they don't, there's still work to be done. Some of the most meaningful change happens not because the moment

is right, but because someone decides to try anyway. To the next generation of idealists, tinkerers, and troublemakers: Don't wait for permission.
Don't wait for the window. Build the thing, write the memo, make the
call. Most of it won't land. Some of it will. And that's enough to change
everything.

Be ready. Your moment will come. And when it does—run fast.

CHAPTER 7

How to Overcome Resistance in Public Agencies

I joined Metro as a change agent in a large bureaucracy at an unusually opportune time—but that didn't make change easy. Far from it. OEI tried and failed many times. But those failures taught us how to navigate resistance and eventually how to win. Along the way, I developed a practical playbook for pushing positive change in systems that were not built for innovation.

Every big idea that we launched in OEI ran into resistance—not just from external stakeholders but from the agency itself. This is how public institutions are designed. Bureaucracies are built to preserve stability and, by their very nature, are not designed to enable useful disruption.[92] Yet, despite this resistance, we made substantial progress.

OEI brought on-demand transit to Los Angeles, delivered a strategic plan that still guides Metro, executed a path defining Pre-Development Agreement, led the charge for a modernized bus network, and advanced congestion pricing. But our biggest wins weren't projects—they were cultural shifts and new processes that continue to influence the agency today.

This didn't happen because I had a magic solution. It happened because I developed strategies to overcome resistance—from relationship building to tactical patience, from creative workarounds to reframing obstacles. You don't need perfect conditions to make progress. What you need is clarity, persistence, and a toolkit for working both within and around the system.

---

[92]German scholar Max Weber defined bureaucracy as an organizational structure characterized by formal rules, standardized processes, clear hierarchies, and impersonal interactions between employees.

So, here's what I learned:

1. Pick your battles and win them.
2. Make friends and collaborate.
3. Build processes, not just projects.
4. Discuss costs and benefits rather than obstacles.
5. Navigate fiefdoms wisely.
6. Find willing collaborators.
7. Pace yourself—you need both urgency and endurance.
8. Do the work up front.
9. Balance naivete with pragmatism.
10. Recognize policy windows.

Pick Your Battles and Win Them

I had the benefit of reporting directly to the CEO, Phil Washington. That gave me a powerful tool—I could call him to resolve various power struggles. At first I did. But I quickly learned that you only get so many swings of the bat. Your boss can't back you on everything without losing credibility or political capital.

In our early projects (Chapter 1)—like podcasts and the Uber-Expo partnership—I leaned heavily on Phil's support. These were unwinnable battles without executive backing, and since we picked them, they became essential to establishing our office's credibility. But every time OEI asked Phil to carry the ball for us, we chipped away at our internal relationships.

By the time we started working on the Recovery Task Force, the support I once relied on wasn't there. Phil was nearing the end of his tenure, and OEI had asked too much. Maybe that effort could have been more successful if we had conserved our political capital and built more trust along the way.

In any bureaucracy—public or private sector—change requires a long-term view. You will find moments when blunt force is necessary. But those moments should be rare. Use executive escalation only for battles that are core to your mission—and only after all other paths have been exhausted.

When setting a strategy be crystal clear—what is a must-win? What is a nice to have? Must-win battles should directly support your highest priorities. And even then, explore every alternative before calling in the heavy hitters. Sometimes a different framing or alternative path can get you to the same outcome without political damage.

Make Friends and Collaborate

Blunt force may seem like a shortcut, but it often backfires. People need to feel part of something before they can put their hearts into it. They can only take ownership after they feel heard and have their concerns considered. That takes time—but it pays off.

I saw this with the Vision 2028 Strategic Plan (Chapter 5). It took far longer than Phil or I might have desired, but our agencywide collaboration led to unanimous Board approval—and laid the groundwork for major initiatives like congestion pricing and improved bus service. The plan worked because we pushed people out of their comfort zones, but we also gave them fair consideration and sufficient empowerment that the plan passed without a hitch.

The Sepulveda Pre-Development Agreement (Chapter 2) was another lesson in patience. I underestimated how long coalition building would take. For a multibillion-dollar project, that alignment was essential. It wouldn't have moved forward without it.

Before launching any initiative, align with your team and leadership on the true timeline. Be honest about what's required. You'll likely face pressure to move faster but hold firm and discuss the trade-offs of accelerated timelines. If you're aiming for lasting change, bringing people along isn't optional, it's the work.

Build Processes, Not Just Projects

Bureaucracies are characterized by routine and procedure. However, public agency processes are rarely created from scratch. Instead, they are patched together over time—shaped by organizational history, leadership changes, one-off crises, and short-term political priorities. What starts as a reaction to a specific problem calcifies into a definite process or "the way things are done." Each step gains a defender, and reforming the process becomes harder than building it in the first place.

That's why real innovation doesn't come from one-off projects. It comes from building new processes that make innovation repeatable. We learned this firsthand through the development of the Unsolicited Proposal Policy (Chapter 2). At first, it was a shortcut to invite outside ideas without rewriting all the procurement rules. But over time it became a codified process that allowed new ideas to be reviewed, vetted, and when promising, implemented.

Investing in process creation takes more time upfront—but it pays dividends. A project might end with a ribbon cutting, but a process keeps opening doors long after you're gone.

Discuss Costs and Benefits Rather Than Obstacles

Humans are typically trained to analyze things by looking for flaws. That mindset—while helpful for risk management—can derail innovation. It leads to conversations about why things can't be done rather than how to make them happen.

I found that reframing ideas in terms of costs and benefits fundamentally changed the dynamic. This was especially true during our work facilitating UPs (Chapter 2). Shifting from a meeting where everyone was telling us why something couldn't be done, toward a meeting where attendees were developing solutions moved conversations from defensive to constructive.

When you hear people fixating on obstacles, ask what it would take to overcome that obstacle and what's the benefit if you do. Often, the resistance isn't about the barrier itself, it's that people aren't yet convinced the outcome is worth the effort.

Navigate Fiefdoms Wisely

Some of our most formidable obstacles were internal fiefdoms, built over many years or decades. These power centers were held by people who had outlasted multiple CEOs, shaped agency policy, and developed expertise. They also controlled critical systems and processes and knew how to defend them.

I found this out when trying to reform fare payment (Chapter 3). Despite technological advancements that made more flexible fare payment options readily available, the CFO (and head of TAP) wasn't willing to engage. In hindsight, I wasted time trying to push forward change where collaboration wasn't possible.

Contrast that with the Sepulveda PDA. It took longer than expected and required significant coalition building, but we eventually found allies across different departments who were open to doing things differently. We learned that fiefdoms can be rigid, but under the right conditions, even entrenched systems can shift.

It's an art to know when to walk away and when to lean in. Not all resistance is unmovable. But it's not all worth fighting either. Overtime we learned to read the signals and prioritize impact over turf.

Find Willing Collaborators

In any large agency, risk aversion runs deep—especially among long-tenured employees with the most to lose. Many have seen change agents flame out and aren't eager to follow. That's why finding allies open to new ideas is essential.

Collaboration only works when both parties are willing. Forcing a partnership wastes time and political capital. I learned this when we tried to work with TAP, and they were the only option for pushing forward our initiative and there was no willingness to engage. For other projects, however, I found that there were many routes we could go. For example, when pushing forward our drone project (Chapter 2) the first department I engaged with said no, but another jumped at the opportunity.

If you're facing resistance, pause. You may have the wrong partner. The right collaborators won't just make work easier; they'll make it possible.

Pace Yourself—You Need Both Urgency and Endurance

Driving change in public agencies means balancing short-term wins with the stamina to deliver lasting impact. It requires advancing long-term goals while taking advantage of near-term opportunities.

OEI struck this balance with on-demand transit (Chapter 4). By moving quickly to secure the federal MOD grant, we launched a short-term pilot that sidestepped early internal resistance to Metro Micro. That initial win gave us the necessary runway to build toward a more permanent, in-house on-demand service.

Quick wins build momentum, but real change requires endurance. Bureaucratic innovation isn't about just acting fast—it's about staying in the game long enough to finish what you started.

Do the Work Up Front

Whether it's building coalitions, or pitching a new idea or controversial project, preparation matters. In public agencies, people are experts in their domains. If you want them to change, you need to earn credibility by knowing what you're talking about.

That means doing your homework. Understand the problems, politics, constraints, and people involved. I often made it OEI's mission to know more about any given topic than anyone else in the room. When OEI succeeded, it was often because we were better prepared than anyone else in the room, like with on-demand transit (Chapter 4). When OEI failed, like when trying to improve Expo Line speeds (Chapter 3), we didn't do enough homework and didn't fully understand the politics or the people.

Preparation won't guarantee a win, but lack of it nearly guarantees a failure. Before launching a new initiative, take the time to dig deep. That investment may be invisible at first, but it's often the difference between stalling out and breaking through.

Balance Naivete with Pragmatism

Naivete was one of OEI's greatest assets. Because I didn't fully understand why things "couldn't" get done, I often pursued ideas that others had written off—and sometimes succeeded because of it. If OEI had been staffed entirely with seasoned insiders, we may have caused less friction—but we also would have aimed lower.

Inexperience sometimes led me to chase lost causes. Having a few embedded veterans helped, but most were self-selecting innovators.

A more structured approach—like placing "innovation liaisons" in each department—may have broadened OEI's reach.

Both the strategic plan and congestion pricing (Chapter 5) required bold thinking from outsiders and grounded execution from insiders. The mix was essential.

Whether building a team or pushing forward change solo, ask yourself if you're being too naive or too jaded. Sometimes a small shift in perspective makes all the difference.

Recognize Policy Windows

The creation of OEI wasn't just about bold ideas—it was about timing. OEI launched in a rare moment when leadership, politics, public interest, and resources aligned in our favor. That kind of convergence doesn't last forever, but it does happen. Recognizing it—and acting while it lasts—is critical.

Phil Washington, our CEO, embodied the right kind of executive leadership. A seasoned outsider with both vision and credibility, he had nothing to prove and wasn't afraid to back controversial ideas. He made OEI central to his agenda and gave us the cover we needed to push boundaries.

Mayor Eric Garcetti offered political support. While more cautious than Phil, he understood that transportation was both an economic and political priority. He backed innovation broadly—from congestion pricing to P3s—and elevated LA's role as a national testbed for mobility.

OEI also benefited from zeitgeists. Congestion was worsening, the sharing economy was booming, and new technology was bringing excitement and attention to the transportation industry. OEI made sense in a moment when the public and private sectors were both asking big questions.

And, crucially, we had resources. Metro was, and is, one of the best funded agencies in the country, buoyed by several voter-approved ballot measures. We didn't have to scrape together dollars to push forward new ideas—funding innovation was actually feasible.

The combination gave OEI a unique platform to make change. But every policy window closes. If you don't recognize the moment you're in, or fail to move before it passes, you'll miss your shot. The trick is to know when the window is open and what to prioritize when it is.

Final Thoughts

Whether you're a CEO, a mid-level manager, or someone just a few years into your public service, we hope these stories and lessons give you the tools—and courage—to move positive change forward. You don't need perfect timing, although it helps. And you definitely don't need permission. What you need is a sense of purpose, a willingness to try, and the resilience to keep going when it gets hard.

Change in government is never easy, but it's always worth trying. I hope that you can learn from what OEI did—our wins, stumbles, and strategies—and that they will help you go further than we did. You can make real progress from wherever you sit.

Above all, never lose sight of why you are here. No one joins public service to get rich. But many stay because it's safe or familiar, or it gives them a sense of power. If you've read this far, I'm guessing you're not one of them. You're here because you believe that government can be a force for good and that through hard work you can help make people's lives better.

I believe that too. And I hope this book helps you do exactly that.

Bibliography

"A Former Red Car Conductor Rides the New Expo Line: 'It Brings Back Memories.'" *LAist*, December 28, 2016. https://laist.com/news /kpcc-archive/before-the-shiny-expo-line-extension-there-was-the.

"Attachment D to Response to Motion by Director Butts to Amend Item 43 with Questions and Instructions." Metro Board Report 2019-0083, February 20, 2019. https://metro.legistar1.com/metro/attachments/6b6f40f5 -b88f-4b5c-8e94-3473ee8e4158.pdf.

"Latest on Metro Micro: Still Few Riders, High Costs." *Streetsblog Los Angeles*, June 21, 2024. https://la.streetsblog.org/2024/06/18/latest-on-metro -micro-still-few-riders-high-costs.

"Metro Partnerships with Rideshare/Ridesourcing Services, Motion by Directors Antonovich and Kuehl." LA Metro Board Archives, April 28, 2016. https://metro.legistar.com/LegislationDetail.aspx?ID=2701761&GUID =8A26E0FE-194E-40B2-9249-F975A668C3EB&Options=ID%7C Text%7C&Search=2016-0375%2C.

"Metro Poised to Waste $8 Million More on Costly 'Metro Micro' Micro-Transit Pilot." *Streetsblog Los Angeles*, June 13, 2023. https://la.streetsblog .org/2023/03/21/metro-poised-to-waste-8-million-more-on-costly-metro -micro-microtransit-pilot.

"Metro Signs Expo + Uberpool Partnership." LA Metro Board Archives, May 18, 2016. https://boardarchives.metro.net/BoardBox/2016/160518_Metro _Signs_Expo_Uberpool_Partnership.pdf

"Personnel/Organizational Restructuring." LA Metro Board Archives, July 23, 2015. https://boardarchives.metro.net/BoardBox/BB2015/2015_07_Jul /150723_Personnel_Organizational_Restructuring_Memo.pdf

"Playa del Rey Street Safety Improvements Court Driver Backlash." *Streetsblog Los Angeles*, June 14, 2023. https://la.streetsblog.org/2017/06/07/playa -del-rey-street-safety-improvements-court-driver-backlash.

"Procurement Lessons Learned: A Line." University of Maryland, 2011. https:// bac.umd.edu/wp-content/uploads/2022/03/A-LIne_Lessons_Learned.pdf.

"TAP Cards and Universal Fare Media in Los Angeles Transit: History & Resources." *Metro's Primary Resources*, August 7, 2024. https://metroprimary resources.info/tap-cards-and-universal-fare-media-in-los-angeles-transit -history-resources/15741/.

About Us—Metro Board. "Los Angeles County Metropolitan Transportation Authority." Accessed May 3, 2025. https://boardagendas.metro.net/about/.

Agranoff, Robert. "Inside Collaborative Networks: Ten Lessons for Public Managers." *Public Administration Review* 66, no. s1 (2006): 56–65. https://doi.org/10.1111/j.1540-6210.2006.00666.x.

All Systems Go for January 30 Opening of Metro Red Line. Los Angeles County Transportation Commission, 1993. https://libraryarchives.metro.net/DPGTL/pressreleases/1993-lactc-pre-merger-press-releases.pdf

American Association of State Highway and Transportation Officials. "Case Study 153." Accessed May 3, 2025. https://planningtools.transportation.org/290/view-case-study.html?case_id=153.

American Society of Mechanical Engineers. "The Disney Monorail System: A National Historic Mechanical Engineering Landmark." December 1986. https://www.asme.org/wwwasmeorg/media/resourcefiles/aboutasme/who%20we%20are/engineering%20history/landmarks/115-disneyland-monorail-system-1959.pdf.

Arthur, W. Brian. "Competing Technologies, Increasing Returns, and Lock-In by Historical Events." *Economic Journal* 99, no. 394 (1989): 116–31. https://doi.org/10.2307/2234208.

Bender, Andrew. "Uber's Astounding Rise: Overtaking Taxis in Key Markets." *Forbes*, April 10, 2015. https://www.forbes.com/sites/andrewbender/2015/04/10/ubers-astounding-rise-overtaking-taxis-in-key-markets/.

Bradley, Ryan. "Walking in L.A.: The Data Driven City." *GOOD*, August 1, 2019. https://www.good.is/articles/walking-in-l-a-the-data-driven-city.

Brakewood, Carrie, Ahmed Ziedan, Sean J. Hendricks, Sean J. Barbeau, and Adam Joslin. "An Evaluation of the Benefits of Mobile Fare Payment Technology from the User and Operator Perspectives." *Transport Policy* 93 (2020): 54–66. https://doi.org/10.1016/j.tranpol.2020.04.015.

Broverman, Neal. "Beverly Hills Finally Loses Its Crazy, Stupid Subway Battle." *Los Angeles Magazine*, September 1, 2023. https://lamag.com/news/beverly-hills-finally-loses-crazy-stupid-subway-battle.

Buhr, Sarah. "Lyft, Now Worth $5.5 Billion, Hops into the Autonomous Car Race with General Motors." *TechCrunch*, January 4, 2016. https://techcrunch.com/2016/01/04/lyft-now-worth-5-5-billion-plans-to-get-into-the-autonomous-car-race-with-general-motors/.

Bustamante, Carlos. "Congestion Pricing: Q&A." UCLA Institute of Transportation Studies, February 20, 2025. https://www.its.ucla.edu/news/for-the-press/congestion-pricing/.

Cervero, Robert. *The Transit Metropolis: A Global Inquiry*. Island Press, 1998.

Chinatown Historical Society of Southern California. Accessed May 3, 2025. https://chssc.org/.

Cosgrove, Jaclyn. "L.A. Makes History with All-Female Board of Supervisors." *Los Angeles Times*, November 5, 2020. https://www.latimes.com/california /story/2020-11-04/l-a-county-makes-history-with-all-female-board-of -supervisors.

Diao, Mi, Haoyue Kong, and Jinhua Zhao. "Impacts of Transportation Network Companies on Urban Mobility." *Nature Sustainability* 4, no. 6 (2021): 494–500. https://doi.org/10.1038/s41893-020-00678-z.

Downs, Anthony. *Still Stuck in Traffic: Coping with Peak-Hour Traffic Congestion.* Brookings Institution Press, 2004.

Dudley, Geoff, David Banister, and Tim Schwanen. "The Rise of Uber and Regulating the Disruptive Innovator." *Political Quarterly* 88, no. 3 (2017): 492–99. https://doi.org/10.1111/1467-923X.12373.

Edmondson, Amy. "Psychological Safety and Learning Behavior in Work Teams." *Administrative Science Quarterly* 44, no. 2 (1999): 350–83. https://doi. org/10.2307/2666999.

Federal Highway Administration. "Edward M. Bassett: The Man Who Gave Us 'Freeway.'" Accessed May 3, 2025. https://www.fhwa.dot.gov/infrastructure /freeway.cfm.

Feigon, Sharon, Colin Murphy, Transit Cooperative Research Program, Transportation Research Board, and National Academies of Sciences, Engineering, and Medicine. *Shared Mobility and the Transformation of Public Transit.* National Academies Press, 2016. https://www.nationalacademies.org/publications/23578

Feldman, Martha S., and Anne M. Khademian. "The Role of the Public Manager in Inclusion: Creating Communities of Participation." *Governance* 20, no. 2 (2007): 305–24. https://doi.org/10.1111/j.1468-0491 .2007.00361.x.

Flynn, James, Charles Thole, Victoria Perk, Julie Samus, Christine Van Nostrand, National Bus Rapid Transit Institute, and Center for Urban Transportation Research. *"Metro Orange Line BRT Project Evaluation."* FTA Report No. 0004. Federal Transit Administration, 2011. https://www .transit.dot.gov/sites/fta.dot.gov/files/FTA_Research_Report_0004 _FINAL_2.pdf.

García, Robert, and Thomas A. Rubin. "The MTA Consent Decree." In *Crossroad Blues: The MTA Consent Decree and Just Transportation.* https://www .shoupdogg.com/wp-content/uploads/sites/2/2015/04/Chapter-12 -Crossroad-Blues-Garcia.pdf.

Goldwyn, Eric, Alon Levy, Elif Ensari, and Marco Chitti. *"Transit Costs Project: Understanding Transit Infrastructure Costs in American Cities."* Transit Costs Project, 2024. https://transitcosts.com/wp-content/uploads/TCP _Final_Report.pdf.

Goodman, Jennifer. "Design-Build Takes Hold in All but 2 States." *Construction Dive*, February 10, 2020. https://www.constructiondive.com/news/design-build-takes-hold-in-all-but-2-states/571951/.

Gordon, Colin. "Costing and Curing Corruption in Public Transit Agencies." *Journal of Financial Crime* 13, no. 4 (2006): 442–55. https://doi.org/10.1108/13590790610707564.

Grose, Jessica. *Why Nothing Works: The Broken Promise of Technology and How We Can Fix It.* Little, Brown Spark, 2025.

Hall, Jonathan D. "Pareto Improvements from Lexus Lanes: The Effects of Pricing a Portion of the Lanes on Congested Highways." *Journal of Public Economics* 158 (2018): 113–25. https://doi.org/10.1016/j.jpubeco.2018.01.003.

Henley, Jon. "Uber Clashes with Regulators in Cities around the World." *The Guardian*, January 31, 2019. https://www.theguardian.com/business/2017/sep/29/uber-clashes-with-regulators-in-cities-around-the-world.

Ilel, Neille. "Metro's Off Peak Podcast." Accessed May 3, 2025. https://www.neille.com/offpeak.

Kille, Lauren W. "Bus versus Rail: Costs, Capacities and Impacts." *The Journalist's Resource*, December 17, 2020. https://journalistsresource.org/economics/bus-versus-rail/.

Killing, Peter, Thomas Malnight, and Tracey Keys. *Must-Win Battles: How to Win Them, Again and Again.* Wharton School Publishing, 2006. https://dl.acm.org/citation.cfm?id=1407343.

Kingdon, John W. *Agendas, Alternatives, and Public Policies.* Updated 2nd ed. Longman, 2011.

Klein, Ezra, and Derek Thompson. *Abundance.* Avid Reader Press, 2025.

Kohler, Brianna. "Expanding L.A. Metro's Fare-Free Transit for Kids and Families." *National League of Cities*, May 14, 2021. https://www.nlc.org/article/2021/05/14/expanding-l-a-metros-fare-free-transit-for-kids-and-families/.

Lencioni, Patrick M. *Silos, Politics, and Turf Wars: A Leadership Fable about Destroying the Barriers That Turn Colleagues into Competitors.* Jossey-Bass, 2006.

Levine, Jonathan. *Zoned Out: Regulation, Markets, and Choices in Transportation and Metropolitan Land Use.* Resources for the Future Press, 2006.

Lewis, Paul. "On the Right Track: Rail Transit Project Delivery Around the World." Eno Center for Transportation, September 2022. https://enotrans.org/wp-content/uploads/2023/02/On-the-Right-Track-Report.pdf.

Los Angeles City Council District 1. "Dodgers Stadium Transportation Study." Accessed May 3, 2025. https://cd1.lacity.gov/press-releases/dodgers-stadium-transportation-study.

Los Angeles County Board of Supervisors. "LA BOS." Accessed May 3, 2025. https://cityselection.lacounty.gov/.

Los Angeles County Metropolitan Transportation Authority. *"A Path Forward: Metro's Recovery Task Force Final Report."* February 2021. https://metro.legistar1.com/metro/attachments/92ebcb28-f344-4ec6 -b0d3-c058cc15c6bb.pdf.

Los Angeles County Metropolitan Transportation Authority. *"Fiscal Year 2025 Adopted Budget Book."* Accessed May 3, 2025. https://www.dropbox.com /scl/fi/5d0ok70douxwuzs5edozw/Fiscal-Year-2025-Adopted-Budget-Book .pdf?rlkey=1jm7cqe0yf5wsyxybgtrsk1ad&e=2&st=wv442xg0&dl=0.

Los Angeles County Metropolitan Transportation Authority. "Los Angeles Aerial Rapid Transit Project Update." File #2022-0316, Executive Management Committee, September 15, 2022. https://metro.legistar.com /LegislationDetail.aspx?ID=5836690&GUID=22349CE5-6682-4B7C -8D22-90E316D25C4C.

Los Angeles County Metropolitan Transportation Authority. "Metro's Partnership with Via: Quarter 1 Report." Board Box, May 28, 2019. https:// boardarchives.metro.net/BoardBox/2019/190530_Partnership_with_Via _Quarter1_Report.pdf.

Los Angeles County Metropolitan Transportation Authority. *"Office of Extraordinary Innovation Mission and Progress Report."* Board Report 2016-0337. Accessed June 16, 2025. https://metro.legistar.com/View Report.ashx?M=R&N=TextL5&GID=557&ID=3132&GUID =LATEST&G=A5FAA737-A54D-4A6C-B1E8-FF70F765FA94&Title =Board+Report.

Los Angeles County Metropolitan Transportation Authority. *"Regional Fare System Plan."* 2010. https://boardarchives.metro.net/Items/2011/02 _February/20110224RBMItem3.pdf.

Los Angeles County Metropolitan Transportation Authority. "Southeast Gateway Line P3 Assessment Update." Board Report 2024-0452, July 18, 2024. https://boardagendas.metro.net/board-report/2024-0452/.

Los Angeles County Metropolitan Transportation Authority. "Twenty-Eight by '28 Initiative." Board Report 2019-0108, February 28, 2019. https:// boardagendas.metro.net/board-report/2019-0108/.

Manville, Michael, Brian D. Taylor, Evelyn Blumenberg, and Andrew Schouten. "Vehicle Access and Falling Transit Ridership: Evidence from Southern California." *Transportation* 50, no. 1 (2022): 303–29. https://doi .org/10.1007/s11116-021-10245-w.

Manville, Michael, and University of California Institute of Transportation Studies. *Measure M and the Potential Transformation of Mobility in Los Angeles.* TransitCenter, 2019. https://doi.org/10.7922/G2VT1Q80.

Manville, Michael, Evelyn Bird, Ifeoma Obi, Jacob Epstein, and Los Angeles County Metropolitan Transportation Authority (LA Metro).

"Measure M: Lessons from a Successful Transportation Ballot Campaign." Eno Center for Transportation, 2019. https://enotrans.org/wp-content /uploads/2023/02/Measure-M-FINAL.pdf.

Mass Transit Magazine. "LA Metro Creates Innovative Office." August 5, 2015. https://www.masstransitmag.com/home/press-release/12099674/los-angeles -county-metropolitan-transportation-authority-metro-metro-creates-innovative -office.

Mintzberg, Henry. *Structure in Fives: Designing Effective Organizations.* Prentice-Hall, 1983.

Moynihan, Donald P. *The Dynamics of Performance Management: Constructing Information and Reform.* Georgetown University Press, 2008.

Murphy, Colin, Sharon Feigon, Albert Benedict, et al. *Shared Mobility and the Transformation of Public Transit.* Edited by Tim Frisbie. Shared-Use Mobility Center, 2016. https://sharedusemobilitycenter.org/wp-content /uploads/2016/04/Final_TOPT_DigitalPagesNL.pdf.

Nelson, Laura J. "L.A. Metro Will Study How to Make Driving More Expensive—in Your Car or in an Uber." *Los Angeles Times*, March 1, 2019. https://www.latimes.com/local/lanow/la-me-ln-congestion-pricing-uber-tax -20190228-story.html.

Nelson, Laura J. "Metro Bus, Train Shutdown Slammed by Riders, Officials." *Los Angeles Times*, June 1, 2020. https://libraryarchives.metro.net/dpgtl /articles/social-equity-justice/20200601-latimes-who-approved-this -riders-officials-criticize-metros-systemwide-shutdown.pdf.

O'Reilly, Charles A., and Michael L. Tushman. "Organizational Ambidexterity: Past, Present, and Future." *Academy of Management Perspectives* 27, no. 4 (2013): 324–38. https://doi.org/10.5465/amp.2013.0025.

Orlove, Raphael. "Silicon Valley Invents Bus." *Jalopnik*, June 19, 2017. https:// www.jalopnik.com/silicon-valley-invents-bus-1796221702/.

Pahlka, Jennifer. *Recoding America: Why Government Is Failing in the Digital Age—and How We Can Do Better.* Metropolitan Books, 2023.

Panagopoulos, Costas, and Joshua Schank. *All Roads Lead to Congress: The $300 Billion Fight over Highway Funding.* Praeger, 2008.

Pierson, Paul. "Increasing Returns, Path Dependence, and the Study of Politics." *American Political Science Review* 94, no. 2 (2000): 251–67. https://doi .org/10.2307/2586011.

Rayle, Lisa, Susan Shaheen, Nelson Chan, Danielle Dai, Robert Cervero, and University of California Transportation Center. *"App-Based, On-Demand Ride Services: Comparing Taxi and Ridesourcing Trips and User Characteristics in San Francisco."* Working Paper, 2014. https://d1wqtxts1xzle7.cloudfront .net/103201966/RidesourcingWhitePaper_Nov2014-libre.pdf.

Rutten, Tim. "Mayor Villaraigosa's 30/10 Plan: Moving Forward." *Los Angeles Times*, March 14, 2019. https://www.latimes.com/archives/la-xpm-2010 -jun-09-la-oe-0609-rutten-20100609-story.html.

Schank, Joshua. *Examining the Cost Effectiveness of Market-Based Policies: The Case of Airside Airport Congestion.* VDM Verlag Dr. Müller, 2010.

Scott, James C. *Seeing Like a State: How Certain Schemes to Improve the Human Condition Have Failed.* Yale University Press, 1998.

Sharp, Steven. "Here Are the 28 Projects That Metro Could Complete before the 2028 Olympics." *Urbanize LA*, November 27, 2017. https://la.urbanize.city /post/here-are-28-projects-metro-could-complete-2028-olympics.

Sharp, Steven. "Monorail or Heavy Rail? Metro Narrows Its Focus in the Sepulveda Pass." *Urbanize LA*, February 17, 2021. https://la.urbanize.city/post /monorail-or-heavy-rail-metro-narrows-its-focus-sepulveda-pass.

Sheehan, Tim. "California High-Speed Rail: Why 2025 Could Make or Break Embattled Bullet Train Project." *Fresno Bee*, January 19, 2025. https://www .fresnobee.com/news/local/high-speed-rail/article298478383.html.

Sinclair, Upton. *I, Candidate for Governor: And How I Got Licked.* Self-published, 1935.

Smart Cities Dive. "The Vision of Jaime Lerner for Curitiba, Brazil." Accessed May 3, 2025. https://www.smartcitiesdive.com/ex/sustainablecitiescollective /vision-jaime-lerner-curitiba-brazil/253266/.

Susannah Luthi. "California Lawmakers Consider Bills That Trade Surveillance for Convenience in Final Sprint." *POLITICO*, August 17, 2021. https://www .politico.com/states/california/story/2021/08/12/california-lawmakers -consider-bills-that-trade-surveillance-for-convenience-in-final-sprint-1389869.

Taylor, Brian D. "Options for the Future of State Funding for Transit Operations in California." Panel Discussion Transcript, SPUR Public Programs, August 2023. https://www.spur.org/sites/default/files/2023-08/Transcript%20 Options%20for%20the%20Future%20of%20State%20Funding.pdf.

The MIT Press Reader. "The Hyperloop: A 200-Year History of Hype and Failure." March 9, 2025. https://thereader.mitpress.mit.edu/the -hyperloop-a-200-year-history-of-hype-and-failure/.

The Times Editorial Board. "Editorial: Finally, a Bus-Lane Building Boom in Los Angeles." *Los Angeles Times*, October 19, 2023. https://www.latimes .com/opinion/story/2023-10-19/finally-a-bus-lane-building-boom-in-los -angeles-metro.

Tidmarsh, Kevin. "Subway or Monorail for the Sepulveda Pass? Metro and Local Residents Weigh Their Options." *LAist*, May 10, 2024. https://laist .com/news/transportation/subway-or-monorail-for-the-sepulveda-pass -metro-and-local-residents-weigh-their-options.

TransitCenter, Steven Higashide, Zak Accuardi, Resource Systems Group (RSG), and Center for Neighborhood Technology. *Who's on Board 2016*. Edited by Jonathan Anbinder, David Bragdon, Jon Orcutt, Shin-pei Tsay, Metropolitan Planning Council, State Smart Transportation Initiative, and Kimberly Williamson. TransitCenter, 2016. https://transitcenter.org /wp-content/uploads/2016/07/TransitCenter-WOB-2016.pdf.

Tusk, Bradley. *The Fixer: My Adventures Saving Startups from Death by Politics*. Portfolio, 2018.

Van Maanen, John, and Edgar H. Schein. "Toward a Theory of Organizational Socialization." *Research in Organizational Behavior* 1 (1979): 209–64.

Wachs, Martin, Peter S. Chesney, Y. H. Hwang, and UCLA Luskin Center for History and Policy. *"A Century of Fighting Traffic Congestion in Los Angeles, 1920–2020."* UCLA Luskin Center, 2020. https://luskincenter.history.ucla .edu/wp-content/uploads/sites/66/2020/10/A-Century-of-Fighting-Traffic -Congestion-in-LA.pdf.

Walker, Jarrett. *Human Transit: How Clearer Thinking about Public Transit Can Enrich Our Communities and Our Lives*. Island Press, 2012.

Weber, Max. "From Max Weber: Essays in Sociology." Translated and edited by H. H. Gerth and C. Wright Mills. *Journal of Philosophy* 43, no. 26 (1946): 722. https://doi.org/10.2307/2019397.

West Virginia University. "About the PRT." *WVU Personal Rapid Transit 50th Anniversary*. Accessed June 12, 2025. https://prt.wvu.edu/about-the-prt.

Westervelt, Marla, Joshua Schank, and Emma Huang. "Partnerships with Technology-Enabled Mobility Companies: Lessons Learned." TRID. Accessed May 3, 2025. https://trid.trb.org/View/1438967.

Wharton, David. "L.A. Officially Awarded 2028 Olympic Games." *Los Angeles Times*, September 13, 2017. https://www.latimes.com/sports/olympics/la -sp-la-olympics-approved-20170913-story.html.

Wilson, James Q. *Bureaucracy: What Government Agencies Do and Why They Do It*. Hachette UK, 2019.

Zahniser, David. "L.A. Reworks Another 'Road Diet,' Restoring Car Lanes in Playa del Rey." *Los Angeles Times*, October 4, 2017. https://www.latimes.com /local/lanow/la-me-ln-mike-bonin-road-diet-20171003-story.html.

About the Authors

Joshua Schank is a Partner with InfraStrategies, a consulting firm that works with transportation organizations across the world on strategy, innovation, and policy. He is also a Research Associate at the Mineta Institute for Transportation at San Jose State University, and a Senior Fellow at the Institute for Transportation Studies at UCLA. He is the former Chief Innovation Officer with the Los Angeles County Metropolitan Transportation Authority (LA Metro), and the former President and CEO of the Eno Center for Transportation, a national transportation think-tank based in Washington, DC. He is the coauthor of *All Roads Lead to Congress: The $300 Billion Fight Over Highway Funding*.

Emma Huang is a Principal Consultant with InfraStrategies, where she helps transit agencies navigate critical challenges—from foundational strategy to implementing innovative service models and policies. She has led the development of major strategic plans including Dallas Area Rapid Transit's 10-year strategic plan, *Point B*, San Mateo County Transit District's plan, *Moving San Mateo County*, and CapMetro's *Strategic Plan 2030*. Prior to joining InfraStrategies, as a manager with Los Angeles Metro's Office of Extraordinary Innovation, Emma spent over six years focused on advancing strategic initiatives for the agency, including the development and implementation of an innovative FTA Mobility-on-Demand partnership with Via, Metro's *Vision 2028* 10-year strategic plan, and Metro's Traffic Reduction Study exploring congestion pricing in Los Angeles County. She holds a Master of Public Policy from UCLA Luskin School of Public Affairs.

Marla Westervelt Berg is a Principal at Cityfi, where she helps governments and private-sector companies—from early-stage start-ups to global firms—navigate the rules, politics, and partnerships that shape innovation in civic space. She was a founding member and Head of Research at LA Metro's Office of Extraordinary Innovation, led global policy at the Coalition for Reimagined Mobility, and built regulatory strategy and data systems from the inside at Bird. Her work bridges public systems and private-sector ambitions to turn civic friction into real-world results. She began her career at the Eno Center for Transportation.

Notes

i. "About Us—Metro Board," Los Angeles County Metropolitan Transportation Authority, accessed May 3, 2025, https://boardagendas.metro.net/about/.

ii. "LA Metro Creates Innovative Office," *Mass Transit Magazine*, August 5, 2015, https://www.masstransitmag.com/home/press-release/12099674/los-angeles-county-metropolitan-transportation-authority-metro-metro-creates-innovative-office.

iii. "Personnel/Organizational Restructuring," LA Metro Board Archives, July 23, 2015, https://boardarchives.metro.net/BoardBox/BB2015/2015_07_Jul/150723_Personnel_Organizational_Restructuring_Memo.pdf.

iv. Costas Panagopoulos and Joshua Schank, *All Roads Lead to Congress: The $300 Billion Fight over Highway Funding* (Praeger, 2008).

v. "Fiscal Year 2025 Adopted Budget Book," Los Angeles County Metropolitan Transportation Authority, accessed May 3, 2025, https://www.dropbox.com/scl/fi/5d0ok70douxwuzs5edozw/Fiscal-Year-2025-Adopted-Budget-Book.pdf?rlkey=1jm7cqe0yf5wsyxybgtrsk1ad&e=2&st=wv442xg0&dl=0.

vi. James C. Scott, *Seeing Like a State: How Certain Schemes to Improve the Human Condition Have Failed* (Yale University Press, 1998).

vii. "All Systems Go for January 30 Opening of Metro Red Line," Los Angeles County Transportation Commission, 1993, https://libraryarchives.metro.net/DPGTL/pressreleases/1993-lactc-pre-merger-press-releases.pdf.

viii. Michael Manville and University of California Institute of Transportation Studies, *Measure M and the Potential Transformation of Mobility in Los Angeles* (TransitCenter, 2019), https://doi.org/10.7922/G2VT1Q80.

ix. "LA BOS," Los Angeles County Board of Supervisors, accessed May 3, 2025, https://cityselection.lacounty.gov/.

x. Robert García and Thomas A. Rubin, "The MTA Consent Decree," in *Crossroad Blues: The MTA Consent Decree and Just Transportation*, accessed May 3, 2025, https://www.shoupdogg.com/wp-content/uploads/sites/2/2015/04/Chapter-12-Crossroad-Blues-Garcia.pdf.

xi. Colin Gordon, "Costing and Curing Corruption in Public Transit Agencies," *Journal of Financial Crime* 13, no. 4 (2006): 442–55, https://doi.org/10.1108/13590790610707564.

xii. Peter Killing, Thomas Malnight, and Tracey Keys, *Must-Win Battles: How to Win Them, Again and Again* (Wharton School Publishing, 2006), https://dl.acm.org/citation.cfm?id=1407343.

xiii. Neille Ilel, *Metro's Off Peak Podcast*, accessed May 3, 2025, https://www
       .neille.com/offpeak.

xiv.   Eric Goldwyn, Alon Levy, Elif Ensari, and Marco Chitti, "Transit Costs
       Project: Understanding Transit Infrastructure Costs in American Cities,"
       Transit Costs Project, 2024, https://transitcosts.com/wp-content/uploads
       /TCP_Final_Report.pdf.

xv.   Los Angeles County Metropolitan Transportation Authority, "Office of
       Extraordinary Innovation Mission and Progress Report," Board Report
       2016-0337, accessed June 16, 2025, https://metro.legistar.com/View
       Report.ashx?M=R&N=TextL5&GID=557&ID=3132&GUID
       =LATEST&G=A5FAA737-A54D-4A6C-B1E8-FF70F765FA94&Title
       =Board+Report.

xvi.   Jon Henley, "Uber Clashes with Regulators in Cities around the World," *The
       Guardian*, January 31, 2019, https://www.theguardian.com/business/2017
       /sep/29/uber-clashes-with-regulators-in-cities-around-the-world#:~:text
       =Uber%20suspended%20operations%20in%20Austin,pass%20
       fingerprint%2Dbased%20security%20checks.

xvii. Mi Diao, Haoyue Kong, and Jinhua Zhao, "Impacts of Transportation
       Network Companies on Urban Mobility," *Nature Sustainability* 4, no. 6
       (2021): 494–500, https://doi.org/10.1038/s41893-020-00678-z.

xviii. Andrew Bender, "Uber's Astounding Rise: Overtaking Taxis in Key
       Markets," *Forbes*, April 10, 2015, https://www.forbes.com/sites
       /andrewbender/2015/04/10/ubers-astounding-rise-overtaking-taxis-in
       -key-markets/.

xix.   Bradley Tusk, *The Fixer: My Adventures Saving Startups from Death by
       Politics* (Portfolio, 2018).

xx.   "Metro Signs Expo + Uberpool Partnership," LA Metro Board Archives,
       May 18, 2016, https://boardarchives.metro.net/BoardBox/2016/160518
       _Metro_Signs_Expo_Uberpool_Partnership.pdf.

xxi.   "Metro Partnerships with Rideshare/Ridesourcing Services, Motion
       by Directors Antonovich and Kuehl," LA Metro Board Archives, April 28,
       2016, https://metro.legistar.com/LegislationDetail.aspx?ID=2701761
       &GUID=8A26E0FE-194E-40B2-9249-F975A668C3EB
       &Options=ID%7CText%7C&Search=2016-0375%2C.

xxii. TransitCenter, Steven Higashide, Zak Accuardi, Resource Systems
       Group (RSG), and Center for Neighborhood Technology, *Who's on
       Board 2016*, ed. Jonathan Anbinder, David Bragdon, Jon Orcutt, et al.
       (TransitCenter, 2016), https://transitcenter.org/wp-content/uploads/2016
       /07/TransitCenter-WOB-2016.pdf.

xxiii. Jessica Grose, *Why Nothing Works: The Broken Promise of Technology and
       How We Can Fix It* (Little, Brown Spark, 2025).

xxiv.   Martha S. Feldman and Anne M. Khademian, "The Role of the Public Manager in Inclusion: Creating Communities of Participation," *Governance* 20, no. 2 (2007): 305–24. https://doi.org/10.1111/j.1468-0491.2007.00361.x.

xxv.   American Association of State Highway and Transportation Officials, "Case Study 153," accessed May 3, 2025, https://planningtools.transportation.org/290/view-case-study.html?case_id=153.

xxvi.   "The Vision of Jaime Lerner for Curitiba, Brazil," *Smart Cities Dive*, accessed May 3, 2025, https://www.smartcitiesdive.com/ex/sustainablecitiescollective/vision-jaime-lerner-curitiba-brazil/253266/.

xxvii. Lauren W. Kille, "Bus versus Rail: Costs, Capacities and Impacts," *The Journalist's Resource*, December 17, 2020, https://journalistsresource.org/economics/bus-versus-rail/.

xxviii. James Flynn, Charles Thole, Victoria Perk, et al., "Metro Orange Line BRT Project Evaluation," FTA Report No. 0004, Federal Transit Administration, 2011, https://www.transit.dot.gov/sites/fta.dot.gov/files/FTA_Research_Report_0004_FINAL_2.pdf.

xxix.   Flynn et al., "Metro Orange Line BRT Project Evaluation."

xxx.   Ryan Bradley, "Walking in L.A.: The Data Driven City," *GOOD*, August 1, 2019, https://www.good.is/articles/walking-in-l-a-the-data-driven-city.

xxxi.   The Times Editorial Board & By The Times Editorial Board, "Editorial: Finally, a Bus-Lane Building Boom in Los Angeles—Los Angeles Times," *Los Angeles Times*, October 19, 2023, https://www.latimes.com/opinion/story/2023-10-19/finally-a-bus-lane-building-boom-in-los-angeles-metro.

xxxii. Neal Broverman, "Beverly Hills Finally Loses Its Crazy, Stupid Subway Battle," *Los Angeles Magazine*, September 1, 2023, https://lamag.com/news/beverly-hills-finally-loses-crazy-stupid-subway-battle.

xxxiii. Los Angeles Union Station, "History," *Union Station Los Angeles*, accessed August 26, 2025, https://www.unionstationla.com/history/.

xxxiv. Susannah Luthi, "California Lawmakers Consider Bills That Trade Surveillance for Convenience in Final Sprint," *POLITICO*, August 17, 2021, https://www.politico.com/states/california/story/2021/08/12/california-lawmakers-consider-bills-that-trade-surveillance-for-convenience-in-final-sprint-1389869.

xxxv.   Goldwyn et al., "Transit Costs Project."

xxxvi. Paul Lewis, "On the Right Track: Rail Transit Project Delivery around the World," Eno Center for Transportation, September 2022, https://enotrans.org/wp-content/uploads/2023/02/On-the-Right-Track-Report.pdf.

xxxvii. Brian D. Taylor, "Options for the Future of State Funding for Transit Operations in California" (panel discussion transcript, SPUR Public Programs, August 2023), https://www.spur.org/sites/default/files/2023-08/Transcript%20Options%20for%20the%20Future%20of%20State%20Funding.pdf.

xxxviii.   Jennifer Goodman, "Design-Build Takes Hold in All but 2 States," *Construction Dive*, February 10, 2020, https://www.constructiondive.com/news/design-build-takes-hold-in-all-but-2-states/571951/.

xxxix.   "Procurement Lessons Learned: A Line," University of Maryland, 2011, https://bac.umd.edu/wp-content/uploads/2022/03/A-LIne_Lessons_Learned.pdf.

xl.   Tim Rutten, "Mayor Villaraigosa's 30/10 Plan: Moving Forward," *Los Angeles Times*, March 14, 2019, https://www.latimes.com/archives/la-xpm-2010-jun-09-la-oe-0609-rutten-20100609-story.html.

xli.   Steven Sharp, "Monorail or Heavy Rail? Metro Narrows Its Focus in the Sepulveda Pass," *Urbanize LA*, February 17, 2021, https://la.urbanize.city/post/monorail-or-heavy-rail-metro-narrows-its-focus-sepulveda-pass.

xlii.   Henry Mintzberg, *Structure in Fives: Designing Effective Organizations* (Prentice-Hall, 1983).

xliii.   Patrick M. Lencioni, *Silos, Politics, and Turf Wars: A Leadership Fable about Destroying the Barriers That Turn Colleagues into Competitors* (Jossey-Bass, 2006).

xliv.   Robert Agranoff, "Inside Collaborative Networks: Ten Lessons for Public Managers," *Public Administration Review* 66, no. s1 (2006): 56–65, https://doi.org/10.1111/j.1540-6210.2006.00666.x.

xlv.   James Q. Wilson, *Bureaucracy: What Government Agencies Do and Why They Do It* (Hachette UK, 2019).

xlvi.   Max Weber, "From Max Weber: Essays in Sociology," trans. and ed. H. H. Gerth and C. Wright Mills, *Journal of Philosophy* 43, no. 26 (1946): 722, https://doi.org/10.2307/2019397.

xlvii.   Amy Edmondson, "Psychological Safety and Learning Behavior in Work Teams," *Administrative Science Quarterly* 44, no. 2 (1999): 350–83, https://doi.org/10.2307/2666999.

xlviii.   Jennifer Pahlka, *Recoding America: Why Government Is Failing in the Digital Age—and How We Can Do Better* (Metropolitan Books, 2023).

xlix.   "TAP Cards and Universal Fare Media in Los Angeles Transit: History & Resources," *Metro's Primary Resources*, August 7, 2024, https://metroprimaryresources.info/tap-cards-and-universal-fare-media-in-los-angeles-transit-history-resources/15741/.

l.   Carrie Brakewood, Ahmed Ziedan, Sean J. Hendricks, Sean J. Barbeau, and Adam Joslin, "An Evaluation of the Benefits of Mobile Fare Payment Technology from the User and Operator Perspectives," *Transport Policy* 93 (2020): 54–66, https://doi.org/10.1016/j.tranpol.2020.04.015.

li.   Los Angeles County Metropolitan Transportation Authority, "Regional Fare System Plan," 2010, https://boardarchives.metro.net/Items/2011/02_February/20110224RBMItem3.pdf.

lii. Paul Pierson, "Increasing Returns, Path Dependence, and the Study of Politics," *American Political Science Review* 94, no. 2 (2000): 251–67, https://doi.org/10.2307/2586011; W. Brian Arthur, "Competing Technologies, Increasing Returns, and Lock-In by Historical Events," *Economic Journal* 99, no. 394 (1989): 116–31, https://doi.org/10.2307/2234208.

liii. "Playa del Rey Street Safety Improvements Court Driver Backlash," *Streetsblog Los Angeles*, June 14, 2023, https://la.streetsblog.org/2017/06/07/playa-del-rey-street-safety-improvements-court-driver-backlash.

liv. David Zahniser, "L.A. Reworks Another 'Road Diet,' Restoring Car Lanes in Playa del Rey," *Los Angeles Times*, October 4, 2017, https://www.latimes.com/local/lanow/la-me-ln-mike-bonin-road-diet-20171003-story.html.

lv. "A Former Red Car Conductor Rides the New Expo Line: 'It Brings Back Memories,'" *LAist*, December 28, 2016, https://laist.com/news/kpcc-archive/before-the-shiny-expo-line-extension-there-was-the.

lvi. Jaclyn Cosgrove, "L.A. Makes History with All-Female Board of Supervisors," *Los Angeles Times*, November 5, 2020, https://www.latimes.com/california/story/2020-11-04/l-a-county-makes-history-with-all-female-board-of-supervisors.

lvii. Los Angeles County Metropolitan Transportation Authority, "Southeast Gateway Line P3 Assessment Update," Board Report 2024-0452, July 18, 2024, https://boardagendas.metro.net/board-report/2024-0452/.

lviii. Michael Manville, Brian D. Taylor, Evelyn Blumenberg, and Andrew Schouten, "Vehicle Access and Falling Transit Ridership: Evidence from Southern California," *Transportation* 50, no. 1 (2022): 303–29, https://doi.org/10.1007/s11116-021-10245-w.

lix. Robert Cervero, *The Transit Metropolis: A Global Inquiry* (Island Press, 1998); Jonathan Levine, *Zoned Out: Regulation, Markets, and Choices in Transportation and Metropolitan Land Use* (Resources for the Future Press, 2006).

lx. Geoff Dudley, David Banister, and Tim Schwanen, "The Rise of Uber and Regulating the Disruptive Innovator," *Political Quarterly* 88, no. 3 (2017): 492–99, https://doi.org/10.1111/1467-923X.12373.

lxi. Colin Murphy, Sharon Feigon, Albert Benedict, et al., *Shared Mobility and the Transformation of Public Transit*, ed. Tim Frisbie (Shared-Use Mobility Center, 2016), https://sharedusemobilitycenter.org/wp-content/uploads/2016/04/Final_TOPT_DigitalPagesNL.pdf.

lxii. Sharon Feigon, Colin Murphy, Transit Cooperative Research Program, Transportation Research Board, and National Academies of Sciences, *Shared Mobility and the Transformation of Public Transit* (National Academies Press, 2016), https://doi.org/10.17226/23578.

lxiii. Lisa Rayle, Susan Shaheen, Nelson Chan, Danielle Dai, Robert Cervero, and University of California Transportation Center, *App-Based, On-Demand Ride Services: Comparing Taxi and Ridesourcing Trips and User Characteristics in San Francisco* (working paper, University of California Transportation Center, 2014), https://d1wqtxts1xzle7.cloudfront.net /103201966/RidesourcingWhitePaper_Nov2014-libre.pdf.

lxiv. Marla Westervelt, Joshua Schank, and Emma Huang, "Partnerships with Technology-Enabled Mobility Companies: Lessons Learned," TRID, accessed May 3, 2025, https://trid.trb.org/View/1438967.

lxv. Joshua Schank, *Examining the Cost Effectiveness of Market-Based Policies: The Case of Airside Airport Congestion* (VDM Verlag Dr. Müller, 2010).

lxvi. Westervelt, Schank, and Huang, "Partnerships with Technology-Enabled Mobility Companies."

lxvii. Sarah Buhr, "Lyft, Now Worth $5.5 Billion, Hops into the Autonomous Car Race with General Motors," *TechCrunch*, January 4, 2016, https:// techcrunch.com/2016/01/04/lyft-now-worth-5-5-billion-plans-to-get -into-the-autonomous-car-race-with-general-motors/.

lxviii. Raphael Orlove, "Silicon Valley Invents Bus," Jalopnik, June 19, 2017, https://www.jalopnik.com/silicon-valley-invents-bus-1796221702/.

lxix. Jarrett Walker, *Human Transit: How Clearer Thinking about Public Transit Can Enrich Our Communities and Our Lives* (Island Press, 2012).

lxx. "Latest on Metro Micro: Still Few Riders, High Costs," *Streetsblog Los Angeles*, June 21, 2024, https://la.streetsblog.org/2024/06/18 /latest-on-metro-micro-still-few-riders-high-costs.

lxxi. "Metro Poised to Waste $8 Million More on Costly 'Metro Micro' Micro-Transit Pilot," *Streetsblog Los Angeles*, June 13, 2023, https://la.streetsblog .org/2023/03/21/metro-poised-to-waste-8-million-more-on-costly-metro -micro-microtransit-pilot.

lxxii. Ezra Klein and Derek Thompson, *Abundance* (Avid Reader Press, 2025).

lxxiii. Carlos Bustamante, "Congestion Pricing: Q&A," UCLA Institute of Transportation Studies, February 20, 2025, https://www.its.ucla.edu/news /for-the-press/congestion-pricing/.

lxxiv. Federal Highway Administration, "Edward M. Bassett: The Man Who Gave Us 'Freeway,'" accessed May 3, 2025, https://www.fhwa.dot.gov /infrastructure/freeway.cfm.

lxxv. John Van Maanen and Edgar H. Schein, "Toward a Theory of Organizational Socialization," *Research in Organizational Behavior* 1 (1979): 209–64.

lxxvi. Charles A. O'Reilly and Michael L. Tushman, "Organizational Ambidexterity: Past, Present, and Future," *Academy of Management Perspectives* 27, no. 4 (2013): 324–38, https://doi.org/10.5465/amp.2013.0025.

lxxvii.   "Personnel/Organizational Restructuring."

lxxviii. Upton Sinclair, *I, Candidate for Governor: And How I Got Licked* (Self-published, 1935).

lxxix.   Jonathan D. Hall, "Pareto Improvements from Lexus Lanes: The Effects of Pricing a Portion of the Lanes on Congested Highways," *Journal of Public Economics* 158 (2018): 113–25, https://doi.org/10.1016/j.jpubeco.2018.01.003.

lxxx.   Anthony Downs, *Still Stuck in Traffic: Coping with Peak-Hour Traffic Congestion* (Brookings Institution Press, 2004).

lxxxi.   Martin Wachs, Peter S. Chesney, Y. H. Hwang, and UCLA Luskin Center for History and Policy, *A Century of Fighting Traffic Congestion in Los Angeles, 1920–2020* (UCLA Luskin Center, 2020), https://luskincenter.history.ucla.edu/wp-content/uploads/sites/66/2020/10/A-Century-of-Fighting-Traffic-Congestion-in-LA.pdf.

lxxxii.   Michael Manville, Evelyn Bird, Ifeoma Obi, Jacob Epstein, and Los Angeles County Metropolitan Transportation Authority (LA Metro), "Measure M: Lessons from a Successful Transportation Ballot Campaign," Eno Center for Transportation, 2019, https://enotrans.org/wp-content/uploads/2023/02/Measure-M-FINAL.pdf.

lxxxiii. Damien Newton, "Santa Monica, Westside Political Leaders Disagree on 'Go Zone' Congestion Pricing Proposal," *Santa Monica Next*, March 29, 2019, https://santamonicanext.org/2019/03/santa-monica-westside-political-leaders-disagree-on-go-zone-congestion-pricing-proposal/.

lxxxiv.   David Wharton, "L.A. Officially Awarded 2028 Olympic Games," *Los Angeles Times*, September 13, 2017, https://www.latimes.com/sports/olympics/la-sp-la-olympics-approved-20170913-story.html.

lxxxv.   Steven Sharp, "Here Are the 28 Projects That Metro Could Complete Before the 2028 Olympics." *UrbanizeLA*, November 27, 2017. https://la.urbanize.city/post/here-are-28-projects-metro-could-complete-2028-olympics.

lxxxvi.   Los Angeles County Metropolitan Transportation Authority, "Attachment D to Response to Motion by Director Butts to Amend Item 43 with Questions and Instructions," Metro Board Report 2019-0083, February 20, 2019, https://metro.legistar1.com/metro/attachments/6b6f40f5-b88f-4b5c-8e94-3473ee8e4158.pdf.

lxxxvii. Brianna Kohler, "Expanding L.A. Metro's Fare-Free Transit for Kids and Families," *National League of Cities*, May 14, 2021, https://www.nlc.org/article/2021/05/14/expanding-l-a-metros-fare-free-transit-for-kids-and-families/.

lxxxviii. Laura J. Nelson, "L.A. Metro Will Study How to Make Driving More Expensive—in Your Car or in an Uber," *Los Angeles Times*, March 1, 2019, https://www.latimes.com/local/lanow/la-me-ln-congestion-pricing-uber-tax-20190228-story.html.

lxxxix. Los Angeles County Metropolitan Transportation Authority, "Twenty-Eight by '28 Initiative," Metro Board Report 2019-0108, February 28, 2019, https://boardagendas.metro.net/board-report/2019-0108/.

xc. Donald P. Moynihan, *The Dynamics of Performance Management: Constructing Information and Reform* (Georgetown University Press, 2008).

xci. John W. Kingdon, *Agendas, Alternatives, and Public Policies*, updated 2nd ed. (Longman, 2011).

xcii. "The Hyperloop: A 200-Year History of Hype and Failure," *MIT Press Reader*, March 9, 2025, https://thereader.mitpress.mit.edu/the-hyperloop-a-200-year-history-of-hype-and-failure/.

xciii. Tim Sheehan, "California High-Speed Rail: Why 2025 Could Make or Break Embattled Bullet Train Project," *Fresno Bee*, January 19, 2025, https://www.fresnobee.com/news/local/high-speed-rail/article298478383.html.

xciv. American Society of Mechanical Engineers, "The Disney Monorail System: A National Historic Mechanical Engineering Landmark," December 1986, https://www.asme.org/wwwasmeorg/media/resourcefiles/aboutasme/who%20we%20are/engineering%20history/landmarks/115-disneyland-monorail-system-1959.pdf.

xcv. Kevin Tidmarsh, "Subway or Monorail for the Sepulveda Pass? Metro and Local Residents Weigh Their Options," *LAist*, May 10, 2024, https://laist.com/news/transportation/subway-or-monorail-for-the-sepulveda-pass-metro-and-local-residents-weigh-their-options.

xcvi. West Virginia University, "About the PRT," *WVU Personal Rapid Transit 50th Anniversary*, accessed June 12, 2025, https://prt.wvu.edu/about-the-prt.

xcvii. Los Angeles County Metropolitan Transportation Authority, "Los Angeles Aerial Rapid Transit Project Update," File #2022-0316, Executive Management Committee, September 15, 2022, https://metro.legistar.com/LegislationDetail.aspx?ID=5836690&GUID=22349CE5-6682-4B7C-8D22-90E316D25C4C.

xcviii. Los Angeles City Council District 1, "Dodgers Stadium Transportation Study," accessed May 3, 2025, https://cd1.lacity.gov/press-releases/dodgers-stadium-transportation-study.

xcix. Laura J. Nelson, "Metro Bus, Train Shutdown Slammed by Riders, Officials," *Los Angeles Times*, June 1, 2020, https://libraryarchives.metro.net/dpgtl/articles/social-equity-justice/20200601-latimes-who-approved-this-riders-officials-criticize-metros-systemwide-shutdown.pdf.

c. Los Angeles County Metropolitan Transportation Authority, "A Path Forward: Metro's Recovery Task Force Final Report," February 2021, https://metro.legistar1.com/metro/attachments/92ebcb28-f344-4ec6-b0d3-c058cc15c6bb.pdf.

ci. LA Metro, "A Path Forward."

Index

www.ingramcontent.com/pod-product-compliance
Lightning Source LLC
Chambersburg PA
CBHW061505180526
45171CB00001B/39